Blackstone's
Police Investigators'

Q&A 2007

Blackstone's
Police Investigators'

Q&A
2007

Paul Connor

OXFORD
UNIVERSITY PRESS

OXFORD
UNIVERSITY PRESS

Great Clarendon Street, Oxford OX2 6DP

Oxford University Press is a department of the University of Oxford.
It furthers the University's objective of excellence in research, scholarship,
and education by publishing worldwide in

Oxford New York

Auckland Bangkok Buenos Aires Cape Town Chennai
Dar es Salaam Delhi Hong Kong Istanbul Karachi Kolkata
Kuala Lumpur Madrid Melbourne Mexico City Mumbai Nairobi
São Paulo Shanghai Taipei Tokyo Toronto

With offices in

Argentina Austria Brazil Chile Czech Republic France Greece
Guatemala Hungary Italy Japan Poland Portugal Singapore
South Korea Switzerland Thailand Turkey Ukraine Vietnam

Oxford is a registered trade mark of Oxford University Press
in the UK and in certain other countries

Published in the United States
by Oxford University Press Inc., New York

British Library Cataloguing in Publication Data

Data available

Library of Congress Cataloging in Publication Data

Data available

Typeset by Laserwords Private Limited, Chennai, India
Printed in Great Britain
on acid-free paper by
Ashford Colour Press Limited, Gosport, Hampshire

ISBN 0-19-920731-3   978-0-19-920731-2

10 9 8 7 6 5 4 3 2 1

Contents

Introduction	vii
Difficulty Value (DV)	ix
Acknowledgements	xi
Revising for the NIE	1
Taking the NIE	11
The 10-Week Revision Programme	23

Part 1 Property Offences — **37**

1. Theft	39
2. Burglary	51
3. Handling	66
4. Robbery	71
5. Deception	76
6. Blackmail	82

Part 2 Assaults, Drugs, Firearms and Defences — **87**

7. Homicide	89
8. Offences Against the Person	97
9. Threats to Kill, Child Abduction, Kidnap and False Imprisonment	106
10. Public Order and Racially Aggravated Offences	113
11. Criminal Damage	121
12. Misuse of Drugs	129
13. Firearms and Gun Crime	139

Part 3 Sexual Offences — **147**

14. The Sexual Offences Act 2003, Rape and Sexual Assault	149
15. Child Sex Offences	163
16. Protection of Children	183
17. Preparatory Offences	188

Contents

Part 4 Evidence   **193**

    18. Presumptions, State of Mind, Criminal Conduct and Bail   195
    19. PACE Codes of Practice, Identification and Interviews   210
    20. Incomplete Offences and Offences Against the Administration of
        Justice and Public Interest   229
    21. Disclosure of Evidence, Documentary Records and Business
        Documents, the Criminal Justice Act 1967 and the Criminal
        Justice and Public Order Act 1994   237

Question Checklist   247

Introduction

On 14 January 2003 the Association of Chief Police Officers approved the 'Initial Crime Investigators' Development Programme' (ICIDP) as a successor to the 'National Foundation Course in Criminal Investigation'. The ICIDP was split into three distinct phases with Phase 1 culminating in 'Trainee Investigators' sitting the National Investigators' Examination. The first National Investigators' Examination (NIE) took place in March 2003 and the examination has been held every three months since that time.

I have provided revision classes and revision advice to Trainee Investigators taking the NIE since December 2002. Initially, this advice was given to Trainee Investigators from West Midlands Police but this quickly expanded and, since that time, I have taught and assisted officers from West Mercia Constabulary, Warwickshire Police, The Metropolitan Police Service, Essex Police, Bedfordshire Police, The Police Service of Northern Ireland and many more. A fact that became clear to me very quickly was that apart from the *Police Investigators' Manual* and accompanying Workbook, there was little, if anything at all, that Trainee Investigators could use to assist them in their efforts to pass the examination. A large amount of material has been written and produced for officers sitting the Sergeant's and Inspector's examinations and many Trainee Investigators have attempted to use this material to assist them with varying degrees of success. However, using this material does not always provide the Trainee Investigator with the right information and can actually be detrimental to study for the NIE.

The aim of this book is to fill the gap in material available for Trainee Investigators as it is principally directed towards Trainee Investigators revising for the NIE. The book is split into the same four sections as the *Police Investigators' Manual* and the questions contained within it are written using that textbook as the basis for the questions.

Every answer is followed by a paragraph reference to *Blackstone's Police Investigators' Manual*. This means that once you have attempted a question and looked at an answer, the Manual can immediately be referred to for help and clarification.

Each question and answer has the same unique number. This should ensure that there is no confusion as to which question is linked to which answer. For example, Question 2.1 is linked to Answer 2.1.

At the back of the book you will find a checklist. This has been designed to help you keep track of your progress when answering the multiple-choice questions. If you fill in the checklist after attempting a question, you will be able to check how many you got right on the first attempt and will know immediately which questions need to be looked at a second time.

I have also included chapters on revising for the NIE and taking the NIE to assist students in their efforts to pass the examination.

I know how hard students have to work to pass the NIE and I applaud your efforts. I sincerely hope that this book will help you in your study and contribute to your successful performance in your forthcoming examination.

Difficulty Value (DV)

All of the multiple-choice questions that you will attempt in this book have been verified by Trainee Investigators studying for the NIE. This has enabled me to attach a 'Difficulty Value' (DV) to each question. In essence, the DV is a measure of how many NIE students would get a question right and it is measured on a scale of 1 to 10. However, if a question has a DV value of less than 2, it is too difficult and at the other end of the scale, if a question has a DV value of more than 8, it is too easy. DV is therefore recorded between the figures of 2 and 8 (as questions with a DV of less than 2 and more than 8 have been removed) and gives the student an idea of how hard/easy the question has proved to his/her peers. The higher the DV, the easier the question.

Acknowledgements

The primary purpose of this book is to provide advice and direction for students taking the National Investigators' Examination and to enable them to test their knowledge against multiple-choice questions based on the *Police Investigators' Manual*.

In order to ensure that the multiple-choice questions in this book were acceptable to NIE students, each of the questions has been tested on groups of between 10 and 40 students who were in the process of studying for the NIE. This has allowed me to allocate a 'Difficulty Value' (DV) to each question. This process also enabled me to eliminate some questions that were unacceptable or modify them to make them acceptable. I could not have accomplished this task without the assistance of many officers from West Midlands Police, West Mercia Constabulary and Essex Police. I wish to thank all the officers who took part in the tests.

Thanks must also go to Jane Kavanagh, Andrea Oliver and Katie Allan, at Oxford University Press. Jane for her help in getting this idea off the ground and Andrea and Katie for dealing with my constant questions and queries and their valuable assistance with the text.

Most of all I would like to thank my wife, Kate, who became a computer widow for over 6 months so that I could complete this book. Your support, encouragement and understanding are the reason these words are in print.

Revising for the NIE

Before any methods of revising for the National Investigators' Examination are suggested, it is vital that students understand that there are no shortcuts to success. Attaining a pass in the NIE will be achieved by many hours of revision and not by the use of any time and effort saving formula advocated in this book.

The primary cause of failing the examination is a lack of revision, so logically the first and most critical question a student should ask is, 'How much should I revise?' This question must then be subdivided and addressed from the dual points of, 'How much time should I revise for?' and 'How much of the content of the Manual and the Workbook should I revise?'

'How much time should I revise for?'

I have carried out a number of surveys with trainee investigators[1] in order to establish what time period a *successful* student will revise for. The initial period was 91 hours but an increase in the size of the syllabus in 2004 led to this figure rising to 112 hours. As a result of the ever-changing syllabus, I advise you to set yourself a 120 hour revision target for the 2007 examinations; this revision target is linked to the '10-week Revision Programme' section of this book.

Having set the target of 120 hours revision, the next factor to consider is over what time period should students revise? The 'Service Level Agreement', between the National Crime Operations Faculty and individual police forces signed up to the ICIDP process, states that students should be provided with the National Investigators' Manual and accompanying Workbook a *minimum* of 12 weeks prior to their examination.[2] This has resulted in many forces distributing the Manual and Workbook to students on their 'Induction Day', usually held on or near to the 12-week deadline. Therefore, students may understandably set a 12-week period over which they will revise for a total of 120 hours, giving an approximate daily target

---

[1] 157 trainee investigators have taken part in four separate surveys between 2003 and 2006.
[2] Paragraph 13.2, page 15 of the 'Service Level Agreement'.

of 1 hour 25 minutes or an approximate weekly target of 10 hours (these figures are a guide).

It is not suggested that students slavishly adhere to a regime of 120 hours revision per day/week as this may not suit the revision style of the individual concerned (a facet of revision covered later in this chapter). The daily/weekly figure is an indication of the task that lies ahead of students studying for the NIE.

Depending on your revision style and general approach to the NIE, it may prove advantageous to obtain the Manual and Workbook at the first available opportunity. The 'Service Level Agreement' only provides a 12-week *minimum* length of time for students to revise. Police forces are not restricted to this time period, i.e. there is nothing stopping individuals obtaining the Manual and Workbook, subject to their availability, before the 12-week period begins. Even obtaining the Manual and Workbook 13 weeks in advance will be an advantage; that extra week can make all the difference as it allows students to spread their revision over a greater period of time. Depending on when a student obtains the Manual and Workbook will obviously affect the average amount of time per day/week that student will have to revise. A student obtaining the Manual and Workbook 16 weeks in advance of the NIE changes the daily/weekly revision time from 1 hour 25 minutes per day/10 hours per week to 1 hour 5 minutes per day/7 hours 35 minutes per week.

I assure you that revising for the NIE has proved to be a demanding test for students in the past. Many NIE students have reported the difficulty of balancing revision for the exam against the heavy workload of a detective not to mention individual social and family commitments. To counter these pressures and to provide time for revision, it is not uncommon for students to take annual leave prior to the exam. This decision, whilst commendable, can have drawbacks. The majority of students making the decision to study during annual leave will arrange for that leave to take place either 1 or 2 weeks in advance of the NIE. The temptation to leave revision until that time is significant. The problem is that by leaving revision until this late stage there is no margin for error; how will the student deal with their leave being cancelled or having to utilise the leave for some other purpose unimagined at the time when they took this decision? The second issue is that there is a great amount of work to do to adequately prepare for the NIE and 1 or 2 weeks might not be enough; how will the student deal with the fact that they underestimated the time it will take to revise or that when they begin to revise the task of reading and answering questions for the best part of 8 hours a day is beyond them? My advice is not to take this chance. Taking annual leave before the exam will undoubtedly help with study but students should begin revising at the first available opportunity, i.e. start when first in possession of the Manual and Workbook.

Starting to revise at the first opportunity is vital; putting revision off makes the task so much harder. To further illustrate this point students should recall how much time per day/week they would have to revise if provided with the Manual and Workbook 12 weeks prior to the NIE. Now consider a hypothetical student who decides not to revise until 6 weeks prior to the NIE. That student will have to revise for 2 hours 40 minutes per day/18 hours 40 minutes per week to catch up with the amount of work required to be successful. Setting aside so much time each day is a challenging activity to say the least and places additional unnecessary pressure on the student.

Having set a target of how many hours revision should be undertaken, the next issue is how that time should be split from the period of initial possession of the Manual and Workbook to taking the NIE.

In the '10-week Revision Programme' section I have set out a detailed approach to revision. This might not suit everybody as we all have our own revision methods and styles. If this is the case the student should consider some of the following general observations with regard to revision.

Taking the 12-week period as an example, the student will be aware that the overall revision target is 120 hours. This target can then be split into a daily target or a weekly target. It has already been suggested that students may not wish to study for 1 hour 25 minutes per day but if this suits the individual then there is no reason not to take this approach. Indeed, many of the successful students who participated in the NIE surveys chose to study by revising for 1 to 2 hours per day. One of the advantages of this approach is that the revision target is broken down into achievable portions. Understandably, many students state that they find it difficult to revise for any longer than 2 hours at a time as the material they are reading is sometimes difficult to learn and their concentration suffers as a direct result. I would recommend that whatever time you set aside for study, you should take a 5-minute break every hour to give your mind a chance to rest. Some students may choose to revise for more lengthy periods of time, perhaps up to 8 hours in one sitting. There is nothing wrong with this approach either as the methods for studying for the NIE are as individual as the student taking the exam. If this method suits the individual style of the student then do not change it for the sake of change.

Students may wish to use a mixture of the two methods. For example, a student may have adopted a study pattern of 1 hour per day/7 hours per week for the first 10 weeks of revision and then in the last 2 weeks of revision the amount of revision is increased to 3 hours 30 minutes/25 hours per week to bring up the required revision period to the desired 120-hour mark. This method has been favoured by many of the students who took part in the NIE survey. The concept of this approach is that as the date of the NIE gets closer students should be looking to 'peak' with their knowledge base. The ideal situation is that the high point of that peak will be the taking of the NIE.

Regardless of the method a student decides to employ for revision purposes I would recommend that when an opportunity arises to revise, they take it. I would go so far as to say even 10 minutes spent reading the Manual is of value and for this reason I would encourage students to take their Manual and Workbook to work as well as reading it at home. When the opportunity to read the Manual and/or Workbook arises it should not be dismissed. Workplace opportunities may be limited with the pressures placed on Trainee Investigators but they may prove advantageous to some students. For example, a student dealing with a suspect for an offence of burglary may take 10 minutes to read the section on burglary before interviewing the suspect and equating the law to the circumstances surrounding the incident they are dealing with. Application of the law surrounding the offence of burglary in reality may assist in the retention of the law to deal with burglary questions in the NIE.

Students should be aware that time spent in revision is time well spent. Whilst it can never be an absolute guarantee of a pass in the NIE, investing the necessary hours of revision certainly lays the foundation for success.

'How much of the content of the Manual and the Workbook should I revise?'

The multiple-choice questions that students will answer in the NIE are based solely on the content of the *Police Investigators' Manual*. The *Police Investigators' Workbook* is designed as a study aid to help students understand the law in practice and to provide examples of such. On that basis, students might consider that the Workbook is unnecessary and omit it from their revision; I would suggest that they should not. It should be used as an additional means of understanding the law contained within the Manual and not ignored. However, as the questions within the NIE are not based on material within the Workbook, there is no need for students to study the Workbook with the intensity required when studying from the Manual.

The examination questions contained in the NIE are written from the content of the *Blackstone's Police Investigators' Manual* and this includes the appendices. It is possible for a student to consider excluding the appendices from their revision as they largely repeat the information contained within the text of the Manual. Students would thereby reduce the amount of material necessary to study from X pages to Y pages. Although this is an attractive option I would recommend that students do not take it. Instead, I would recommend that students still revise the appendices of the Manual but revise them as an alternative to reading the corresponding chapters within the Manual. For example, there are chapters within the Manual on 'Identification', 'Interviews' and 'Disclosure of Evidence', all of which have corresponding appendices (Codes C, D, E, F; Disclosure: Criminal Procedure and Investigations Act 1996; and Code of Practice under Part II. Instead of revising from the chapter within the Manual alone, I recommend that the student read the chapter from the Manual and then the next time they decide to read on that particular subject, read the appendix that relates to it instead. This approach will have a positive result in that revision involves the constant reading and re-reading of the same material and regardless of how hard a student concentrates there may come a time when rather than actually reading and remembering the material, the student begins to 'scan' the text because he/she has read it so many times. Although (for example) the chapter on 'Identification' and the appendix on 'Code D' relate to the same material, they are expressed differently and in a different order. This difference may not only assist the student to understand the subject but also to eliminate the danger of 'scanning' the text due to those differences.

As has already been stated, the questions in the NIE are based on the content of the Manual alone. On that basis, the whole of the Manual is testable. This fact may lead students to consider methods of cutting down on the content they will have to revise. One approach often considered is that students can cut out certain sections that they deal with regularly in the workplace because of that workplace knowledge; this would be a mistake. The fact that a student deals with thefts, burglaries and assaults on a daily basis will not, alone, provide them with the requisite knowledge on those subjects in order to answer questions correctly in the NIE. The practical application of the law and the theoretical application of the law, whilst closely related, are not always the same. A student should not treat these areas with contempt purely because of their workplace familiarity with the subject. Conversely, students may look at certain sections and consider that the likelihood of dealing with such an incident in the workplace is insignificant and therefore so is the requirement to know the subject for the purposes of the exam. Do not think that this is the case. Purely because an offence is not an everyday occurrence in a student's workplace does not mean that it is never committed or that it is unimportant; if it is included in the Manual it is as testable as the crimes that make up 95% of a CID officer's daily routine.

Having examined the issues surrounding 'How much should I revise', I will now turn to some methods of revising.

Methods of revising

The prospect of revising from the *Police Investigators' Manual* can be an over-whelming one for students. Many have not revised for a police examination since their initial training and this can, in some cases, be in excess of 10 years prior to taking the NIE. Even students familiar with the format of multiple-choice-examinations as their initial training period was not that long ago or perhaps because they have taken the Sergeants' examination at some time find the task daunting. One of the primary difficulties faced by all students, regardless of their experience, is deciding on an approach to revising from the Manual; having set the time they will study for, how will they study?

Perhaps the most important point to make at this stage is that nobody is expect-ing the student to remember, word for word, the whole of the *Police Investigators' Manual*. I would go so far as to say that this task is near impossible. The task for the student is to retain enough information from their revision in order to pass the NIE; whether the student gets 99% or 48.57% is irrelevant as a pass is a pass.

There are no absolute rules when it comes to methods of revision as all students differ in the way they revise and retain information. However, I am often asked about alternative revision systems by students seeking to maximise the benefit of the time they will invest in the task. One method of approaching your revision is advanced in the '10-week Revision Programme' section but there are several other approaches that may be preferable to you. Below are several tried and tested meth-ods of revision used by *successful* students who have revised for the NIE (they are in no order of popularity or effectiveness).

1. Reading through the text of the Manual in order (beginning to end)

Many students favour this method because it is simple and effective. Students will read and re-read the same text continually, a task that can become tiresome and heighten the danger of 'scanning' the text rather than actually reading it and tak-ing in the detail. To counter this I suggest students consciously slow down their reading speed; take more time reading the definitions and 'keynote' explanations of the law in action. It is far better to take time and therefore ensure comprehen-sion rather than race through the text in an effort to finish reading the Manual as soon as possible.

2. Reading through the text and 'highlighting' relevant point and words

A version of method 1, this method naturally draws the attention of the student to important elements of legislation highlighted by that student. Used correctly, this method can make referring to the Manual a speedier process. However, students should not overuse the 'highlighter' as the end result is often half or whole pages of the Manual highlighted with no discernible relevant points as the page turns into a mass of bright pink, yellow, blue or green.

3. Begin revising from the student's perceived weakest area

For example, a student may consider their weakest area to be 'Sexual Offences' or 'Evidence' and start their revision by reading and re-reading that particular section. One of the advantages of this method is that by dealing with the difficult from the outset, the task of revision will become easier as the student progresses through their revision to areas of strength, such as 'Property Offences'. A disadvantage is that in beginning with an area of weakness, the student may become demoralised at an early stage of the revision process.

4. Begin revising from the student's perceived strongest area

This is the exact act opposite of method 2 with the opposite advantage and disadvantage, i.e. starting from an area of strength will boost the confidence of the student at an early point in their revision but leaving the difficult area(s) until last may demoralise the student in the run-up to the NIE.

> I would raise a note of caution with regard to methods 3 and 4. These methods operate on the student's *perceived* areas of weakness or strength and the student is sometimes incorrect as to their ability. For example, a student may believe that 'Property Offences' is an area of strength when in fact this is not the case and on closer examination of the text it is an area of weakness and vice versa. Students should be aware of the detrimental effect this may have.

5. Read a section in the Manual, make short notes from that section and then revise from the short notes

Another popular choice with students, this method condenses the Manual into smaller more manageable portions and allows the student to draw their own attention to significant points. Making notes from the text sometimes helps to cement knowledge in the mind of the student as the exercise involves reading the text, making a mental decision on relevant points, writing down those points and then re-reading them. I would not recommend a total abandonment of the Manual after the notes have been written as there is always the danger that in making the notes, a student may inadvertently miss out a vital part of a definition or explanation.

6. *Reading the Manual from cover to cover (to understand the nature and difficulty of the task of revising), constantly re-reading the Manual and taking part in study sessions with another student(s)*

Some students have been successful by meeting with a fellow student or students and testing each other on their knowledge of the Manual. The element of competition can act as a spur for students to work hard and answer more questions correctly than their colleague(s). It also enables students to discuss difficulties with certain areas of law and help each other to understand those areas; one student's weak area is another's strong area. It is not always possible to meet with a fellow student but this should not preclude the use of this method as there is nothing wrong with students asking their tutor constables or work colleagues to test them.

7. *Split the Manual into the four component sections and set aside a time period in which to study each part*

An example of this method is the student who sets aside 12 weeks to study and splits those 12 weeks into four 3-week sections. Each 3-week section is devoted to studying one section of the Manual, for example 'Sexual Offences'. The student will study according to his or her own preferred revision method. This method is successful as the Manual can be a barrier to effective revision because of its size. Breaking it down into component sections can diffuse that barrier. The drawback with this method is that some sections are far larger than others, for example, 'Evidence' is at least three times longer than any of the other sections of the Manual and may, as a consequence, require considerably more time to study effectively. However, there is no reason why the student could not alter the split of the revision period to reflect this and any other factors that affect the student's revision programme.

8. *Read the whole book and make crammer cards on offences. Alternate between reading the crammer cards and reading the Manual*

A version of method 5 but instead of notes, the student will revise from cards with the very basic details of the chosen offences written on those cards. Using cards in this manner can really help with revision as the student will only have the card to concentrate on rather than a full page of A4 from the Manual or notes that they have written. As with method 5, students should not exclusively use the cards they have written because they may miss out certain details from the Manual in the process.

Whatever method a student employs, I would recommend that some form of testing knowledge, e.g. answering multiple-choice questions, follows revision from the Manual. I have known many students whose knowledge of the Manual was certainly good enough to pass the NIE, however, they did not test that knowledge by answering questions. The result of this is that in the NIE, the student who has not practised multiple-choice questions can become disorientated by the complexity of the questions and the choice put before them. The result of this has, in many cases, been failure.

Do not

Having examined alternative revision methods it is also advisable to mention methods that students should not employ in their revision.

1. Do not use any other legal textbooks to revise from

Although students may be tempted to utilise other legal textbooks (aside from the Manual) to enhance their knowledge, there is a high risk that such a method will only confuse the student. The law is not always black and white, it is sometimes grey and accordingly, different legal textbooks will often have different interpretations of the law. This might be a bonus if the student was answering essay type questions where the answer is expected to discuss different opinions but it is an obstruction to answering a multiple-choice exam question, as only one answer from the four choices is right. If the student reads from other texts there is a strong chance that when answering questions in the NIE they will feel that two or three of the options could be correct. In addition, questions in the NIE are often worded to mirror the text of the Manual. If the student has read from other sources then their ability to recognise the correct option will be adversely affected.

2. Do not use the 'Police National Legal Database' (PNLD) as a primary revision tool

This facility is an excellent professional tool for police officers to use in the workplace. However, like using other legal texts it may conflict with the Manual and confuse the student rather than enlighten. The further difficulty with the PNLD is that it is constantly updated with new law and procedures and this new law may contradict the law that is written in the Manual. There is a possibility that the law that was correct when your Manual was printed has since been superseded by a new Act of Parliament or by a stated case and is now no longer correct. Whilst it is desirable to maintain your professional knowledge by keeping up to date with legal developments, this can have a negative effect on your revision. Students then ask, 'what should I answer if this question comes up in the exam?' The answer to that question is that you answer according to the Manual regardless of whether it is right or wrong. This confusion can be avoided if the PNLD is used occasionally as a reference tool and not as a major part of revision.

On that last point, students are often concerned about changes in the law where the Manual is inconsistent with those changes. This is also a concern for the examiners who construct the examination. If the examiners are aware of a contradiction in the law, it is unlikely that a multiple-choice question relating to that law will be set in the NIE, in order to avoid confusion. However, there is always the possibility that such questions may inadvertently be set (as has occurred in several OSPRE® examinations) and hence my advice as above.

3. Do not answer multiple-choice questions ONLY

I have known several students who have told me that their learning style meant that answering multiple-choice questions was the way they preferred to learn and that they had never looked at the Manual. One student (who used this method) came out of the NIE and told me that she had ticked every question she had guessed; she had 65 ticks and failed the examination. I think that makes my point.

In conclusion, if the student has a revision method or pattern that they find works for them then my advice is simple; use it. Every student is different and will learn in a different way and at a different pace. One fact I am sure of is that 99.9% of students get the result their efforts deserve; students must revise to succeed.

Taking the NIE

In order to pass the NIE, students will have to spend many hours revising to expand their knowledge of the law. This preparation for the examination is an absolute necessity; without it students invite failure. I am sure any hard work will not be wasted but in order to maximise the benefit of any revision students carry out, they should also know *how* that knowledge will be tested.

Students need to understand exactly what they will be doing when they sit the examination. This is a small but nevertheless vitally important part of preparation. Becoming familiar with the technicalities of a multiple-choice question (MCQ) examination is part of a professional and ordered approach to the task; in addition, it will increase the student's confidence regarding the examination.

The aim is for students to sit down at the time of the examination knowing what their target is and how they will achieve it. The only unknown factor should be the precise content of the examination; everything else should be recognisable to the student. This chapter will deal with the examination format so that the process should not catch students unaware.

Do not underestimate the danger of ignoring this part of preparation as in doing so students run the risk of panic setting in at the beginning of or during the examination. This could have a devastating effect on performance. I am not trying to train students as examination writers, but I believe just a little time invested in this task will serve students well. I know very few people who have no nerves before sitting such an examination; students can reduce those nerves and therefore improve performance by becoming accustomed to the MCQ examination format.

The standard MCQ style

Before we look at differing styles of MCQs, students need to familiarise themselves with some terms relating to the subject that they may be unfamiliar with. This section is only for information.

Look at the question below:

You have arranged that WILSON, a suspect for robbery, will attend your station along with his solicitor. WILSON arrives with his solicitor and you arrest him for the offence. After the custody officer has completed the custody record and before you interview WILSON, his solicitor presents a pre-prepared statement written by WILSON that relates to the robbery. WILSON's solicitor suggests that his client does not need to be interviewed by the police as the statement represents all his client is willing to say.	STEM
As the interviewing officer, what action will you take?	LEAD-IN
A Inform the solicitor that any statement made by WILSON to the solicitor is subject to legal privilege and as a result it cannot be introduced to the investigation. B Point out to the solicitor that the contents of the statement will be considered but that the decision to interview rests with the police. C Confirm that the statement represents all WILSON wants to say. If that is the case then he may not be questioned about the robbery unless it is to clear up any ambiguity. D WILSON and his solicitor should sign and date the statement. You should seize the statement and treat it as if it were a 'written statement under caution' by the defendant.	OPTIONS

The terms used on the highlighted side of the table are the only technical MCQ terms used in this chapter.

Individual forces should provide students with a booklet entitled the 'Guide to the National Investigators' Examination' that explains the rules and syllabus of the examination. There is a great deal of important information contained in the guide. For now, I want to concentrate on the style of the questions in the NIE. The guide illustrates a typical example of the style of MCQ that students will face when they take the examination. Below is a further example:

BREEN plans an armed robbery on a security van that regularly picks up cash at a local bank. He enlists the help of FISH and TODD who agree to actually carry out the armed robbery while BREEN waits for them at a rendezvous point. BREEN has no intention of taking part in the commission of the armed robbery itself.

> Unknown to BREEN, the security company has been 'tipped off' about the rob-
> bery and changes the day of collection so that the security van does not arrive
> at the bank. FISH and TODD leave empty handed.
>
> Does BREEN commit Statutory Conspiracy contrary to s. 1 Criminal Law Act
> 1977?
>
> A No, BREEN has no intention of taking part in the actual armed robbery itself.
> B Yes, BREEN commits the offence as soon as he plans the robbery and before
> he enlists the help of FISH and TODD.
> C No, the commission of the offence is impossible because the security van
> would never arrive at the bank.
> D Yes, BREEN has agreed on a course of conduct that will involve the commis-
> sion of an offence.

The correct answer is **D**. BREEN does not have to take part in the offence to be guilty of conspiracy as he has agreed on a course of conduct that will involve the commission of an offence by one or more parties to the agreement, making answer A incorrect. Answer B is incorrect as at this stage BREEN is only planning the offence and is the only person involved; you need at least two parties to commit statutory conspiracy. Answer C is incorrect as you can conspire to commit the impossible under s. 1(1)(b) of the Criminal Law Act 1977.

Although this is the typical style of examination question, there are some MCQs that do not conform to the above archetypal layout. These different MCQs are responsible for one of the most common misconceptions about the NIE and indeed any type of OSPRE® examination; that the question style is complex and detailed. This is not the case. The content might be somewhat difficult and that is reasonable; after all, students would not expect the examination to be easy. However, the style of question students will face in the NIE is *exactly* as the two examples I have just given. In other words, a 'stem' giving you the facts of the question, the 'lead-in' directing you to the area of law to be tested and finally four clear 'options' that are viable alternative solutions to the problem.

MCQ styles that are not used in the NIE

There are a number of valid ways of compiling MCQs. Some of them are excluded from the standard best practice for question setting in the NIE.

MCQs where the answer options are effectively presented in two stages (as in the PARKER example below) are generally excluded and students will not come across this style of question in the NIE.

This type of question can be presented in a way that does fall within the NIE style. An example of the two-stage approach and how that question could be amended to fit within the NIE style is in the AGNEW example below.

PARKER breaks into a warehouse intending to steal anything of value that he can find. He forces a door and gets into the warehouse but finds nothing during his search. Frustrated at his lack of success, PARKER damages a toilet inside the warehouse before he leaves.

What offences does PARKER commit?
(i) Burglary contrary to s. 9(1)(a) Theft Act 1968.
(ii) Burglary contrary to s. 9(1)(b) Theft Act 1968.
(iii) Attempted theft contrary to s. 1 Criminal Attempts Act 1981.
(iv) Criminal damage contrary to s. 1(1) Criminal Damage Act 1971.

A (i), (ii) and (iv) only.
B (ii) and (iii) only.
C (i) and (iv) only.
D (ii), (iii) and (iv) only.

MCQs using roman numerals as options are not contained in the examination. They unnecessarily complicate matters and are very confusing for the student. Not only does this type of MCQ test students' knowledge of the law but also it tests their ability to select the correct option. Mistakes are easily made when students are under pressure and it is possible that the correct answer is known but the wrong option is picked because of the complicated layout of the question. Students will be relieved to know that this style of question is out of favour with NIE examiners. In case you were wondering, the answer to the above question is C.

Also removed from the examination are questions that follow the style below:

In which, if either, of the following cases has an offence of 'Obstruct Police' contrary to s. 89, Police Act 1996, been committed?

(i) STEVENS is caught in a speed trap. After he is given a speeding ticket he doubles back and drives 200 metres away from the speed trap. He holds out a homemade sign that states, 'All drivers slow down—Police speed trap ahead!'

> (ii) INGLETON is stopped by PC CONNOLLY who believes INGLETON may have seen the direction that an armed robber has run off in. INGLETON refuses to answer any of the questions put to him by the officer.
>
> A (i) only.
> B (ii) only.
> C Both.
> D Neither.

Once more, a complicated type of question because it effectively asks the student to answer two questions at once and again, I can state that this style of question will not be in the examination. The answer to this question is A.

What students *may* see in the examination is a version of the last style of question, an example of which is below (I have put the (i), (ii), 'Both' and 'Neither' options by the side to illustrate my point:

> AGNEW and CLARKE decide to break into a house. AGNEW is in possession of a screwdriver to force the window and CLARKE is in possession of a knuckle-duster just in case the occupier causes any trouble. CLARKE knows about the screwdriver but AGNEW has no idea that CLARKE has a knuckle-duster with him. The two men break into the house but are arrested while inside searching for property.
>
> Who, if anyone, is guilty of aggravated burglary?
> A AGNEW alone commits aggravated burglary. ((i) only)
> B CLARKE alone commits aggravated burglary. ((ii) only)
> C CLARKE and AGNEW commit the offence. (Both)
> D Neither AGNEW nor CLARKE commits aggravated burglary. (Neither)

The answer to this question is B.

Questions with longer sets of facts take longer to process

The next point I want to make relates to the length of the MCQ. This is important as it links to a central element of the examination-time.

It is plain that not all MCQs will be of exactly the same length. The unwritten rule is that the MCQ should not be more than 250 words long. There is no lower limit but to test a student's knowledge and so that the question makes sense and is written following the correct style, it is unlikely that the MCQ will be less than

50 words long. For example the six questions in this chapter range from 103 to 210 words long, with an average of 144 words per question.

So why is this relevant? It is relevant because students have to know how long it takes to read a question, consider the facts, come to a conclusion and mark their answer on the question paper. Students have 120 minutes to complete the 80-question NIE, that's an average of 90 seconds per question. It might not sound a long time but it is. The time it takes to consider the facts and come to a decision is what many students worry about but the main factor affecting how long it takes to answer a question is a student's reading of time.

It is important not to worry if it is taking a little longer than 90 seconds to answer each question, as it is likely that students will be able to make up for lost time as the examination progresses. A strict 90 seconds per question approach will probably work against students rather than for them as answering questions is not an exact science. Some questions will be easy, others will not. However, regardless of the difficulty of the question, the one factor that will impact on time is the length of the MCQ.

Examine the question below and time how long it takes to answer it:

The Crime and Disorder Act 1998 took existing offences and then set out circumstances under which those offences would be deemed to be 'aggravated'.

Which of the offences below is covered by that legislation?
A Riot, contrary to s. 1, Public Order Act 1986.
B Violent Disorder, contrary to s. 2, Public Order Act 1986.
C Affray, contrary to s. 3, Public Order Act 1986.
D Fear or provocation of violence, contrary to s. 4, Public Order Act 1986.

This question has 76 words in it. You, like many other students, will have started to consider the answer as you were reading through the MCQ, but how long did it take you to actually deal with the question in its entirety? The following table shows the results from a sample of 10 police officers:

Allocated time per question	=	90 seconds
Read time (how long it took just to read the MCQ)	=	15 seconds
Consideration of question and marking the answer	=	21 seconds
Total time to answer question	=	36 second
Spare time (to make up for previous/carry on to next MCQ)	=	54 seconds

It is important to bear in mind that these are averages and you may have taken more time or maybe even less to answer this question. The point is that this length of question gives you one of two things; the chance to catch up on your time if you are behind your average of 90 seconds per question schedule or alternatively the chance to bank time for when you meet the more lengthy and complex MCQs. The answer to the question is D.

Now examine the question below and time how long it takes you to answer it:

LONSDALE is a volunteer worker. He visits the homes of senior citizens in his area and carries out a variety of maintenance work on their houses; he does not charge anyone for the work he carries out. KELLY, a 35-year-old, is not very good at 'Do-It-Yourself' and so contacts LONSDALE. KELLY lies to LONSDALE and tells him that her 85-year-old grandmother needs some work doing on her roof and gives LONSDALE her own home address. KELLY lives alone and would not be entitled to LONSDALE's help unless she was over 65. LONSDALE visits KELLY's house and carries out the work for no charge.

Has KELLY committed the offence of obtaining services by deception (contrary to s. 1 Theft Act 1978)?

A Yes, as the deception used by KELLY has caused LONSDALE to provide services that KELLY would not normally be entitled to.

B No, it is not an offence for KELLY, by deception, to cause LONSDALE to provide services without charge.

C Yes, the fact that LONSDALE provides the services free of charge is immaterial and KELLY would be guilty of the offence in these circumstances.

D No, the offence of obtaining services by deception can never be committed where there is no economic loss to the victim.

This question contains 210 words. Let us examine how our 10 police officers fared with the question:

Allocated time per question	=	90 seconds
Read time (how long it took just to read the MCQ)	=	53 seconds
Consideration of question and marking the answer	=	23 seconds
Total time to answer question	=	76 seconds
Spare time (to make up for previous/carry on to next MCQ)	=	14 seconds

Our 10 candidates managed to complete the question in less than 90 seconds but this may not be the case under examination conditions. There is always that question that takes longer than average, either because it is complicated or perhaps because you find it difficult. You must be prepared for this to happen and do not panic if you spend longer than 90 seconds on a particular question. Do not let this play on your mind during the examination. Deal with the question and move on. It may be worth taking a more measured approach to reading the question so ensuring that you do not have to repeatedly read through the elements of it in order to make sense of the answer options. This question is part of the section on deception and a full answer is included in the relevant answers section.

Binary questions

Answer the question below:

> RICARDO's wife is chronically ill and is in considerable and relentless pain. She continually begs RICARDO to kill her and end her suffering. This continues for several months. One evening after enduring her pleas, RICARDO eventually decides that he will kill his wife. He waits until she falls asleep and then calmly strangles her. At no stage did RICARDO ever lose control of his behaviour.
>
> Would RICARDO be able to rely on the defence supplied by s. 3 of the Homicide Act 1957?
>
> A Yes, if the prolonged behaviour by his wife could be shown to have affected his judgement.
> B No, as there is no loss of control by RICARDO.
> C Yes, if the jury decides that a reasonable person might have acted as RICARDO did under the same circumstances.
> D No, as the defence is only available when the defendant panics or acts out of fear.

Normally, the standard MCQ asks one question of a candidate, i.e. which of the four options below is correct? I call this style of question the 'binary question' because it is one question that is a combination of two questions:
1. Do you know what s. 3 of the Homicide Act is?
2. If you do, which of the options below is correct?

This style of MCQ is still acceptable and *may* be included in your examination. If you find yourself dealing with such a question and you know that you do not know what s. 3 of the Homicide Act 1957 is, what can you do? The only option is to synthesise an answer using the information contained in the stem, the lead-in and the options. For example:

The stem tells you that RICARDO has killed his wife, therefore the question probably relates to either manslaughter or murder.

The lead-in talks about a defence. Your Manual deals with three defences—diminished responsibility, provocation and suicide pact—it is not the latter.

The options talk about prolonged behaviour, loss of control, the reasonable person and panic and fear. These are unlikely to be associated with diminished responsibility.

Therefore, s. 3 of the Homicide Act 1957 must be the defence of provocation.

Of course, if you did not know the three defences to murder then you would have found this question all the more difficult. Even if you did know them, then you would have to know more about the section to accurately answer the question. However, working out the subject matter from the question content might help you eliminate one or even two of the options and therefore give you a better chance of obtaining a correct answer. The answer to this question is B.

Having considered the question styles that will and will not present themselves to the student taking the NIE, we should turn to some other important issues to consider with regard to the examination.

Verification questions

The NIE contains 80 MCQs but students are only marked from 70; the remaining 10 MCQs are verification questions. Verification questions are placed into the examination randomly, i.e. not all 10 are placed at the beginning, middle or end of the examination. It is necessary to test verification questions in order to access their suitability for future examinations. The fact that these questions are not marked may tempt students to guess which questions within the NIE are the verification questions and pay less attention to them as a result. I would advise against this course of action. As the verification questions are placed randomly in the examination it is very difficult to accurately decide whether a question is a verification question or not. If a student guesses incorrectly then they may lose a mark from a question that counts towards the result and this must be discouraged. It is a far better policy to treat every single question as a question that counts rather than guessing if it is a verification question.

Pass mark

The pass mark for the NIE has been set at 49%. However, this mark is unattainable due to the fact that only 70 questions from the 80 that students answer are marked (see 'verification questions' above). The actual pass park for the exam is 48.57%. This means that a student can pass the examination if they answer 34 of the 70 marked questions correctly. It is important to know what is required to pass the examination as this gives the student a target to aim for. The actual target to *guarantee* a pass is to get 44 questions right out of 80. Getting 44 questions right would mean that a student would pass the NIE even if they had answered all 10 of the verification questions correctly within those 44 correct answers (44/80 – 10 = 34 = 48.54% = Pass). Research[3] shows that the average student loses 5 questions to the verification process so it is vital that students do not rely on luck to get them through the NIE. The further away from the target of 44 correct questions the student is, the greater the chance of failure.

Begin immediately

When the examiner informs you that you may be begin, *do not* read through all the questions before you start the examination. Start answering the questions straight away. Reading through questions is suitable for essay type examinations but any student taking this course of action in the NIE will squander a large proportion of the examination time. Apart from wasting time, it will be no benefit to the student, as, by the time they have read question 80, they will most certainly have forgotten question 1. I know of two occasions when this approach has been taken and both resulted in failure for the student involved.

Do not change your answers

Research[4] has shown that more students change correct answers to incorrect answers than incorrect answers to correct answers. In other words, a student's first answer is often correct. Unless the student is checking their answers and realises they have made an error or misunderstood the question, it is better to stick with the original answer.

---

[3] Carried out on 284 NIE students taking an 80-question 'mock' examination between 2003 and 2006.

[4] Carried out on 284 NIE students taking an 80-question 'mock' examination between 2003 and 2006.

Do not miss questions out

During the NIE it is almost inevitable that the student will come across a question that causes them some difficulty. This will probably be because the question is complicated and/or the student has some knowledge, but not quite enough, to answer the question. A student may invest 90+ seconds trying to answer this question before deciding to leave it to the end of the examination. Invariably, the student will mark the question paper next to the question but will not mark an answer on the answer sheet. I would advise that the student *should* answer the question, even if it is their best guess. This is because, when the student returns to the question at the end of the examination, they will still have to read the question again to familiarise themselves with the circumstances. This eats into any time the student has to check their answer paper. If the student runs out of time then at least there is a mark against that question rather than a blank space that will receive no mark. The other danger of leaving a gap in the answer paper is that such an action can accidentally lead to the student filling in the wrong answer boxes to a question. This is an easy mistake to make when answering MCQs and can lead to failure purely because of the student's error.

Do not be an 'administration failure'

Perhaps the worst reason for failing the exam is making some type of error that could have easily been avoided. The student has prepared for the NIE by investing time and effort in their revision only to ruin their chances of success by a lack of consideration of the very basic detail surrounding the examination. There are several possible ways that students can become what I term 'administration failures'; some thought should be given to the factors below to ensure that you do not fall into this category.

1. Do you know the venue for your examination?

Find out where your examination is going to be held and make sure that you are aware how you will get there, i.e. your route and mode of transport.

2. Give yourself plenty of time to get to the examination venue

Regardless of whether you are familiar with the venue for the examination or not, you should ensure that you will arrive in plenty of time. The NIE is held at various test centres across the country and you will be told that you *must* be at the test centre 30 minutes before the examination begins. You will be allowed into the examination room 15 minutes before the NIE begins and you cannot afford to be late. The examination invigilators are under strict instructions that students arriving after this time will not be allowed into the examination room. If necessary, carry out a 'dry run' to the venue at the same time as you will need to on the day of the examination. Whatever time it takes to get to the venue, I suggest you add an hour to it and you have your start time. The last thing that a student needs is to be refused access because they are late. Even if the student arrives close to the cut-off time because of traffic congestion they will be flustered and not in the best frame of mind to sit the examination. It is far better to be at the venue early and relaxed.

3. *Take and use a 6" ruler in the examination*

As you answer each question, place the ruler underneath the A, B, C and D box that relates to that question. This will prevent you from accidentally placing your answer against the wrong question number. It will not add any significant time to the time it takes to answer the questions.

> I am a strong believer in luck and I find the harder I work the more I have of it.
>
> Benjamin Franklin (1706–90)

The 10-Week Revision Programme

I created this programme in June 2005 for a student who had failed their first attempt at the National Investigators' Examination (scoring 28.6% in the process). The student was extremely upset and naturally concerned that a second failure would mean removal from the CID[1] and that her previous efforts had gone unrewarded. Unlike some trainers and supervisors, I have always been aware of the pressure that this examination brings, but this student's predicament highlighted the fact that the stakes in the NIE can be high and that failure and, ultimately, removal from the ICIDP has the potential to be extremely damaging to the student concerned. This is particularly true when the student genuinely wants to pass and is willing to work but simply does not know how to go about it.

When I questioned the student, the reason for this failure became obvious to me. Although the student had done some revision (although not enough in my opinion) it had been carried out in a very haphazard fashion. This factor was far more to blame for the student's failure than the lack of revision. The student was flitting from one subject to the next using no apparent logical methodology in the process. The student lacked one of the central elements required for success in any examination:

An Ordered Approach

An ordered approach to revision is essential from the outset. That order is obtained by being able to answer three questions:
 (i) What do I need to revise for this examination (what is the syllabus)?
 (ii) How much time (in total) do I have to revise it?
 (iii) How will I organise (i) and (ii)?

---

[1] Depending on your force policy, you will be allowed either two or three attempts to pass the National Investigators' Examination. Failure at attempt two or three ordinarily means that you will be removed from the ICIDP and consequently you will be removed from your post.

Many students, not only the 28.6% failure mentioned above, have a disordered approach because they do not have an answer to question (iii). This has a negative effect on revision and damages morale, both of which can be fatal or at least damaging to their result. I realised that I was going to have to provide my student with an answer to question (iii) because they could not find it themselves and would inevitably fail again. My aim therefore, was to provide a revision programme that ensured my student revised the whole syllabus in time for their next examination and would present them with an improved chance of success. I achieved that aim. My student passed on their second attempt with a mark of 78.5%. The student later told me that they had increased the amount of revision carried out (something else I told them to do) but had benefited immensely from the programme I had created as it provided an ordered framework into which the student's revision efforts were placed.

I decided that rather than wait for future students to fail before the programme was made available, I would provide it to them at the outset, *when it is most required*. The programme was provided to West Midland's officers in December 2005 (sitting the NIE in March 2006) and proved to be a great success. It has since been provided to West Midland's and Essex officers sitting the June and September 2006 NIE. Since December 2005, over 200 officers have field-tested the programme and I have yet to receive any negative feedback about it.

I am not saying that you must use this programme or that it guarantees success (any such claim would be unwarranted). What I am asking you to consider is that over 200 of your peers have found it extremely beneficial and, based on that fact, you might consider if it could be of use to you. Alternatively, if you have a method that works for you, stick with it; do not change just for the sake of change.

Should you choose to follow this programme, please remember the following points:

- You will probably need a larger version of the Revision Log. If you do, you can create your own in a variety of ways (enlarging and photocopying the example given, using MSWord or Excel to create your own log or even just using lined paper with columns drawn in).
- The programme targets 120 hours revision because my research suggests that this is an optimum revision period for the average NIE student (see 'Revising for the NIE').
- Just because the programme starts approximately 11 weeks before the examination does not mean that you should leave your revision until the start date—you can begin revising at any time and the sooner the better!

- Once you start the programme, stick with it. You must follow my instructions and do not worry whether or not my methodology works—it does.
- Be disciplined in your approach and keep an accurate record of your revision time.

Following the Programme—Week 1 Example

In the first week of the programme you are set revision from pages 3 to 17 from the Property section of the Investigators' Manual.

**For the whole week do nothing else but study
the material contained in these pages!**

The subjects covered are theft, burglary and aggravated burglary. All of these subjects have corresponding sections in the Investigators' Workbook.

1. Begin your revision by answering the multiple-choice questions on 'Theft' contained in the Workbook (it does not matter if you have no knowledge whatsoever of the subject you are being tested on—your best guess will be fine).
2. When you have answered the multiple-choice questions read the section on 'Theft' contained in the Manual (once only).
3. After you have read the 'Theft' section in the Manual, complete the Workbook section on 'Theft'.
   *To get the most out of the Workbook you **must** try to complete any written exercises you are asked to. If you do not know the answer to a question, do not worry as all of the exercises have an explanation. Do not fall into the trap of telling yourself, 'I know that' when you do not and then not bother writing anything down in the space provided. Practising self-deception with regard to the level of your knowledge might make you feel secure when you are reading the Workbook but it will not help you to learn. Being honest with yourself about your own knowledge level will be far more beneficial in terms of passing the NIE.*
4. Attempt the 'Recall Questions' at the end of the 'Theft' section.
5. When you are satisfied with your answers, return to the Manual and read the section on 'Theft' for the second time.
6. When you have finished reading the 'Theft' section for the second time, return to the Workbook and make your second attempt at the multiple-choice questions. When you have finished, check your answers.

After checking your answers, you should attempt the multiple-choice questions on the subject you are revising in this Q&A, e.g. answer the questions on theft.

Be prepared to perform badly at first but do not give up because of this perform-ance; it is quite normal. Your knowledge and ability will steadily increase as you move through the stages and if you follow the above instructions I am confident that you will finish the process with a good level of knowledge. Remember that this process will provide you with a good *foundation* of knowledge but in order to maintain that level you should briefly revisit the subject from time to time.

Repeat these steps with burglary and aggravated burglary.

Follow the same process each week

You will see that some weeks demand that you cover far more material than in others. This is intentional as the programme aims to make your knowledge base stronger in the three areas of Property Offences, Assaults and Defences and Sexual Offences than in Evidence. Evidence is by no means ignored (three weeks' revision) but my analysis of the NIE since June 2004 shows that a stronger knowledge of Property Offences, Assaults and Defences and Sexual Offences will provide you with a greater chance of success.

The Manual contains subjects with no corresponding section in the Workbook. For these sections you should use the multiple-choice questions from this Q&A to check your knowledge of the subjects.

Answer Questions—Read Manual Material—Answer Questions (2nd attempt)

If you cannot find any questions on the subject:

Read It—Read It Again—Read It Again

You only finish when the week actually ends, not when you have done everything once. If you have completed all of the questions you can find, finished all of the exercises and questions in the workbook, answered all of the questions in this Q&A and obviously know the subject backwards, fine. Read it again and again and again, no matter how boring you think it is or how well you think you know it!

Take a Break

Half-way through the revision programme I have included a one-week break from revision (more if you are taking the NIE in March 2007). Take it and do not revise during this time. If you ceaselessly push yourself from the moment you obtain your Investigators' Manual you are in danger of 'burning out' before you actually sit your examination. Taking the examination in this condition is highly likely to result in failure. Imagine you are in a gym lifting a weight with your arm. You will lift it so many times before you stop and rest, but after the rest you can complete more repetitions of the exercise. If you do not stop lifting the weight and keep pushing, you will end up injured and unable to move your arm and unable to complete the exercise. Your mind is exactly the same. Give your mind a total break from the difficult exercises you are asking it to complete on a daily basis and when you return to your revision you will do so refreshed and better able to deal with the final push to the examination.

Keeping Track

Each day you should enter the amount of time you have revised for in your Revision Log. This includes '0' minutes when you have not managed to study.

The log does not demand that you slavishly adhere to completing 90 minutes a day, every day, but exists so that you can see where you are in terms of hitting your 120 hour target and how far ahead or behind schedule you are. Some days you will pass the target, some days you will not, but the log will not lie about your commitment to revision. By regularly filling the log in and being honest about the amount of time you have spent revising, you can create internal pressure on yourself to get ahead or catch up. I recommend that you put this somewhere in your home where you will see it every day, do not put it inside a cupboard so you can hide away from your lack of revision. If you are married, have a partner, have children, place it somewhere where they can see it and get them to remind you of how you are doing to create external pressure. Getting ahead of schedule allows you to pick a day or days off when you will be too busy to study because of work or social commitments.

If you reach your 120 hours target before the last day of the revision programme, well done BUT DON'T STOP. The finishing post is passed when you sit down to take your examination, not when you have completed 120 hours revision.

Revision Programme

Your revision programme start date depends on when you are sitting the NIE.

March 2007 NIE	Start Date = 11th December 2006
June 2007 NIE	Start Date = 19th March 2007
September 2007 NIE	Start Date = 18th June 2007
November 2007 NIE	Start Date = 10th September 2007

Those of you who are taking the NIE in March 2007 will notice that the revision programme starts earlier than you might expect. This is because I have built in a

2006 Christmas revision break. Of course, if you want to revise over Christmas you may, but I consider this to be not only difficult but also unpleasant and wonder if you will actually accomplish much in this time. The choice is yours. As a result of the additional Christmas break, weeks 2 and 3 are shorter but ask more of you in terms of minutes revised in order to catch up. As March 2007 candidates have a different programme I have had to set their schedule out separately.

March 2007 NIE

Week	Start	Finish
1	11/12/06	17/12/06
2	18/12/06	23/12/06
Break	24/12/06	01/01/07
3	02/01/07	07/01/07
4	08/01/07	14/01/07
5	15/01/07	21/01/07
Break	22/01/07	28/01/07
6	29/01/07	04/02/07
7	05/02/07	11/02/07
8	12/02/07	18/02/07
9	19/02/07	25/02/07
10	26/02/07	04/03/07

June, September and November 2007 NIE

Week	June 2007 NIE		September 2007 NIE		November 2007 NIE	
	Start	Finish	Start	Finish	Start	Finish
1	19/03/07	25/03/07	18/06/07	24/06/07	10/09/07	16/09/07
2	26/03/07	01/04/07	25/06/07	01/07/07	17/09/07	23/09/07
3	02/04/07	08/04/07	02/07/07	08/07/07	24/09/07	30/09/07
4	09/04/07	15/04/07	09/07/07	15/07/07	01/10/07	07/10/07
5	16/04/07	22/04/07	16/07/07	22/07/07	08/10/07	14/10/07
Break	23/04/07	29/04/07	23/07/07	29/07/07	15/10/07	21/10/07
6	30/04/07	06/05/07	30/07/07	05/08/07	22/10/07	28/10/07
7	07/05/07	13/05/07	06/08/07	12/08/07	29/10/07	04/11/07
8	14/05/07	20/05/07	13/08/07	19/08/07	05/11/07	11/11/07
9	21/05/07	27/05/07	20/08/07	26/08/07	12/11/07	18/11/07
10	28/05/07	03/06/07	27/08/07	02/09/08	19/11/07	25/11/07

Now that you have your start date and know your overall schedule, you should address the issue of what exactly you will have to cover as each week passes.

Week 1

Property

Paragraph 1.1.1 up to and including paragraph 1.3.1

Week 2

Property

Paragraph 1.4 up to and including paragraph 1.11.1

Week 3

Assaults, Drugs, Firearms and Defences

Paragraph 2.1.1 up to and including paragraph 2.7.4.1

Week 4

Assaults, Drugs, Firearms and Defences

Paragraph 2.8 up to and including paragraph 2.12.11

Week 5

Sexual Offences

The whole section

Week 6

Evidence

Paragraph 4.1 up to and including paragraph 4.4.16.4

Week 7

Evidence

Paragraph 4.5.1 up to and including paragraph 4.6.12.2

Week 8

Evidence

Paragraph 4.7.1 up to and including paragraph 4.13.10

Week 9

Property

The whole section (again)

Week 10

Multiple-Choice Questions

In week 10 you should attempt to answer every question in the Workbook and every question in this Q&A. If you have access to questions from an independent source, you should attempt these as well. In this final week you are going over *ALL* of your knowledge in the same way that you will be tested in your examination. Please make sure that all the questions you answer are written in the correct format (see the chapter on 'Taking the NIE').

Revision Log (Time)

The last part of the Revision Programme is your daily log. You *MUST* ensure that this is filled in every day, regardless of the fact that you may not have completed any revision (for those days enter '0' minutes). The whole idea is that you can see how on or off target you are with your revision and make sure that you are not falling behind, or racing too far ahead.

I have set you an overall target of 120 hours revision. In the main, this is split into 90 minute daily targets until the final 10 days where I have increased your minimum daily target to 3 hours a day (you *should* be increasing at this stage of your revision to 'peak' for the examination). Please don't worry if you are not hitting 90 minutes each day; try to make up for it by hitting your weekly target instead.

March 2007 NIE Candidates

Your Revision Planner is different as I have programmed in two breaks. This is catered for by an increase in the amount of minutes you will have to revise in weeks two and three. You should then be back on target to finish 120 hours by the 4th of March 2007.

June, September and November NIE Candidates

Your Revision Planner is simpler as it only has one break.

All schedules will finish one day before the examination. It is your decision as to what to do with that day. My personal advice would be to revise whatever you want and try to put the books down at a reasonable time and attempt to get a good night's sleep (easier said than done).

Start Date	
My 'Total Revision Target' is:	7200 minutes (120 hrs)
My 'Daily Target' is:	90 minutes (1 hr 30 mins) (Week 10 = 3 hrs +)
My 'Weekly Target':	630 minutes (10 hrs 30 mins) (Week 10 = 21 hrs +)
The latest I will complete my revision by is:	

March 2007 NIE Planner

Date	Revision Schedule (Mins)	'Today I revised for'	My Running Total	+ or −
11/12/06	90			
12/12/06	180			
13/12/06	270			
14/12/06	360			
15/12/06	450			
16/12/06	540			
17/12/06	630			
18/12/06	730 (100 mins)			
19/12/06	830 (100 mins)			
20/12/06	930 (100 mins)			
21/12/06	1030 (100 mins)			
22/12/06	1130 (100 mins)			
23/12/06	1170 (140 mins)			
24/12/06				
25/12/06				
26/12/06				
27/12/06				
28/12/06				
29/12/06				

Date	Revision Schedule (Mins)	'Today I revised for'	My Running Total	+ or −
30/12/06				
31/12/06				
01/01/07				
02/01/07	1290 (120 mins)			
03/01/07	1410 (120 mins)			
04/01/07	1530 (120 mins)			
05/01/07	1650 (120 mins)			
06/01/07	1770 (120 mins)			
07/01/07	1890 (120 mins)			
08/01/07	1980			
09/01/07	2070			
10/01/07	2160			
11/01/07	2250			
12/01/07	2340			
13/01/07	2430			
14/01/07	2520			
15/01/07	2610			
16/01/07	2700			
17/01/07	2790			
18/01/07	2880			
19/01/07	2970			
20/01/07	3060			
21/01/07	3150			
22/01/07				
23/01/07				
24/01/07				
25/01/07				
26/01/07				
27/01/07				
28/01/07				
29/01/07	3240			
30/01/07	3330			
31/01/07	3420			
01/02/07	3510			

Date	Revision Schedule (Mins)	'Today I revised for'	My Running Total	+ or −
02/02/07	3600			
03/02/07	3690			
04/02/07	3780			
05/02/07	3870			
06/02/07	3960			
07/02/07	4050			
08/02/07	4140			
09/02/07	4230			
10/02/07	4320			
11/02/07	4410			
12/02/07	4500			
13/02/07	4590			
14/02/07	4680			
15/02/07	4770			
16/02/07	4860			
17/02/07	4950			
18/02/07	5040			
19/02/07	5130			
20/02/07	5220			
21/02/07	5310			
22/02/07	5400			
23/02/07	5580			
24/02/07	5760			
25/02/07	5940			
26/02/07	6120			
27/02/07	6300			
28/02/07	6480			
01/03/07	6660			
02/03/07	6840			
03/03/07	7020			
04/03/07	7200			

June, September and November NIE Planner

Whatever your start date is, enter it on the first day and then fill in the rest of the date column.

Date	Revision Schedule	'Today I revised for'	My Running Total	+ or −
	90			
	180			
	270			
	360			
	450			
	540			
	630			
	720			
	810			
	900			
	990			
	1080			
	1170			
	1260			
	1350			
	1440			
	1530			
	1620			
	1710			
	1800			
	1890			
	1980			
	2070			
	2160			
	2250			
	2340			
	2430			
	2520			
	2610			
	2700			

Date	Revision Schedule	'Today I revised for'	My Running Total	+ or −
	2790			
	2880			
	2970			
	3060			
	3150			
	3240			
	3330			
	3420			
	3510			
	3600			
	3690			
	3780			
	3870			
	3960			
	4050			
	4140			
	4230			
	4320			
	4410			
	4500			
	4590			
	4680			
	4770			
	4860			
	4950			
	5040			

Date	Revision Schedule	'Today I revised for'	My Running Total	+ or −
	5130			
	5220			
	5310			
	5400			
	5580			
	5760			
	5940			
	6120			
	6300			
	6480			
	6660			
	6840			
	7020			
	7200			

This may seem like a lot of trouble to go to but accurately recording how much time you have revised will prove to be extremely beneficial to your examination preparation.

To summarise you need to:

- Adopt an ordered approach to your revision by understanding what you have to revise and how long you have to do the revision and then *organise* yourself to accomplish these tasks.
- Choose a revision method that works for you.
- Be meticulous in your revision.
- Show discipline and do not attempt self-deception; you will pay for it in the long run.

And remember, the only place that success comes before work is in a dictionary.

PART ONE

Property Offences

QUESTIONS

Question 1.1

BOYLAN and HAMILL are employed in a small shop and regularly chat to each other. During one such conversation, BOYLAN asks if HAMILL will help her with a problem. She tells HAMILL that over 12 months ago she lent £2,000 to IRONS, another shop employee and that since then IRONS has flatly refused to pay any part of the money back. BOYLAN offers HAMILL £200 to act on her behalf and recover the loan from IRONS. HAMILL tells BOYLAN not to worry and that he will somehow resolve the situation. After work, HAMILL goes to IRONS's home and breaks into and takes IRONS's car, worth £3,000, from the drive. He takes the car to BOYLAN's house and presents it to BOYLAN as payment of the loan.

With regard to s. 2 of the Theft Act 1968, which of the statements below is correct?

A HAMILL's actions would not be dishonest if he honestly believes that he has a right in law to deprive IRONS of the car on behalf of BOYLAN.

B HAMILL must have a reasonable belief that he has a right in law to act as he did. If this is not the case then he has acted dishonestly.

C Section 2 of the Theft Act 1968 only allows an individual to appropriate property on behalf of himself and not, as in this case, on behalf of a third person.

D HAMILL's behaviour is dishonest as it falls below the standards of reasonable and honest people.

Question 1.2

CANHAM is a committed anti-vivisectionist and is a long-standing member of the Animal Liberation Front. He breaks into a laboratory and releases a variety of animals used for testing medicines. CANHAM personally believes that freeing the animals from captivity is not dishonest but an ethically and morally correct and proper decision. He does realise that according to the ordinary standards of reasonable and honest people what he has done would be considered dishonest. As he leaves the laboratory he is caught and arrested. At his trial, CANHAM maintains that his behaviour was not 'dishonest'.

Considering the ruling in *R* v *Ghosh*, which of the statements below is correct?

A A jury must take into account the fact that CANHAM's behaviour has not been dishonest according to his own moral values and in such a situation he should be acquitted of the charge.

B The only test the jury will apply is whether CANHAM's actions were dishonest according to the standards of reasonable and honest people.

C In such a situation, if s. 2 of the Theft Act 1968 is not applicable or helpful, the decision regarding whether CANHAM was dishonest or not is a matter for the judge to decide.

D CANHAM's actions can still be dishonest as what he did will be tested against the standards of reasonable and honest people along with the fact that he knew his actions were dishonest by those standards.

Question 1.3

MILSOM is shopping in his local supermarket when he notices that a member of staff has left a price-labelling machine on a display stand. He thinks it will be funny to create new price labels for goods in the store and cause chaos as a result. MILSOM walks round the store placing new and cheaper price labels on a wide variety of goods. MILSOM's only intention is to create confusion, not to benefit him or any other customers in the supermarket.

Which of the statements below is correct with regard to MILSOM's actions?

A Although MILSOM swaps price labels, he is not assuming all the rights of the owner. To do this effectively, he must pay for the goods.

B MILSOM's actions fall short of a full appropriation. This can only be accomplished by a combination of label swapping and the removal of an item from the shelf.

C It does not matter what MILSOM's further intention is, his conduct would constitute an appropriation.

D In order for MILSOM to appropriate property, he must have a dishonest intention. As this is not present, he does not appropriate.

Question 1.4

PC TROTMAN starts an attachment to the CID. He is told to take over the workload of a colleague who has retired. A few days later, PC TROTMAN approaches you with numerous reports that have been recorded as thefts. He believes that several of these reports do not represent offences of theft, as there are some elements of the offence missing.

In which one of the reports below will you tell the officer that there has been an offence of theft?

A JOBLING was stopped in a stolen Mercedes. He had bought the car in good faith, paying a reasonable price for it but refused to hand it back to the original owner when he found out it was stolen.

B YU speaks little English. He shows ADEY, a taxi driver, a written address and gives him £10. The fare should be £9.50. ADEY indicates that this is not enough and takes a £50 note. YU permits him to do so.

C PIT was arrested for stealing a caravan. The caravan was never recovered by the police and was left in a lay-by while PIT was interviewed. When he was released and before the true owner recovered the caravan, PIT took the caravan again.

D RODWELL was stop searched and found in possession of a £1,000 gold ring stolen in a theft. RODWELL states that when he innocently found the ring he believed he would never find the true owner.

Question 1.5

EALES rents a house under a tenancy agreement from his local council. EALES is short of money and decides to sell off several items from the house to help him through his cash crisis.

At what stage, if at all, does EALES first commit an offence of theft?

A When he picks flowers from the front garden of the house to sell commercially at a car-boot sale.

B When he severs a large amount of topsoil to sell to his neighbour.

C When he removes a fireplace to sell at a nearby second-hand shop.

D As EALES is in possession of the land under a tenancy agreement, he cannot steal land, things forming part of the land or severed from it or fixtures or structures let are to be used with the land.

Question 1.6

LONGWORTH is a medical student with a keen interest in human anatomy. To satisfy her desire for experimentation she enters a university laboratory and takes a whole human body and several amputated and preserved body parts.

Which of the statements below is correct?

A LONGWORTH would be guilty of the theft of the human body and of the body parts.

B LONGWORTH would only be guilty of the theft of the human body.

C LONGWORTH would be guilty of the theft of the body parts.

D LONGWORTH would not be guilty of theft as human bodies and body parts are not property for the purposes of s. 4 of the Theft Act 1968.

Question 1.7

GRATTON is a registered charity collector and is collecting in a shopping precinct. WHITBREAD approaches GRATTON and places a £20 note into his collecting tin. Moments later, WHITBREAD realises that he will not have enough cash to buy a computer game and returns to speak with GRATTON. He asks GRATTON for the money back but GRATTON refuses. WHITBREAD grabs hold of the collecting tin, removes the £20 and gives the tin back to GRATTON.

For the purposes of s. 5 of the Theft Act 1968, has WHITBREAD taken property 'belonging to another'?

A No, for although the money is no longer in WHITBREAD's direct control, he still retains a proprietary right or interest in the property.

B Yes, where money is given to charity collectors it becomes the property of the charitable trustees at the moment it goes into the collecting tin.

C No, as GRATTON is only the representative of the charity, 'ownership' of the money would remain with WHITBREAD until it is officially handed to the relevant charitable trustees.

D Yes, because you can steal property belonging to yourself. The money may be WHITBREAD's but it 'belongs' to GRATTON.

Question 1.8

DENYER opens a garden centre specialising in water features. One large fountain has a sign next to it that says, 'Make a wish, all donations go to local charity'. After a couple of months the centre is having financial problems. DENYER decides to collect the coins in the fountain and place the cash into the company bank account instead of giving it to charity. DENYER intends to replace the charity funds if her business survives the difficult period.

Has DENYER committed the offence of theft?

A Yes, DENYER has received and retained money to use in a specific way. She has contravened this obligation and is guilty of theft.

B No, as DENYER intends to replace the money she cannot commit the offence of theft.

C Yes, but only if she is unable to repay the money to the nominated charity.

D No, ownership of the money has been transferred to DENYER who has a moral and not a legal obligation to pass the money onto a local charity.

Question 1.9

PAREKH is a wages clerk working at a small insurance company and calculates the wages of all the staff including his own. One day he is particularly busy and mistakenly adds £50 to his weekly wage. At the end of the week the additional money is paid into his bank account but PAREKH does not realise the extra payment was as a result of his error, thinking instead that it was payment for overtime he had worked. PAREKH's employer discovers the error and demands that PAREKH pay back the money; PAREKH refuses.

Considering s. 5 of the Theft Act 1968, does PAREKH commit theft?

A Yes, as PAREKH is under an obligation to return the money and an intention not to return it amounts to an intention to permanently deprive.

B No, an employee who is mistakenly credited with extra money in his/her bank account cannot be prosecuted for theft.

C Yes, in such circumstances an employee will be liable for stealing the extra money if he/she keeps it.

D No, as this section only applies where someone other than PAREKH has made a mistake.

Question 1.10

While visiting a council art gallery, POINTON removes a painting worth £30,000 from the premises. When he takes the painting, his intention is to return it provided the council make a £3,000 donation to a local charity. The incident receives a large amount of press coverage that causes POINTON to panic. He returns the picture to the gallery the next day.

Considering the offence of theft only, which of the statements below is correct?

A Although POINTON does not intend the gallery to permanently lose the painting, he treats the painting as if it were his own and therefore commits theft.

B This is not theft as there is no intention to permanently deprive the gallery of the painting at the time of the appropriation.

C POINTON commits theft as he may not be able to return the painting in the circumstances he imagines and this amounts to treating the painting as his own.

D Theft cannot be committed in these circumstances as at no stage does POINTON intend to permanently deprive the gallery of the picture.

Question 1.11

QUILTEY is walking his dog in a park when he finds £300 in £10 notes on the footpath. QUILTEY believes that the person to whom the money belongs cannot be discovered by taking reasonable steps and decides to keep the money. The money was lost by GILL 20 minutes before QUILTEY found it. GILL reported the loss at a police station near to the park where the money was lost.

Is s. 2 of the Theft Act 1968 applicable in these circumstances?

A Yes, because QUILTEY has not taken reasonable steps to discover the person to whom the property belongs.

B No, and as s. 2 is not applicable, the issue of whether QUILTEY was dishonest or not will have to be decided by reference to the ruling in *R v Ghosh*.

C Yes, as it is QUILTEY's belief that is important, not the fact that he did or did not go on to take reasonable steps to find the owner of the property.

D No, as QUILTEY does not appropriate the property in the belief that he has a right in law to deprive a person of it.

Question 1.12

BEST becomes friendly with BROOK. BROOK is in her 70s and of limited intelligence. Over a period of time, BEST persuades BROOK to provide him with cash from her bank account and after some 6 months, BROOK has given BEST £30,000. This is done with the consent of BROOK who has made an absolute gift of the money to BEST. BROOK's son finds out about BEST's activities and reports the matter to the police.

Considering the law with regard to 'appropriation', which of the statements below is correct?

A In a prosecution for theft it will be necessary to prove that the taking of the property was done without the owner's consent.

B BEST cannot appropriate property belonging to another because BROOK has made an absolute gift of the money to BEST.

C In these circumstances, it is immaterial whether the act of appropriation was done with BROOK's consent or authority.

D As BEST consented to the appropriation, BROOK does not commit the offence of theft.

Question 1.13

The term 'property' is defined under s. 4 of the Theft Act 1968.

Which of the following comments is correct with regard to that term?

A A person cannot steal land, or things forming part of land in any circumstances.

B A person's characteristics and their administrative data (such as a national insurance number) would constitute property.

C A trademark is 'property' and is capable of being stolen.

D Confidential information can be classed as property.

Question 1.14

The term 'belonging to another' is defined by s. 5 of the Theft Act 1968.

Which of the below statements is INCORRECT with regard to that term?

A Property can be 'stolen' from any person who has possession or control or a right or interest in that property.

B In determining whether a person has 'possession' of property, the period of possession can be finite (i.e. for a given number of hours, days, etc).

C It is not necessary to show who does own the property, only that it belongs to someone other than the defendant.

D In proving theft, you do not need to show that the property belonged to another at the time of the appropriation.

ANSWERS

Answer 1.1

Answer **A** — Section 2 of the Theft Act 1968 provides three instances where appropriation of property will not be regarded as dishonest. This question centres on s. 2(1)(a) which states appropriation will not be dishonest 'if he appropriates the property in the belief that he has in law the right to deprive the other of it, on behalf of himself or of a third person'. The belief of the defendant need only be honest and not reasonable, therefore answer B is incorrect. The appropriation can take place on behalf of a third person, making answer C incorrect. Answer D is incorrect as it relates to the ruling in *R* v *Ghosh* [1982] QB 1053 and although relevant to the issue of dishonesty, it does not form any part of s. 2 of the Act.

Investigators' Manual, paras 1.1.3, 1.1.4   **DV = 4**

Answer 1.2

Answer **D** — Plainly, A is incorrect; to attribute dishonesty on the basis of the moral beliefs of the defendant would be unsound. The test is whether, according to the ordinary standards of reasonable and honest people, what was done was dishonest and if it was, whether the defendant realised, making answer B incorrect. Answer C is incorrect as the jury makes the decision of whether the defendant was dishonest.

Investigators' Manual, para. 1.1.4   **DV = 4**

Answer 1.3

Answer **C** — Appropriation under s. 3 of the Theft Act 1968 is an assumption by a person of the rights of an owner and there is no requirement for a dishonest intention, making answer D incorrect. There have been a number of cases involving the swapping of price labels but after *R* v *Gomez* [1993] AC 442, the House of Lords concluded that the mere swapping of the price labels on goods amounted to an 'appropriation', this eliminates answers A and B. This was the case regardless of any further intentions of the defendant.

Investigators' Manual, para. 1.1.5   **DV = 5**

Answer 1.4

Answer **B** — Answer A is incorrect because although the buyer of the car 'appropriates' property, this has been done in good faith and for value and, as per s. 3(2) of the Theft Act 1968, this will not amount to theft. Answer D is incorrect as although an appropriation has taken place it is not accompanied by circumstances of dishonesty as per s. 2(1)(c) of the Theft Act 1968. Answer C is incorrect as although stolen property can be 'appropriated', the same property cannot be stolen again by the same thief (*R* v *Gomez* [1993] AC 442). The same stated case dealt with answer B. It is immaterial that the owner of the property permits or consents to an appropriation; it is still theft.

Investigators' Manual, paras 1.1.3, 1.1.5   **DV = 3.5**

Answer 1.5

Answer **C** — Under s. 4(2)(c) of the Theft Act 1968, a tenant can appropriate fixtures or structures let to be used with the land, i.e. the fireplace. This makes answer D incorrect. Answers A and B are incorrect as a tenant cannot steal things forming part of the land (the flowers) or the land itself (the topsoil) when he/she is in possession of the land.

Investigators' Manual, para. 1.1.6   **DV = 5**

Answer 1.6

Answer **C** — A person cannot steal a human body. Human bodies are not classed as property under the Theft Act 1968 (*Doodeward* v *Spence* (1908) 6 CLR 406) unless some work has been carried out on the body for preservation or for a scientific purpose. This makes answers A and B incorrect. This conclusion was reached in *R* v *Kelly* [1999] QB 621, where body parts taken from the Royal College of Surgeons were classed as stolen. This makes answer D incorrect.

Investigators' Manual, para. 1.1.7   **DV = 3**

Answer 1.7

Answer **B** — In *R* v *Dyke* [2002] Crim LR 153, it was stated that the moment money given by members of the public to charity collectors goes into the collecting tin, it becomes the property of the relevant charitable trustees. So once the money is in the tin, it no longer 'belongs' to WHITBREAD making options A and C incorrect. Option D is also incorrect because, whilst you can steal your own property, the money does not belong to WHITBREAD.

Investigators' Manual, para. 1.1.8 **DV = 7**

Answer 1.8

Answer **A** — Section 5(3) of the Theft Act 1968 states that when a person receives property from another and is under an obligation to deal with that property in a particular way, the property shall be regarded (as against him) as belonging to the other. An 'obligation' is a legal one not a moral one. This makes answer D incorrect. Section 6(2) of the Theft Act makes it clear that regardless of an intention to repay, a person parting with property under a condition as to its return that may not be possible commits theft, making answers B and C incorrect.

Investigators' Manual, para. 1.1.9 **DV = 3**

Answer 1.9

Answer **D** — This section only applies where someone other than the defendant has made a mistake. For that reason answers A and C are incorrect. Answer B is incorrect as s. 5(4) explicitly covers this scenario should the error come from someone other than the defendant. If that were the case then PAREKH would commit theft.

Investigators' Manual, para. 1.1.10 **DV = 2**

Answer 1.10

Answer **A** — If there is an intention to permanently deprive at the time of the appropriation then an offence of theft will be committed. The intention to permanently deprive is defined in s. 6(1) of the Theft Act 1968 and states that a person who appropriates property without meaning the other to permanently lose it has this intention if their intent is to treat the thing as their own regardless of the others rights. POINTON's intention to 'ransom' the painting (regardless of his motives) would be caught by this section, making answers B and D incorrect. Answer C is incorrect as it relates to s. 6(2) of the Theft Act 1968 where someone parts with property belonging to another under a condition as to its return which he may not be able to perform and does not relate to this scenario.

Investigators' Manual, para. 1.1.11 **DV = 4**

Answer 1.11

Answer **C** — Section 2 of the Theft Act relates to dishonesty, in particular what is *not* dishonest rather than what is. There are several circumstances where a defendant will not be dishonest and one of those (s. 2(1)(a)) is where the person appropriates property in the belief that he has a right in law to deprive the other of it. There are three other circumstances including (s. 2(1)(c)) if the person appropriates the property in the belief that the person to whom the property belongs cannot be discovered by taking reasonable steps. This makes answer D incorrect as a belief in the right in law is not the only time a person will/will not be dishonest. It also makes answer B incorrect as the ruling in *R v Ghosh* is only used when s. 2 is not applicable or helpful and s. 2(1)(c) clearly relates to the circumstances of this question. Answer A is incorrect as it is the defendants *belief* at the time of the appropriation that is important, not that the defendant went on to take reasonable steps to discover the person to whom the property belongs.

Investigators' Manual, paras 1.1.3, 1.1.4   **DV = 6**

Answer 1.12

Answer **C** — In a prosecution for theft it is unnecessary to prove that the taking was without the owner's consent (*Lawrence v Metropolitan Police Commissioner* [1972] AC 626), making answer A incorrect. It is immaterial whether the act of appropriation was done with the owner's consent or authority (*R v Gomez* [1993] AC 442), making answer D incorrect. In *R v Hinks* [2000] 3 WLR, the court held that even though the complainant had made an absolute gift of property, retaining no proprietary interest in the property or any right to resume or recover it, an appropriation can still take place. This makes answer B incorrect.

Investigators' Manual, para. 1.1.5   **DV = 4**

Answer 1.13

Answer **C** — Answer A is incorrect as although a person cannot steal land *in general,* there are several circumstances under s. 4(2) of the Act that are exceptions to this rule. Answers B and D are incorrect as a person's characteristics and administrative data and confidential information (*Oxford* v *Moss* (1978) 68 Cr App R 183) are not intangible property for the purposes of the Theft Act 1968.

Investigators' Manual, paras 1.1.6–1.1.7   **DV = 3.5**

Answer 1.14

Answer **D** — Answers A, B and C are all correct. Answer D is incorrect as you *must show* that the property belonged to another at the time of the appropriation.

Investigators' Manual, para. 1.1.8   **DV = 5.5**

2 | Burglary

QUESTIONS

Question 2.1

WILKIN is a tramp with a long record for burglary offences. He breaks into a garden shed but is arrested as he is leaving the shed with a mower in his hands. He tells the arresting officer that he was going to sell the mower to buy drink. In interview WILKIN states that initially, he never intended to take anything from the shed, stealing the mower was just an idea he had once he was inside. The reason he entered the shed was that he was looking for shelter.

What offence is WILKIN guilty of?

A As WILKIN was only looking for shelter, he commits Theft (contrary to s. 1 of the Theft Act 1968) when he steals the mower.

B WILKIN commits Burglary (contrary to s. 9(1)(a) of the Theft Act 1968) as soon as he enters the shed.

C WILKIN commits Burglary (contrary to s. 9(1)(b) of the Theft Act 1968) when he steals the mower.

D WILKIN commits Burglary (contrary to s. 9(1)(a) of the Theft Act 1968) when he steals the mower.

Question 2.2

CATER asks her neighbour, TEW, to look after her house while she is away on holiday. CATER gives TEW a key to her house and tells him he is welcome to go into the house and watch the satellite TV system, situated in the lounge, anytime he likes while she is away. TEW decides to steal from the house and at 2.00am one morning, while CATER is on holiday, he uses the key to get into CATER's house. He goes into the main bedroom and steals all of CATER's jewellery. TEW is aware that CATER would never have consented to this activity.

Which of the statements below is correct with regard to TEW?

A As CATER has given TEW permission to enter the premises, he is not a trespasser and in these circumstances would be guilty of theft rather than burglary.

B TEW is guilty of burglary but if the jewellery were in the same room as the satellite TV, then TEW would be guilty of theft alone.

C As TEW is the temporary owner of the property, he has a 'charge' on it and its contents and cannot be guilty of any offence in these circumstances.

D As TEW has gone beyond a condition of entry, he is a trespasser and would be guilty of burglary.

Question 2.3

HILLEN is the 'nominated driver' on a stag night. While he drinks orange juice all evening, his four friends get extremely drunk in a pub. All five decide to go to a nightclub and are all walking along a street when the four drunken men decide to drag HILLEN into a house for a joke. The four men kick open the door of a house and throw HILLEN into the hallway against his will. HILLEN gets up and decides that while he is in the house he may as well make it worth his while, intending to steal something from the house. He spots £50 on a table in the hallway, takes the money and leaves.

What offence does HILLEN commit?

A HILLEN commits Burglary (contrary to s. 9(1)(a) of the Theft Act 1968) when he forms the intent to steal from the house.

B HILLEN commits Theft (contrary to s. 1 of the Theft Act 1968) when he steals the money from the hallway.

C HILLEN commits Burglary (contrary to s. 9(1)(b) of the Theft Act 1968) when he steals the money from the hallway.

D HILLEN commits Burglary (contrary to s. 9(1)(b) of the Theft Act 1968) but would have a defence in these circumstances.

Question 2.4

Whilst having a drink at his local pub, GOMEZ goes into the toilet. He notices a man trying to put money into a contraceptive machine (also in the toilet) that will not accept the coins because it is full of money. GOMEZ decides to hide in the cubicles until the pub closes and then break into the machine to steal the cash. When GOMEZ eventually breaks into the machine he makes so much noise that the police are called and catch him in the act.

What offence does GOMEZ commit?

A GOMEZ commits Theft (contrary to s. 1 of the Theft Act 1968) when he breaks into the machine.

B GOMEZ commits Burglary (contrary to s. 9(1)(a) of the Theft Act 1968) when he decides to hide in the cubicle.

C GOMEZ commits Burglary (contrary to s. 9(1)(a) of the Theft Act 1968) when he breaks into the machine.

D GOMEZ commits Burglary (contrary to s. 9(1)(b) of the Theft Act 1968) when he breaks into the machine.

Question 2.5

HAYDEN goes into his local store to do some shopping. While he is walking around the shopping area he notices that the door to the staff room is ajar and that there is an open safe containing several bundles of cash inside it. HAYDEN decides to steal the cash and hides behind a large cardboard display in the corner of the shopping area, intending to come out when the shop is closed. The shop closes and HAYDEN comes out from behind the display. He walks across the shopping area to the staff room door and enters the staff room. Once inside the staff room he approaches the open safe and steals the cash contents. To get out, HAYDEN has to force a fire exit at the rear of the staff room.

At what stage does HAYDEN become a trespasser for the purposes of burglary?

A When he decides to steal the cash and hides behind the cardboard display.

B When he comes out from behind the display after the shop has closed.

C When he enters the staff room and approaches the safe.

D When he forces the fire exit to get out of the store.

Question 2.6

SOUTHALL decides to burgle a stately home. He visits the home during the day to look at the security arrangements and sees that apart from some security cameras there is a warning sign telling people to 'Beware of the Dog!' He returns later the same night to burgle the stately home. In his possession he has a piece of meat containing a large quantity of Valium (used to incapacitate any guard dog inside the home) and a screwdriver he intends to use to force a window and gain entry. SOUTHALL uses the screwdriver to force a window and enters the stately home with both the screwdriver and the meat in his possession.

Does SOUTHALL commit an aggravated burglary?

A No, in these circumstances neither of the articles in his possession relate to an aggravated burglary offence.

B Yes, but only in respect of the drugged meat. This would be classed as a 'weapon of offence' as it is designed to incapacitate.

C Yes, both items are classed as 'weapons of offence' in these circumstances. The drugged meat is designed to incapacitate and the screwdriver could be adapted to cause injury.

D No, although both items are 'weapons of offence', SOUTHALL would actually have to use one or both of them to cause injury or incapacitate before the full offence is committed.

Question 2.7

CRADDOCK intends to break into and steal from ELVIN's house. CRADDOCK knows that ELVIN is 80 years old but does not wish to take any chances and so before he goes to the house he decides to take a piece of cord with him to tie up ELVIN, should he be in. He breaks into the house and enters the lounge with the cord ready in his hands. He searches the lounge but finds nothing worth taking so he goes through the lounge door into the dining room. In the dining room is ELVIN who has come from his bedroom after hearing the noise of the break-in. CRADDOCK decides to steal from the dining room and ties his hands with the cord before committing theft.

At what stage does CRADDOCK first commit the offence of aggravated burglary?

A When, before he goes to the house, he decides to take the piece of cord with him to tie up any occupants.

B When he enters the house after forcing the ground floor lounge window.

C When he enters the dining room (another part of the building).

D When he uses the cord to tie the hands of the occupant and commits theft.

Question 2.8

KYRIACOU has made a grappling hook that, if pushed through a letterbox, will enable her to take hold of letters from the floors of houses. She intends to take any money or valuable goods from the letters she manages to seize. She goes to a house and puts the grappling hook through the letterbox of a porch at the front of the house. Unfortunately for KYRIACOU the grappling hook is not long enough to reach some of the letters on the floor and she has to put her hand through the letterbox to reach the letters. She manages to hook the letters and pulls them through the letterbox.

Which of the statements below is correct?

A The front porch of a house would not be classed as a building for the purposes of burglary; KYRIACOU commits theft.

B When KYRIACOU uses the grappling hook she does not commit burglary. It is only when her hand goes through the letterbox that this offence is committed.

C These circumstances would not qualify as an 'effective and substantial' entry for the purposes of burglary; KYRIACOU has committed theft.

D Using the grappling hook as an extension of her body means that KYRIACOU has 'entered' premises and would be guilty of an offence of burglary.

Question 2.9

KEYS owns a builders' merchants and is owed £5,000 by BEATON. KEYS phones BEATON and demands the money; BEATON tells KEYS he will not pay a penny and that KEYS will have to take it from him. KEYS goes to BEATON's home and breaks in, intending to find some or all of the £5,000. KEYS' honest belief is he is legally entitled to act in this way because of BEATON's debt. There is no money in the house and so he goes to the building site where BEATON is working. He enters an unfinished house and demands the money from BEATON. When BEATON refuses, KEYS assaults him, breaking BEATON's arm.

Which of the statements below is correct?

A KEYS only commits burglary when he breaks into BEATON's house with intent to steal.

B KEYS only commits burglary when he inflicts grievous bodily harm on BEATON.

C KEYS commits burglary when he breaks into BEATON's house and also when he inflicts grievous bodily harm on BEATON.

D At no stage does BEATON commit the offence of burglary.

Question 2.10

The GARTONs go on holiday for a week in a houseboat and constantly move around the country's canal system, never staying in one location for more than a day. They moor the boat and go to 'The Hen' pub for lunch. When they return to the boat some 3 hours later, they find that it has been broken into and a video camera has been stolen.

Would the houseboat be classed as a 'building' for a burglary offence?

A Yes, the term 'building' would apply to an inhabited vessel and it would also apply when the person living in or on the vessel is not there as well as times when he/she is.

B No, the term 'building' should be given its everyday meaning as a structure of some permanence. As the houseboat is continually moored in different places it is not permanent and cannot be a 'building' for the purposes of burglary.

C No, a vehicle or vessel can only be a building if a person has a habitation in it. In these circumstances, the houseboat was empty when the offence took place and therefore it is not a 'building'.

D Yes, but the houseboat would be classed as an 'other building' rather than a 'dwelling' and as such the maximum sentence for this offence would be 10 years' imprisonment.

Question 2.11

LAMONT and HEWITSON break into a house intending to steal from it. They are seen putting stolen property from the break-in into a car, the police are called and both men are arrested. When LAMONT is searched he is found to have a household knife in his coat pocket. The arresting officer asks LAMONT why he has the knife and LAMONT replies, 'For self-defence because there's a drug dealer who is after me'. HEWITSON had no idea that LAMONT had a knife in his possession.

Has an offence of aggravated burglary been committed?

A Yes, LAMONT commits the offence. HEWITSON would have to know of the existence of the knife and its purpose to be guilty of aggravated burglary.

B Yes, both men commit the offence. The mere fact that LAMONT has a weapon is all the evidence that is required.

C No, neither man commits the offence. LAMONT does not intend to use the knife in the course of the burglary and HEWITSON has no knowledge of its existence.

D No, the knife is not a weapon of offence because it is not an article made or adapted for use of causing injury or incapacitating a person.

Question 2.12

HULBERT breaks into a house using a screwdriver to force a downstairs window. He walks into the lounge and starts searching for items to steal. As he searches, the owner of the house, WEEDON, confronts him. HULBERT threatens WEEDON with the screwdriver, telling her to leave him alone or he will stab her with the screwdriver. WEEDON backs away from HULBERT into a hallway. HULBERT decides to rape WEEDON and follows her into the hallway, threatening her with the screwdriver as he does so. He rapes WEEDON in the hallway then, worried about leaving a witness, he stabs WEEDON in the throat with the screwdriver. He returns to the lounge, steals a DVD player and leaves.

At what point does HULBERT first commit an aggravated burglary?

A When he threatens WEEDON with the screwdriver in the lounge.

B When he decides to rape WEEDON and follows her into the hallway.

C When he stabs WEEDON in the throat with the screwdriver.

D When he returns to the lounge and steals the DVD player.

Question 2.13

RULE and HOQUE intend to steal from O'HALLORAN's house. The two men go to the back garden of the house where RULE smashes a window to the kitchen. He makes so much noise that O'HALLORAN comes outside and challenges the two men. HOQUE instantly picks up a piece of wood from the back garden and starts to hit O'HALLORAN on the head with it intending to cause grievous bodily harm to him.

O'HALLORAN runs away from the house, followed by HOQUE who is still hitting him with the piece of wood. RULE climbs into the kitchen and steals cash from the house.

Have RULE and HOQUE committed an offence of aggravated burglary?

A Yes, both men commit the offence as a piece of wood can be a weapon of offence and its use in these circumstances has enabled entry to the premises.

B No, the piece of wood can never be an offensive weapon for the purposes of aggravated burglary.

C Yes, but only HOQUE commits the offence as he intends to cause O'HALLORAN grievous bodily harm.

D No, when the burglary is committed nobody actually enters the premises with a weapon of offence.

Question 2.14

DARE decides to steal from the offices of a printing firm owned by SHEA. Thinking there might be a security guard on the premises he takes a pair of handcuffs with him in case he needs to incapacitate the guard. At 5.00am when DARE gets to the offices, it becomes obvious that there is no security guard so he throws the handcuffs away. He breaks into the offices and begins searching. Minutes later DARE is confronted by SHEA who has come to work early. In order to escape, DARE picks up a pair of scissors and threatens SHEA to stay back or he will be stabbed. SHEA backs away from DARE. Still holding the scissors, DARE picks up a cash-box and makes off.

Which of the statements below is correct?

A   As the handcuffs are designed to incapacitate, DARE would commit an offence of aggravated burglary when he goes to the offices intending to steal.

B   DARE is guilty of burglary but not aggravated burglary. The handcuffs were disposed of prior to entry and the scissors are used only to assist in his escape.

C   When DARE steals the cash-box he commits an offence of aggravated burglary.

D   When DARE picks up the scissors and threatens SHEA he commits an offence of aggravated burglary.

Question 2.15

BUCKNALL (a TV engineer) visits GRETTON's house to repair her television. BUCK-NALL arrives at GRETTON's house and is shown into the downstairs lounge where the television is. GRETTON tells BUCKNALL that she is going out to visit a friend and that he should make his own way out when the television is fixed. While GRETTON is out, BUCKNALL decides to steal from GRETTON's house.

At what stage, if at all, does GRETTON commit burglary?

A   When he takes £500 in cash from a moneybox on top of the television in the lounge.

B   When he goes into GRETTON's upstairs bedroom intending to steal but only if there is anything worth stealing in the bedroom.

C   When he enters GRETTON's upstairs study and steals her home computer.

D   GRETTON does not commit burglary, as he is never a trespasser.

Question 2.16

LLOYD visits DERMOT's house to pick up a drill. DERMOT invites LLOYD into his house and asks him to wait in the hall while he fetches the drill. While waiting, LLOYD spots an envelope on the hall window ledge; he can see it contains cash. LLOYD quickly picks up the envelope and puts it in his pocket. DERMOT returns with the drill, hands it to LLOYD and LLOYD leaves. The envelope contains £2,000. A few minutes later, DERMOT discovers the envelope has gone. He chases after LLOYD and accuses him of taking the envelope. LLOYD pushes DERMOT over and runs away.

With regard to the Theft Act 1968 only, what offence does LLOYD commit?

A LLOYD commits theft (contrary to s. 1 of the Theft Act 1968).

B LLOYD commits burglary (contrary to s. 9(1)(b) of the Theft Act 1968).

C LLOYD commits burglary (contrary to s. 9(1)(a) of the Theft Act 1968).

D LLOYD commits robbery (contrary to s. 8 of the Theft Act 1968).

Question 2.17

The offence of burglary (contrary to s. 9(1)(a) of the Theft Act 1968) can be committed in a variety of ways.

In which of the below situations has such an offence been committed?

A HEDGELAND breaks into a house intending to cause actual bodily harm against MOORE. MOORE is not in the house so HEDGELAND does not carry out the offence.

B PANG breaks into a garage intending to commit an offence of taking a conveyance (contrary to s. 12 of the Theft Act 1968).

C TAMM breaks into a warehouse intending to steal but finds nothing worth taking. Out of spite, TAMM turns on all the warehouse lights committing an offence of abstract electricity (contrary to s. 13 of the Theft Act 1968).

D YOUNGER breaks into a garden shed looking for shelter. Once inside he commits criminal damage (contrary to s. 1(1) of the Criminal Damage Act 1971) to several gardening tools stored inside the shed.

Question 2.18

LEAVY intends to break into a house to steal property. In his pocket he is carrying a screwdriver which he intends to use to cause injury against anyone who tries to prevent him from escaping. LEAVY forces a downstairs lounge window and enters the house. Once inside the lounge he steals several ornaments before being disturbed by the householder. LEAVY pulls out the screwdriver and threatens the householder who is not afraid and approaches LEAVY. LEAVY stabs the householder causing him grievous bodily harm.

At what point, if at all, does LEAVY first commit an offence of aggravated burglary (contrary to s. 10 of the Theft Act 1968)?

A When he initially breaks into the house.

B When he actually steals the ornaments.

C When he stabs the householder him causing grievous bodily harm.

D The offence of aggravated burglary is not committed in these circumstances.

ANSWERS

Answer 2.1

Answer **C** — Breaking into the garden shed clearly makes WILKIN a trespasser for the purposes of the offence of burglary. However, his lack of intent to commit any of the ulterior offences of theft, grievous bodily harm, rape or criminal damage when he entered the shed means that he cannot be guilty of an offence under s. 9(1)(a) of the Theft Act 1968, making B and D incorrect. Although WILKIN does commit theft, he has entered as a trespasser and stolen, falling into the category of a burglary under s. 9(1)(b) of the Theft Act 1968 and making answer C correct.

Investigators' Manual, paras 1.2.1–1.2.5 **DV = 8**

Answer 2.2

Answer **D** — Answer C is incorrect as looking after property in such a manner would not prohibit the person in 'charge' of the property being guilty of theft should they treat it as TEW has done. CATER's permission for TEW to enter was granted 'conditionally'; that is, to watch the satellite TV. This conditional permission has been violated and that violation turns TEW into a trespasser (*R v Jones and Smith* [1976] 3 All ER 54), making answer B incorrect. TEW's intention to steal from the premises from the outset and his entry as a trespasser makes him guilty of burglary under s. 9(1)(a) of the Theft Act 1968. Even if the jewellery were in the same room as the satellite TV, TEW is a trespasser with intent to steal the moment he enters the house, this makes answer A incorrect.

Investigators' Manual, para. 1.2.1 **DV = 3**

Answer 2.3

Answer **B** — Answers A, C and D are incorrect because HILLEN is never a trespasser for the purposes of burglary. A crime is committed when there is a meeting of *mens rea* with *actus reus* but that *actus reus* must be voluntary. HILLEN's entry to the house must be deliberate or reckless and so, as he was not responsible for being thrown into the house by his drunken friends, the *actus reus* of burglary must be eliminated. Once inside the house he decides to steal—HILLEN is now guilty of theft.

Investigators' Manual, paras 1.2.1, 4.3.2, 4.3.2.1 **DV = 2.5**

Answer 2.4

Answer **A** — Answers B, C and D are all incorrect as at no time is GOMEZ a trespasser for the purposes of burglary. When GOMEZ initially goes into the pub toilets he is a legitimate customer and therefore not a trespasser. His decision to hide and break into the machine will not make him a trespasser even if he has gone beyond the implied permission given by the landlord as this decision is made after entry to the toilets.

Investigators' Manual, para. 1.2.5   **DV = 4.5**

Answer 2.5

Answer **C** — Initially, HAYDEN is not a trespasser as he enters the shop as a genuine and honest customer and with the implied permission of the shop owner. Even when he decides to hide and steal, he remains in the part of the shop he has legitimate access to and so cannot be a trespasser as his intention has been formed after he has entered, making answer A incorrect. Answer B is also incorrect as when he moves from behind the display he still remains in a part of the building he had legitimate access to and once again he will not be a trespasser. The offence of burglary would be committed when he moves into the staff room as at this point he enters part of a building as a trespasser with intent to steal, making answer D incorrect as a result.

Investigators' Manual, para. 1.2.5   **DV = 7**

Answer 2.6

Answer **A** — One way an aggravated burglary can be committed is when a person enters premises in possession of a weapon of offence. A screwdriver is not a weapon of offence 'per se' and SOUTHALL would have to intend for the screwdriver to be used as such for this item to fall into the category of offensive weapon. This makes answer C incorrect. Drugged meat to incapacitate a dog is not an offensive weapon as the weapon must be to incapacitate a person, making answer B incorrect. Answer D is incorrect as neither of the items is a weapon of offence.

Investigators' Manual, paras 1.3, 1.3.1   **DV = 5**

Answer 2.7

Answer **B** — There are two questions to ask to obtain the correct answer to this question: (i) is the cord a weapon of offence? (ii) what type of burglary is this? The piece of cord intended to tie up any occupants is a weapon of offence as it is intended to incapacitate a person. This is a burglary under s. 9(1)(a) of the Theft Act 1968 as CRADDOCK intends to break in and steal from the house and burglary is committed when he enters with that intent. Where these two points meet is where the aggravated burglary is first committed.

Investigators' Manual, paras 1.3, 1.3.1   **DV = 8**

Answer 2.8

Answer **D** — Answer A is incorrect, as the front porch of a house would be classed as a building or part of a building. Although *R v Collins* [1973] QB 100, stated that entry must be 'effective and substantial', this does not mean that the defendant needs to get the whole of their body into premises and any part of the body would be sufficient making answer C incorrect. A person may use an object as an extension of himself or herself to enter which makes B incorrect.

Investigators' Manual, para. 1.2.1   **DV = 8**

Answer 2.9

Answer **B** — If KEYS honestly believes that he has a right in law to deprive a person of property then he is not dishonest and cannot commit theft. Therefore, if there is no theft, KEYS does not commit burglary at BEATON's house, making answers A and C incorrect. An unfinished house is a building for the purposes of burglary and KEYS has entered as a trespasser and committed grievous bodily harm satisfying the requirements for an offence under s. 9(1)(b) of the Theft Act 1968, making answer D incorrect.

Investigators' Manual, paras 1.1.3, 1.2.1, 1.2.2, 1.2.5   **DV = 6**

Answer 2.10

Answer **A** — Section 9 of the Theft Act 1968 defines a building and states that the word 'building' applies to inhabited vehicles or vessels (the houseboat) and applies to those vehicles or vessels at times when they are unoccupied (when the GARTONs go for a meal).

Investigators' Manual, para. 1.2.2   **DV = 8**

Answer 2.11

Answer **A** — Answer D is incorrect as the definition of a weapon of offence is in-complete; you should add 'or intended by the person having it with him for such use'. On this basis, the knife will become a weapon of offence. The fact that LA-MONT had the weapon of offence in his possession for some other purpose than to use during the course of the burglary is irrelevant. The harm this section aims to protect the public from is that a burglar may be tempted to use such a weapon to injure someone during a burglary, making answer C incorrect. Finally, answer B is incorrect as HEWITSON must know of the existence of the knife and, because it is not an offensive weapon per se, its purpose.

Investigators' Manual, paras 1.3, 1.3.1   **DV = 4**

Answer 2.12

Answer **C** — The screwdriver is not a weapon of offence until HULBERT intends to use it in this way and this intention is accompanied by an offence under s. 9(1)(a) or 9(1)(b) of the Theft Act 1968. When HULBERT threatens WEEDON with the screw-driver, it instantaneously changes from a screwdriver to a weapon of offence but while he remains in the lounge an aggravated burglary can only be committed if he commits or attempts to commit one of the offences under s. 9(1)(b) of the Theft Act 1968, i.e. theft or grievous bodily harm. It cannot be under s. 9(1)(a) as he has already entered the premises when the intention regarding the use of the screw-driver is formed. When HULBERT decides to rape WEEDON and moves from the lounge to the hall, he does not commit burglary as his intention is to rape and this offence was removed from the definition of burglary by the Sexual Offences Act 2003. The offence of aggravated burglary is first committed when HULBERT stabs WEEDON, as at this point he has entered the hall as a trespasser and committed GBH.

Investigators' Manual, paras 1.3, 1.3.1   **DV = 6**

Answer 2.13

Answer **D** — The inclusion of an article intended by a person to cause injury or incapacitate within the definition of a weapon of offence means that absolutely anything can instantaneously become a weapon of offence in the hands of the burg-lar, making answer B incorrect. This is a burglary under s. 9(1)(a) of the Theft Act 1968 and so to become an aggravated burglary the weapon of offence must be with the offender at the time of entry. This is not the case. The fact that entry has been gained because of the use of the piece of wood against O'HALLORAN is irrelevant, RULE is the only person entering the premises and he does not have any weapon at the time of entry, making answer A incorrect. HOQUE does not commit the offence as he never enters the premises, therefore answer C is incorrect.

Investigators' Manual, paras 1.3, 1.3.1   **DV = 8**

Answer 2.14

Answer **C** — Although handcuffs are a weapon of offence, DARE disposes of them prior to entry and so cannot commit aggravated burglary because he does not have the weapon in his possession at the time of entry, making answer A incorrect. At this stage, DARE is guilty of burglary alone. When he picks up the scissors they become a weapon of offence, but a mere threat to use them does not make his burglary aggravated so answer D is incorrect. As DARE then commits a theft by stealing the cash-box he commits a burglary under s. 9(1)(b) and is in possession of an offensive weapon when he does so. This makes him guilty of aggravated burglary so answer B is incorrect.

Investigators' Manual, paras 1.3, 1.3.1   **DV = 4**

Answer 2.15

Answer **B** — To work out when BUCKNALL commits burglary you must decide when he becomes a trespasser. At point 'A', GRETTON has invited BUCKNALL into her lounge to fix her TV. BUCKNALL has no intent to commit one of the trigger offences for burglary 9(1)(a) (**DIT**—Damage, Inflicting GBH, Theft) so cannot be a trespasser for burglary 9(1)(a) at this point. When GRETTON leaves, BUCKNALL decides to steals from the lounge but this stealing does not make him a trespasser for the purposes of burglary 9(1)(b). BUCKNALL must have entered the lounge as a trespasser; it is not enough that stealing from the lounge is against the wishes of the householder. You are either a trespasser when you enter a building or part of a building or you are not and you cannot become a trespasser *in that part of the building* just because you steal. At point 'A' BUCKNALL is a thief, not a burglar. At point 'B' BUCKNALL has moved from one part of a building to another (the upstairs bedroom) with the intention to steal (a 9(1)(a) burglary). He has gone beyond the conditional entry permission given by GRETTON and as a consequence he becomes a trespasser. The fact that he enters with the intention of stealing is all that is required and it is immaterial whether he enters with the idea to steal if there is 'anything worth stealing' (*R* v *Walkington* [1979] 1 WLR 1169). As a consequence, answers C and D are incorrect.

Investigators' Manual, paras 1.2–1.2.5 **DV = 5**

Answer 2.16

Answer **A** — LLOYD cannot commit burglary because he is never a trespasser. DERMOT invited him into his house and, when he entered, LLOYD had no criminal intentions, making answers B and C incorrect. No robbery has been committed because the force has been used after the property has been appropriated, making answer D incorrect.

Investigators' Manual, paras 1.1.2, 1.2–1.2.5, 1.5 **DV = 8**

Answer 2.17

Answer **C** — Answer A is incorrect as actual bodily harm is not a trigger offence for the purposes of s. 9(1)(a). Answer B is incorrect as an intent to steal will not include an intention to commit an offence of taking a conveyance (no intent to permanently deprive). Answer D is an offence of criminal damage. Answer C is a burglary as the offender breaks in with the intention of stealing. The fact that the offender goes on to commit an offence of abstracting electricity out of spite is immaterial.

Investigators' Manual, paras 1.2–1.2.5 **DV = 3.5**

Answer 2.18

Answer **A** — At point 'A' LEAVY has committed a burglary contrary to s. 9(1)(a) of the Theft Act 1968 and has with him a weapon of offence (his intent to use it to cause injury make it a weapon of offence), making this an aggravated burglary. It does not matter that he only intended to use it to assist in his escape.

Investigators' Manual, para. 1.3 **DV = 8**

3 | Handling

Question 3.1

FENSHAW is a collector of rare records. He visits a car-boot sale to see if there are any bargains available. While browsing at a stall run by REAY, he spots a record that he knows would cost over £1,000 from his normal reputable source. He asks REAY how much the record costs and REAY tells him he can buy the record for £30. FENSHAW remarks that this is a bargain to which REAY replies 'Easy come and easy go'. FENSHAW buys the record.

If FENSHAW were later arrested for handling stolen goods, what state of mind would be required for a prosecution to succeed?

A FENSHAW would have to know or believe the record to be stolen goods.

B FENSHAW would have to presume that the record was stolen goods.

C FENSHAW would have to think it probable that the record was stolen goods.

D FENSHAW would have to suspect that the record was stolen goods.

Question 3.2

GOODCHILD steals a car from TURVEY and sells it to CLIFF for £2,000. This is a cheap price for the car and although CLIFF is suspicious of GOODCHILD, she buys the car nevertheless. CLIFF drives the car for several days and eventually finds papers in the car belonging to TURVEY. CLIFF telephones TURVEY who tells her that the car is stolen. CLIFF quickly hangs up and retains the car for two days while she decides what she will do. Realising that she may lose the car if she returns it to TURVEY, CLIFF sells the car to MARTINEZ for £500.

At what stage, if at all, does CLIFF commit the offence of handling stolen goods?

A When CLIFF buys the car for £2,000 from GOODCHILD.

B When CLIFF retains the car knowing it is stolen.

C When CLIFF sells the car to MARTINEZ.

D CLIFF does not commit the offence in these circumstances.

Question 3.3

VENN breaks into a house and steals a quantity of jewellery. He takes the jewellery to AUSTEN and tells him about the burglary. AUSTEN gives VENN £100 for the jewellery. VENN uses the money to buy a games console. AUSTEN exchanges the jewellery for two tickets to a football match. He keeps one ticket for his own use and gives the other to PEERS as a birthday present. PEERS knows nothing about the origin of the ticket.

Which of the below would be regarded as 'stolen goods' for the purposes of handling stolen goods?

A The £100 given to VENN and the games console he buys with the money.

B The jewellery in the hands of AUSTEN alone.

C All of the property except for the jewellery in the hands of VENN and the ticket in the hands of PEERS.

D The jewellery and both tickets in the hands of AUSTEN.

Question 3.4

GREEN orders a computer from a company owned by FORD. FORD dispatches the computer using a postal firm but the computer is stolen in transit. Two months later, SMITH is arrested in possession of the computer and is charged with an offence of handling stolen goods. The prosecution wish to serve a statutory declaration on SMITH under s. 27 of the Theft Act 1968 as proof that the computer was stolen.

Which of the statements below is correct?

A Only GREEN can make the declaration and a copy of it must be given to SMITH at least 3 days before the trial.

B Either GREEN or FORD can make the declaration and a copy of it must be given to SMITH at least 7 days before the trial.

C Only FORD can make the declaration and this must be given to SMITH at least 14 days before the trial.

D Only GREEN can make the declaration a copy of which must be given to SMITH at least 21 days before the trial.

Question 3.5

POPPITT contacts HUNN and tells him that he plans to steal a lorry full of designer clothes. HUNN tells POPPITT that he will store the goods after the theft and then sell them on for a share of the proceeds that will go to POPPITT.

Which of the statements below is correct with regard to the offence of handling stolen goods?

A Even though HUNN's actions are merely preparatory to the receiving of stolen goods, he commits the offence as he has arranged to receive them.

B HUNN commits an offence of handling stolen goods as the act of receiving does not require the physical reception of the goods.

C HUNN does not commit an offence of handling stolen goods in these circumstances.

D HUNN commits the offence of handling stolen goods as he has arranged to act for the benefit of another.

Question 3.6

DEAKIN has been charged with offences of handling stolen goods and theft. DEAKIN has a previous conviction for handing stolen goods that is 6 years old and a previous conviction for theft that is 4 years old.

Would the prosecution be able to use s. 27 of the Theft Act 1968 to prove that DEAKIN knew or believed the goods to be stolen goods?

A No, as both convictions are over 12 months old.

B Yes, but only in relation to the conviction for theft.

C No, as DEAKIN has been charged with theft as well as handling stolen goods.

D Yes, both previous convictions could be used.

ANSWERS

Answer 3.1

Answer **A** — Section 22 of the Theft Act 1968 states that a person can only handle stolen goods if he/she 'knows or believes' the goods to be stolen. Any other state of mind, including suspicion, will not suffice, making answers B, C and D incorrect.

Investigators' Manual, para. 1.4   **DV = 8**

Answer 3.2

Answer **D** — CLIFF must know or believe the goods to be stolen and mere suspicion will not suffice, making answer A incorrect. To commit an offence of handling stolen goods, the retention, removal, disposal or realisation must be by or for the benefit of another. Retaining the car and then disposing of it is only done for the benefit of CLIFF so the offence is not made out, making answers B and C incorrect.

Investigators' Manual, paras 1.4, 1.4.6   **DV = 2.5**

Answer 3.3

Answer **C** — 'Stolen goods' under s. 24 of the Theft Act 1968, are those that directly or indirectly represent the stolen goods in the hands of the thief or the handler, or the originally stolen goods themselves. The jewellery in the hands of VENN would not be considered as goods as he is the original thief. The £100 given to VENN and the games console he buys with the money indirectly represent the stolen goods in the hands of the thief. The jewellery in the hands of AUSTEN is the original stolen goods in the hands of the handler. The tickets exchanged for the jewellery indirectly represent the stolen goods in the hands of the handler. The ticket passed on to PEERS ceases to be 'stolen goods' as PEERS is in innocent possession of the ticket and has no idea as to its origin. Therefore, answers A, B and D are incorrect.

Investigators' Manual, para. 1.4.1   **DV = 4.5**

Answer 3.4

Answer **B** — Section 27 of the Theft Act 1968 allows a declaration of proof that goods were stolen to be made in proceedings for any theft or handling stolen goods from that theft. The declaration can be made by the person who dispatched the goods (FORD) or the person who failed to receive the goods (GREEN) and is admissible if a copy of the statement is given to the person charged (SMITH) at least 7 days before the hearing or trial. This makes answers A, C and D incorrect.

Investigators' Manual, para. 1.4.3   **DV = 4**

Answer 3.5

Answer **C** — Although the conduct mentioned in answers A, B and D would qualify as activities associated with the offence of handling stolen goods, the offence will only be committed if the goods are stolen. If the goods have yet to be stolen, as in this case, then the offence is not committed.

Investigators' Manual, para. 1.4.1   **DV = 8**

Answer 3.6

Answer **C** — Section 27 of the Act can be used to prove that the defendant knew or believed the goods to be stolen goods if he/she (i) had in his possession, or has undertaken or assisted in the retention, removal, disposal or realisation of, stolen goods from any theft taking place not earlier than 12 months before the offence charged; and (ii) evidence that he has within five years preceding the date of the offence charged been convicted of theft or of handling stolen goods. Therefore the conviction for handling stolen goods cannot be used, making answer D incorrect. Answer A is incorrect in relation to the time limits regarding the previous convictions. The prosecution may only use s. 27 if the defendant is being proceeded against in relation to a charge of handling stolen goods alone and not any other offence. As DEAKIN has been charged with theft in addition to handling stolen goods, the power under s. 27 cannot be used, making answer B incorrect.

Investigators' Manual, para 4.1.3.3   **DV = 4**

4 | Robbery

Question 4.1

CREW, MUSGROVE and BYER play cards together on a regular basis. As a result, BYER falls into debt, owing CREW and MUSGROVE £500 each. One evening, BYER is drinking in a bar when CREW and MUSGROVE approach him. CREW places the tip of a knife against BYER's face and MUSGROVE says, 'Give us all you have or your face might not have a future'. BYER hands over his wallet and all his gold jewellery. CREW and MUSGROVE believe they are legally entitled to the property but realise they are not entitled to use force to get it.

Which of the statements below is correct?

A CREW and MUSGROVE commit robbery. It does not matter that they believe in a right to take the property; they have used force in order to obtain it.

B The beliefs of CREW and MUSGROVE are immaterial as gambling debts are not legally enforceable. This is a robbery.

C There is no dishonesty by CREW or MUSGROVE and as a robbery involves theft and therefore dishonesty, the offence of robbery is incomplete.

D Only CREW is guilty of robbery as he is the only person actually using force against BYER.

Question 4.2

ASGHAR and CULLEM are pickpockets. On a train station platform ASGHAR nudges into GLENN knocking him off-balance and into CULLEM who steals a wallet from inside GLENN's jacket. GLENN realises the wallet has been stolen and tells ASGHAR and CULLEM he is going to inform the police. CULLEM produces a flick-knife and threatens GLENN with it, telling him to keep quiet or he will be stabbed.

At what point, if at all, has the full offence of robbery been committed?

A When ASGHAR nudges into GLENN knocking him off-balance.
B When CULLEM steals the wallet from inside GLENN's jacket.
C When CULLEM threatens GLENN with the flick-knife.
D At no time has an offence of robbery has been committed.

Question 4.3

DEIGHTON is part of a football crowd who become involved in a street brawl with a group of rival supporters. During the course of the fight, DEIGHTON punches and kicks WATTON to the floor, knocking WATTON unconscious. Even though WATTON is unconscious and can offer DEIGHTON no resistance, DEIGHTON continues to punch WATTON about the head and face with his right fist while he removes WATTON's wallet with his left hand.

Has DEIGHTON committed robbery?

A Yes, as DEIGHTON has used force on WATTON immediately before a theft was committed.
B No, WATTON was unconscious during the theft so DEIGHTON cannot put or seek to put him in fear of being then and there subjected to force.
C Yes, at the time the theft takes place, DEIGHTON has used force against WATTON.
D No, DEIGHTON's use of force against WATTON was not in order to commit theft.

Question 4.4

The police receive information that ROCK will steal the takings from a shop owned by MAN. MAN wishes to help and volunteers to run the shop on his own at the time of the offence. Three police officers are waiting in a small room behind the till when ROCK enters the shop. ROCK produces a toy pistol and points it at MAN demanding the takings. Although MAN hands over some cash from the till, he does not believe he will be subjected to force because there are police officers nearby and he realises the gun is a fake.

Which of the statements below is correct with regard to these circumstances?

A The force used during a robbery should at least amount to an assault. As MAN does not apprehend the immediate infliction of force there can be no robbery.
B This is not a robbery as the police were nearby and MAN realised the gun was a fake. Therefore, MAN cannot fear that ROCK would be able to use force on him or even threaten to do so.

C ROCK's state of mind is irrelevant to the offence of robbery. Whether ROCK intended to put MAN in fear of force being used or not is an objective decision to be made by a jury.

D The fact that MAN could have successfully resisted if he wished is immaterial. The offence of robbery is committed because ROCK seeks to put MAN in fear of being subjected to force.

Question 4.5

HONEYBOURNE owns and operates a hot dog stand and has had a particularly good day's business at a music festival. As he is counting his takings, he is approached by ORDISH who produces an imitation firearm and says, 'Hand over the money!' ORDISH intends HONEYBOURNE to believe the gun is real and that he will be shot if he does not do as ORDISH demands. HONEYBOURNE does not believe he will be subjected to force as he used to be in the army and realises that the gun is not real. He laughs at ORDISH and tells him if he wants to rob people he should get a real gun. ORDISH flees empty handed.

Why has NO OFFENCE of robbery (contrary to s. 8 of the Theft Act 1968) taken place?

A Because ORDISH did not actually use force against HONEYBOURNE.

B Because ORDISH has not actually stolen the takings.

C Because HONEYBOURNE realised the gun was a fake and did not fear that he would be subjected to force.

D Because ORDISH did not verbally threaten HONEYBOURNE with violence.

ANSWERS

Answer 4.1

Answer **C** — One of the essential elements of an offence of robbery is that there must be a theft. Theft in robbery is the same as s. 1 of the Theft Act 1968 and the defences under s. 2 will therefore apply. The honest belief of CREW and MUS-GROVE means that they are not dishonest. This principle stems from *R* v *Robinson* [1977] Crim LR 173, CA, where it was held that all the defendant had to show was an honest belief in the entitlement to the property and not an honest belief in an entitlement to take it in the way he did. The fact that gambling debts are legally unenforceable does not affect the above.

Investigators' Manual, paras 1.1.3, 1.5   **DV = 6.5**

Answer 4.2

Answer **B** — A theft has taken place and immediately before the theft, force has been used, making answer D incorrect. When CULLEM threatens GLENN with a flick-knife it is not in order to steal but to deter him from reporting the matter, making answer C incorrect. When force is used, no theft has taken place and so the full offence is incomplete, making answer A incorrect, although this may be an attempted robbery. Although the use of force in nudging into GLENN may appear minimal it is nevertheless a use of force (*R* v *Dawson and James* (1976) 64 Cr App R 170).

Investigators' Manual, para. 1.5   **DV = 5**

Answer 4.3

Answer **D** — An offence of robbery is committed when the offender not only uses force against the victim immediately before or at the time of stealing but also in order to do so. Therefore, if the violence has no connection with the offence of theft and is effectively an unnecessary and sadistic activity it is not a robbery. Answer A is incorrect as the force used is because of a fight and not in order to commit theft. Answer C is incorrect for the same reason. Answer B is incorrect as the definition also includes the direct application of force as a means of committing the offence as well as the threat of its use.

Investigators' Manual, para. 1.5   **DV = 4**

Answer 4.4

Answer **D** — There is no requirement that the force used during a robbery should amount to an assault, making answer A incorrect. The fact that the victim does not resist or is unafraid because of the surrounding circumstances is of no consequence, the offence is still committed, so answer B is incorrect. It is enough that the offender puts or seeks to put the victim in fear of force being used at that time and so the state of mind of the offender is significant. It is not an objective decision made by the jury and so answer C is incorrect.

Investigators' Manual, para.1.5   **DV = 7.5**

Answer 4.5

Answer **B** — Although many robbery offences will involve the use of force, the offence can just as easily be committed without it by the use of a threat, i.e. the defendant puts or seeks to put any person in fear of being then and there subjected to force, therefore, answer A is incorrect. Putting a person in such fear does not require a verbal threat of violence as actions (pointing an imitation forearm at the intended victim) can satisfy this part of the offence, making answer D incorrect. The fact that the victim is not in fear of the threat is immaterial as it is the intention of the defendant that is important, making answer C incorrect. The offence has **not been** committed as there was no actual theft; this is an *attempt* robbery.

Investigators' Manual, para. 1.5   **DV = 6**

5 Deception

Question 5.1

PC YOUNG is seeking advice from PC PARKS regarding an offence of obtaining property by deception (contrary to s. 15 of the Theft Act 1968). DC THORLEY overhears the advice given by PC PARKS and needs to correct the advice given by the officer.

In relation to the advice given by PC PARKS, which of the comments below is INCORRECT?

A When a person, by deception, dishonestly obtains property belonging to another, it must be with the intention of permanently depriving the other of it.

B 'Obtaining' as defined under s. 15(2) is very broad and includes enabling another to retain property.

C You must prove a connection between the deception practised and the obtaining of the property.

D A defendant practising a deception to enable himself to retain property would commit the offence.

Question 5.2

Six months ago, THORP lent a lawnmower to WING and has never had it returned. THORP believes that WING has in fact sold the lawnmower. THORP tells WING that she intends to cut down a tree in her garden and asks if she may borrow WING's chainsaw for that purpose; WING agrees. THORP has no intention of using the chainsaw. Instead, believing in a civil legal entitlement to compensation for her lawnmower, THORP sells the chainsaw at a car-boot sale.

Considering 'dishonesty' relating to deception offences, which of the statements below is correct?

A THORP has not acted dishonestly as any of the special provisions under s. 2 of the Theft Act 1968 apply to deception offences.
B Only a belief that she has a right in law to deprive the other of property will allow THORP to claim she was not dishonest.
C Whether THORP was dishonest or not will be the subject of an *R v Ghosh* direction to a jury.
D THORP's intention to deceive WING is proof that she had dishonest intentions.

Question 5.3

VENABLES is a keen gardener and wants to join an exclusive allotment club. The club he wants to join allocates a piece of land to each member for the period of their natural life but it is only open to residents of a particular area. VENABLES does not live in the area so he knows he will be refused. He forges several letters that state he resides in the area and as a result he is allowed to join the club and is given an allotment to use for the rest of his life.

Has VENABLES committed an offence of obtaining property by deception contrary to s. 15 of the Theft Act 1968?
A VENABLES does not commit the offence, as he has not 'obtained' property.
B VENABLES has committed the offence as 'obtaining' includes possession or control and land can be 'property' for deception offences.
C The offence is not committed because land is not 'property' under the Theft Act 1968.
D There is no offence of obtaining property by deception because VENABLES cannot 'permanently deprive' the allotment club of the land.

Question 5.4

LING has a £1,000 overdraft but wants an increase to £3,000 to go on holiday. LING lies to her bank manager stating that she has had a wage rise and wants to raise her overdraft limit accordingly. The bank manager states that he needs proof that what she says is true. LING gets her friend, JENSEN, to phone the bank manager and lie to him. JENSEN tells the bank manager that she is LING's employer and that LING has had a wage rise. As a result, the bank manager raises LING's overdraft limit to £3,000. LING fully intends to repay the overdraft but as it turns out, she never actually uses the increased overdraft.

Considering the offence of obtaining a pecuniary advantage by deception only, which of the statements below is correct?

A JENSEN commits the offence as it includes obtaining a pecuniary advantage for another as well as one's self.

B LING would need to use the extended overdraft facility for the offence to be complete.

C As LING intended to pay back the overdraft there is no dishonesty and therefore no offence.

D There is no offence of obtaining a pecuniary advantage by deception as this offence only applies to bank loans and not to bank overdrafts.

Question 5.5

LONSDALE is a volunteer worker. He visits the homes of senior citizens in his area and carries out a variety of maintenance work on their houses; he does not charge anyone for the work he carries out. KELLY, a 35-year-old, is not very good at 'Do-It-Yourself' and so contacts LONSDALE. KELLY lies to LONSDALE and tells him that her 85-year-old grandmother needs some work doing on her roof and gives LONSDALE her own home address. KELLY lives alone and would not be entitled to LONSDALE's help unless she was over 65. LONSDALE visits KELLY's house and carries out the work for no charge.

Has KELLY committed the offence of obtaining services by deception (contrary to s. 1 Theft Act 1978)?

A Yes, as the deception used by KELLY has caused LONSDALE to provide services that KELLY would not normally be entitled to.

B No, it is not an offence for KELLY, by deception, to cause LONSDALE to provide services without charge.

C Yes, the fact that LONSDALE provides the services free of charge is immaterial and KELLY would be guilty of the offence in these circumstances.

D No, the offence of obtaining services by deception can never be committed where there is no economic loss to the victim.

Question 5.6

NAWAZ lives with his disabled mother. The bathroom in the house they live in requires major alterations to allow NAWAZ's mother to stay there. NAWAZ's local council agree to carry out £10,000 worth of alterations using materials NAWAZ will supply. Before the work begins on the house, NAWAZ's mother dies. NAWAZ fails to tell the council about his mother's death and allows the council to fit the bathroom.

What offence does NAWAZ commit?

A Obtaining property by deception (s. 15 of the Theft Act 1968).
B Obtaining a pecuniary advantage by deception (s. 16 of the Theft Act 1968).
C Obtaining services by deception (s. 1 of the Theft Act 1978).
D Evasion of liability by deception (s. 2 of the Theft Act 1978).

ANSWERS

Answer 5.1

Answer **D** — Be aware that the *incorrect* comment is required. Options A, B and C are all correct advice. Option D is incorrect as a defendant practising a deception to enable *himself/herself* to retain property would not commit the offence of deception under s. 15 of the Act. The deception practised must be to 'dishonestly *obtain* property *belonging to another'*.

Investigators' Manual, para. 1.7.1 **DV = 3.5**

Answer 5.2

Answer **C** — None of the special provisions of s. 2 of the Theft Act 1968 directly apply to deception offences, making answers A and B incorrect. The presence of an intention to deceive is not necessarily proof that the defendant is dishonest (*R v Clarke* [1996] Crim LR 824), making answer D incorrect.

Investigators' Manual, para. 1.6 **DV = 5**

Answer 5.3

Answer **B** — A person is classed as obtaining property if they obtain ownership, possession or control of the property, making answer A incorrect. The limitations regarding 'property' that apply to other areas of the Theft Act 1968 do not apply to this offence, making it an offence to obtain land in this manner and making answer C incorrect. Section 6 of the Theft Act 1968 (the intention to permanently deprive) is applied as per s. 1 of the Theft Act and VENABLES' activities would certainly fall within this section, making answer D incorrect.

Investigators' Manual, para. 1.7.1 **DV = 8**

Answer 5.4

Answer **A** — A person who by any deception, dishonestly gains for himself *or another* any pecuniary advantage commits this offence. The pecuniary advantage regarding banks relates to overdraft facilities and not to loans, making answer D incorrect. To commit an offence under this section, the defendant does not have to be shown to have in fact benefited by his/her actions, only that the deception brought about the opportunity to do so. The full offence of obtaining a pecuniary advantage by deception is committed as soon as the borrowing arrangement is granted by the banker, so that it does not matter if the facility is never exercised (*R* v *Watkins* [1976] 1 All ER 578), making answer B incorrect. It is entirely irrelevant that LING intends to repay the overdraft; this does not negate the commission of the offence, making answer C incorrect.

Investigators' Manual, para. 1.7.2   **DV = 8**

Answer 5.5

Answer **B** — Section 1(2) of the Theft Act 1978 states, 'it is the obtaining of services where the other is induced to confer a benefit by doing some act, or causing or permitting some act to be done, on the understanding that the benefit has or will be paid for'. This means that answer C is incorrect as it is not an offence for KELLY, by deception, to cause LONSDALE to provide services without charge. Answer A is incorrect as although it is a correct statement of fact, it is incorrect in law for the above reason. There does not have to be an economic loss for the offence to be committed, making answer D incorrect.

Investigators' Manual, paras 1.8.1, 1.8.1.1   **DV = 2**

Answer 5.6

Answer **C** — This question relates to the circumstances in *R* v *Rai* (2000) 1 Cr App R 233 and is mentioned in your Manual under the sub-heading of 'Words or Conduct'. He does not commit an offence of obtaining property by deception as no 'property' is obtained, making answer A incorrect. He does not obtain a pecuniary advantage as this offence relates only to offences where a deception allows an opportunity to borrow by way of overdraft, take out insurance or being given the opportunity to earn greater money in employment or to win money by betting, making answer B incorrect. He does not commit evasion of liability because there is no existing liability to pay, nor will there be a liability in the future.

Investigators' Manual, paras 1.6.1, 1.8.1   **DV = 7**

6 | Blackmail

QUESTIONS

Question 6.1

LONGSTAFF needs money to fund his drug habit. He waits in the car park of a supermarket and watches McCOY park her car and enter the supermarket with her 3-month-old daughter. LONGSTAFF follows McCOY into the store. While McCOY is shopping, LONGSTAFF approaches her and tells her that it is dangerous to park where she has. He demands that she hand over her purse or he will wait by her car and stab her and her daughter when they return to the car. McCOY hands over her purse and LONGSTAFF runs away.

At what stage, if at all, is the offence of blackmail complete?

A When LONGSTAFF tells McCOY that it is dangerous to park where she has.
B When LONGSTAFF makes the demand for the purse.
C When McCOY hands over her purse to LONGSTAFF.
D No offence of blackmail is committed; this is a robbery.

Question 6.2

GARWOOD has placed a large bet on the outcome of a local Sunday league football match. Two days before the match is due to take place he finds out that the team he has backed have lost four of their star players after they were involved in a car accident. Worried that he will lose his money, GARWOOD approaches the referee of the match. GARWOOD tells the referee, 'If you don't call off the game my friends will rape your wife'. The referee takes no notice of GARWOOD and two days later the game goes ahead. GARWOOD loses his bet.

Considering the offence of blackmail (contrary to s. 21 of the Theft Act 1968) only, which of the statements below is true?

A GARWOOD does not commit the offence because he did not 'gain' any money.

B GARWOOD does not commit the offence because the threat is that his friends rather than GARWOOD would rape the referee's wife.

C As the game went ahead, GARWOOD commits an offence of attempted blackmail.

D In these circumstances GARWOOD commits the offence as he intended to keep what he already had (his original bet).

Question 6.3

GILCHRIST has just started a new job at a bank when she is approached by BAXTER who tells her that he knows she used to be a prostitute and that if she does not have sexual intercourse with his friend, HUMPHRIES, he will inform the bank manager and she will probably be sacked. GILCHRIST reluctantly agrees to BAXTER's demand and has sexual intercourse with HUMPHRIES.

Is this an offence of blackmail (contrary to s. 21 of the Theft Act 1968)?

A Yes, because BAXTER makes the unwarranted demand with a view to gaining a benefit for another.

B No, because 'gain' is to be construed as extending only to a gain in money or other property.

C Yes, as a 'gain' refers to anything at all and not necessarily something with a monetary value.

D No, because BAXTER did not make the demand with a view to gain for himself.

Question 6.4

BRIDALE, FORD and HILL all work at the same bank. BRIDALE and FORD are having an affair and need somewhere that they can meet and have sex. BRIDALE approaches HILL and tells him that unless he hands over the keys to his flat and leaves the flat for one night a week, he (BRIDALE) will inform the management that HILL has been stealing from the tills. HILL believes that BRIDALE will carry out his threat and does as BRIDALE demands.

Would this constitute an offence of blackmail (contrary to s. 21 of the Theft Act 1968)?

A Yes, as the gain and loss of property can be temporary.

B No, because BRIDALE did not threaten HILL with any form of violence.

C Yes, but only because HILL actually believes BRIDALE will carry out his threat.

D No, as the gain and loss must both be of a permanent nature.

ANSWERS

Answer 6.1

Answer **B** — The offence of blackmail is completed when the demand with menaces is made as the offence of blackmail is aimed at the making of the demands rather than the consequences of them. Answers A and C are incorrect because at point A, no demand has been made, although this would form part of the menace. At point C the offence has already been committed. Answer D is incorrect, as although blackmail and robbery are closely linked, a robbery cannot occur where the threat to use force is not immediately before or at the time of the theft.

Investigators' Manual, paras 1.5, 1.11, 1.11.1 **DV = 5**

Answer 6.2

Answer **D** — There is no such offence as 'attempted blackmail', making answer C incorrect. It is immaterial whether the menaces relate to action to be taken by the person making the demand, making answer B incorrect. 'Gain' for the purposes of blackmail includes a gain by keeping what one has, making answer A incorrect.

Investigators' Manual, paras 1.11, 1.11.1 **DV = 4**

Answer 6.3

Answer **B** — The demand can be made with a view to gain for another, making answer D incorrect. The 'gain' must be in money or other property, making answers A and C incorrect.

Investigators' Manual, paras 1.11–1.11.1 **DV = 6**

Answer 6.4

Answer **A** — Answer B is incorrect as there is no requirement for violence to form any part of the demand with menaces. Answer C is incorrect as there is no need for the victim of the offence to actually believe the threat by the offender (even if the victim did not believe the threat, the offence would be committed). The gain or loss in blackmail can be in money or in other property (the flat) and this gain and loss can be either permanent or temporary. HILL has lost his flat for one evening a week—the temporary loss of property, making answer D incorrect and answer A correct in the process.

Investigators' Manual, paras 1.11–1.11.1   **DV = 6.5**

PART TWO

Assaults, Drugs, Firearms and Defences

7 | Homicide

QUESTIONS

Question 7.1

FOZIA despises her husband, ALI. For years, ALI has subjected FOZIA to repeated physical and verbal abuse, making her life a misery. One night FOZIA is severely beaten by ALI. The attack proves to be 'the last straw' for FOZIA. After the attack FOZIA decides that enough is enough and plans to kill ALI. She waits for him to fall asleep and attacks him with a claw hammer. She strikes ALI five times about the head, causing serious injuries but not, as she intended, ALI's death.

Which of the statements below is correct?

A FOZIA has committed an attempted murder but because she suffered abuse over a prolonged period, she may raise the 'special defence' of provocation.
B FOZIA has committed an attempted murder and would be able to use any of the 'special defences' provided by the Homicide Act 1957.
C FOZIA's intention to kill ALI provides the *mens rea* needed to support a charge of attempted murder but she would not be able to use any 'special defences'.
D FOZIA has committed an attempted murder but could raise diminished responsibility as a defence if she can prove she was suffering from 'battered wives' syndrome'.

Question 7.2

PIGGOT and LAY both own burger bars. They pitch next to each other in a prime location on a bridge over a subway near a local football ground on match days. The pair become involved in an argument about stealing trade from each other and PIGGOT, in a fit of rage, picks up a tray of canned drinks from the counter of LAY's burger bar and throws the tray over the bridge. The tray of drinks strikes YEO, who is walking along the subway to the match, and kills him.

Does PIGGOT commit the offence of manslaughter?

A   Yes, as long as PIGGOT foresaw the risk of somebody being harmed.

B   No, as PIGGOT does not have the *mens rea* for assault.

C   Yes, the risk of someone being harmed will be judged objectively.

D   No, as PIGGOT's initial action was not directed or aimed at a person.

Question 7.3

CHALLINOR and BARNSLEY, both British citizens, are on holiday in Cuba (a country not forming part of the Commonwealth). The two men are having dinner when an argument takes place over who will pay for the meal. CHALLINOR loses his temper, picks up a steak knife from the table and stabs BARNSLEY in the chest. BARNSLEY immediately dies from his injuries.

Could CHALLINOR be tried in this country for the offence of murder?

A   No, as the offence was committed outside the jurisdiction of the English courts CHALLINOR would have to be tried in Cuba under Cuban law.

B   Yes, any British citizen who commits a murder anywhere in the world may be tried in England and Wales.

C   No, the Offences Against the Person Act 1861 makes it clear that such offences may only be tried in this country if the act is committed in a country belonging to the Commonwealth.

D   Yes, but this is only because both CHALLINOR and BARNSLEY are British citizens.

Question 7.4

STEWARD is 7 months pregnant when MORRELL, her boyfriend, finds out that she has had an affair and the child may not be his. MORRELL attacks STEWARD intending to cause her serious harm. He hits her head with a baseball bat and fractures STEWARD's skull in the process. The attack does not injure the unborn child. STEWARD is rushed to hospital where, as a result of the attack, she prematurely gives birth. The child is born alive but subsequently dies 3 days after the incident.

Considering the law regarding murder and manslaughter only, what is MORRELL's criminal liability regarding the child?

A   In these circumstances, MORRELL has no criminal liability regarding the child.

B   MORRELL can only face criminal charges relating to the child if he intended to kill STEWARD.

C   As MORRELL intended to cause serious harm to STEWARD, he is guilty of the murder of the child.

D MORRELL's intention to cause serious injury to STEWARD may support a charge of manslaughter of the child.

Question 7.5

BUSHELL is involved in a fight with GREY. BUSHELL intends to cause grievous bodily harm to GREY and does so. BUSHELL is arrested and convicted for the s. 18 wounding and receives a 15-year jail sentence. Four years after the attack, GREY dies as a direct consequence of the injuries received during the fight with BUSHELL.

With regard to the law relating to murder, which of the statements below is correct?

A BUSHELL cannot be charged with murder as the *mens rea* needed for a murder conviction is the intention to kill only.

B As GREY has died more than 3 years after receiving his injuries, the consent of the Attorney General is needed before bringing a prosecution.

C If convicted of murder, BUSHELL must be sentenced to life imprisonment unless there are exceptional circumstances surrounding the case.

D BUSHELL cannot be charged with murder as he has already been convicted of an offence committed under the circumstances connected with the death.

Question 7.6

APPLETON is employed by 'Jays Heating Ltd' to fit a central heating system in CURTIS's house. The company director, HUNTER, failed to check if APPLETON had any formal qualifications to fit the system; APPLETON does not. As a consequence he fails to connect a vital part of the system. The result of this failure is that CURTIS dies from leaking fumes. Sergeant JENNINGS investigates the incident.

Which of the comments below is incorrect?

A In these circumstances APPLETON may be guilty of manslaughter by gross negligence.

B Manslaughter could be committed in these circumstances as it is the only criminal offence at common law capable of being committed by negligence.

C APPLETON could not be prosecuted for manslaughter unless he has committed an unlawful act.

D As a limited company is an entirely separate 'legal' person, 'Jays Heating Ltd' is capable of committing the offence of manslaughter.

Question 7.7

BALDRY and LODGE are jointly charged with an offence of murder. At the trial for the offence, BALDRY's defence team submit that when she committed the offence she was suffering from pre-menstrual symptoms and consequently her defence will be one of 'diminished responsibility'.

Considering the defence of 'diminished responsibility', which of the statements below is **INCORRECT**?

A In these circumstances, the burden of proving 'diminished responsibility' lies with the defence.

B If BALDRY's defence is successful and she is found guilty of manslaughter as a consequence, LODGE cannot be convicted of murder.

C Pre-menstrual symptoms would constitute a substantial impairment of mental responsibility.

D A minor lapse of lucidity would not be enough to prove this defence.

Question 7.8

DCs MORA, PERCOX, RUSSELL and POOLE are seconded to a murder enquiry and are discussing the offence. During their discussion, several statements are made regarding the offence of murder.

Which one of their statements is correct?

A DC MORA states that if a victim of an alleged murder dies more than a year and a day after receiving their injury, then the consent of the Attorney General is required before bringing a prosecution.

B DC PERCOX states that a defendant who successfully advances the defence of 'provocation' will be acquitted of the offence of murder.

C DC RUSSELL states that in order to prove an offence of murder, the prosecution must show some degree of premeditation on the part of the defendant.

D DC POOLE states that the term 'unlawful killing' includes occasions where someone fails to act after creating a situation of danger.

Question 7.9

Section 5 of the Domestic Violence, Crime and Victims Act 2004 creates an offence of causing or allowing the death of a child or vulnerable adult.

What does the term 'child' mean for the purposes of this offence?

A A 'child' is a person under the age of 10 years old.

B A 'child' is a person under the age of 14 years old.

C A 'child' is a person under the age of 16 years old. ⟵

D A 'child' is a person under the age of 18 years old.

ANSWERS

Answer 7.1

Answer **C** — FOZIA's *mens rea* to kill ALI is the only state of mind that would support a charge of attempted murder. Regardless of the motives FOZIA has to commit the offence, she does not kill ALI and would, therefore, only be liable for that offence. The 'special defences' of diminished responsibility, provocation and suicide pact are only available to a defendant who is responsible for murder, making answers A, B and D incorrect.

Investigators' Manual, paras 2.1.2, 2.1.3–2.1.3.2   **DV = 3**

Answer 7.2

Answer **C** — This is an offence of manslaughter by an unlawful act. To prove the offence there must be (i) an inherently unlawful act by the defendant, (ii) evidence that the act involved the risk of somebody being harmed (a risk that will be judged objectively, making answer A incorrect) and (iii) proof that the defendant had the required *mens rea* for the unlawful act which leads to the death of the victim. The unlawful act does not have to be aimed or directed against a person, it can be aimed at property, making answer D incorrect. Answer B is incorrect for the same reason; the *mens rea* required is for the specific act carried out by the defendant, in this case, theft of the tray of drinks and not necessarily the offence of assault.

Investigators' Manual, paras 2.1.4, 2.1.4.1   **DV = 5**

Answer 7.3

Answer **B** — Under the provisions of the Offences Against the Person Act 1861, any British citizen who commits a murder anywhere in the world may be tried in England or Wales. Jurisdiction is not an issue, making answer A incorrect. Whether the country where the offence took place is a part of the Commonwealth or not, makes no difference, so answer C is incorrect. The only issue relating to origin is if the defendant, not the victim, is a British citizen, making answer D incorrect.

Investigators' Manual, para. 2.1.2   **DV = 6.5**

Answer 7.4

Answer **D** — This is a complex area of the law touching on the doctrine of transferred malice. The answer also depends on the state of mind of the offender. If, as in this case, the defendant only intends to cause serious harm to the mother and as a result of the attack the baby dies after being born, then it is possible, after the ruling in *Attorney General's Reference (No. 3 of 1994)* [1998] AC 245, to charge the defendant with manslaughter. If the defendant intended to kill the mother then this intention could be sufficient to bring a charge of murder.

Investigators' Manual, para 2.1.2   **DV = 8**

Answer 7.5

Answer **B** — Answer A is incorrect as the *mens rea* for murder is an intention to kill or an intention to cause grievous bodily harm. Answer C is incorrect as the sentence for murder is a mandatory life sentence regardless of the surrounding circumstances. If a defendant has already been convicted of an offence relating to the incident that causes the eventual death of the victim it will not prevent a charge of murder being made against the defendant. The consent of the Attorney General is required for such action (s. 2(2)(a) of the Law Reform (Year and a Day Rule) Act 1996), making answer D incorrect.

Investigators' Manual, paras 2.1.2–2.1.2.2   **DV = 5**

Answer 7.6

Answer **C** — Note that the *incorrect* statement is required. Answers A, B and D are all correct statements of fact in relation to the law of manslaughter. Answer C is incorrect as involuntary manslaughter can be committed by unlawful act or by gross negligence.

Investigators' Manual, paras 2.1.4–2.1.4.2   **DV = 4**

Answer 7.7

Answer **B** — Note that the *incorrect* statement is required. Answers A, C and D are all correct statements of law. Answer B is incorrect as if one defendant successfully raises the defence it will not affect the question of whether the killing amounted to murder in the case of any other party to it (s. 2(4) of the Homicide Act 1957).

Investigators' Manual, para. 2.1.3.1   **DV = 3**

Answer 7.8

Answer **D** — Statement A is incorrect as the consent of the Attorney General is only required if the victim dies more than three years after receiving their injury or if the defendant has already been convicted of an offence committed under the circumstances connected with the death. Statement B is incorrect as a successful special defence plea reduces the offence from murder to voluntary manslaughter. Statement C is incorrect as premeditation is not required to prove an offence of murder.

Investigators' Manual, paras 2.1.2–2.1.3   **DV = 4**

Answer 7.9

Answer **C** — For the purposes of an offence under s. 5 of the Act, a 'child' is a person under the age of 16 years old.

Investigators' Manual, para. 2.1.5   **DV = 5**

8 | Offences Against the Person

Question 8.1

GUNNING is walking his dog in a park. Although he knows his dog is bad-tempered there is nobody else in the park and so he lets his dog off its lead and allows it to run free. Just after GUNNING lets his dog free, O'HARE walks into the park. Because GUNNING has omitted to keep his dog on the lead, the dog runs towards O'HARE. O'HARE is frightened of the dog and believes it will bite him. GUNNING runs up to his dog and puts it back on the lead. O'HARE says, 'You bloody idiot, if your dog wasn't with you I'd kick your head in!' GUNNING is annoyed by the comment and lets his dog off the lead again saying, 'Bite him boy!' The dog bites O'HARE.

At what point, if at all, is an assault committed?

A   When, because of GUNNING's omission, his dog causes O'HARE to believe he will be bitten.
B   When O'HARE threatens GUNNING.
C   When GUNNING sets his dog on O'HARE.
D   An assault has not taken place in these circumstances.

Question 8.2

ILLINGWORTH makes a series of telephone calls to FENNEL over a period of several days. One day, he makes 14 phone calls within a one-hour period. When FENNEL answers the phone, ILLINGWORTH remains silent, sometimes for several minutes. ILLINGWORTH suffers psychiatric harm as a result.

Which of the following comments is true?

A   ILLINGWORTH could only be charged with a s. 47 assault, as psychiatric injuries can never amount to a s. 20 assault.

B No assault is committed because 'silence' would not constitute the act needed for the *actus reus* of an assault.

C ILLINGWORTH could be charged with a s. 20 assault as serious or really serious harm includes psychiatric injury.

D No assault is committed unless the victim and the defendant are face to face when the threats take place.

Question 8.3

LAKER is a prostitute. She is contacted by SAINSBURY, a sado-masochist, who tells her that he wishes to beat her for his sexual gratification. LAKER agrees to SAINS-BURY's offer and meets him in a hotel room where, during sexual intercourse, SAINSBURY punches LAKER in the face and breaks two of her front teeth. A member of staff at the hotel hears LAKER crying out and calls the police who arrive just as SAINSBURY is paying LAKER for her services.

Considering the defence of 'consent', which of the statements below is correct?

A As LAKER has consented to the use of force, it cannot be unlawful and no assault or battery is committed.

B All assaults that result in more than transient harm will be unlawful unless there is good reason for allowing the plea of 'consent'.

C Consensual activity between LAKER and SAINSBURY would not be classed as a matter for criminal investigation.

D The European Court of Human Rights has held that consensual sado-masochistic injuries may not justifiably be made the subject of criminal law.

Question 8.4

PC TERNAN is dealing with a road traffic collision and asks CHIPMAN, who was driving one of the vehicles involved, to provide a breath specimen. CHIPMAN immediately produces a hip-flask full of whisky and drinks a large quantity of the contents. PC TERNAN immediately arrests CHIPMAN for an offence of obstruct police (contrary to s. 89(2) of the Police Act 1996). At this point, CHIPMAN punches PC TERNAN in the face. CHIPMAN is taken to a police station and brought before the custody officer, PS LUGOWSKI, who asks for the circumstances of the arrest. Before PC TERNAN can say anything, CHIPMAN punches PS LUGOWSKI in the face.

With regard to the offence of assault police (contrary to s. 89(1) of the Police Act 1996), which of the comments below is correct?

A CHIPMAN has committed the offence against PC TERNAN and PS LUGOWSKI.

B CHIPMAN has committed the offence against PS LUGOWSKI only.

C CHIPMAN has committed the offence against PC TERNAN only.
D CHIPMAN has not committed the offence against either officer as the arrest was unlawful.

Question 8.5

ELVIN is a store detective who witnesses YEUNG stealing a bottle of whisky from a supermarket. ELVIN arrests YEUNG outside the supermarket at which point YEUNG punches ELVIN in the face and runs off. ELVIN chases after YEUNG and catches her 200 metres away where the two begin fighting. GILLIGAN sees the struggle and believes that ELVIN is trying to rob YEUNG. GILLIGAN punches ELVIN in the face and as a result YEUNG manages to escape.

Who, if anyone, has committed the offence of assault with intent to resist arrest (contrary to s. 38 of the Offences Against the Person Act 1861)?
A Only YEUNG commits the offence.
B Only GILLIGAN commits the offence as he is preventing the lawful apprehension of another.
C Both YEUNG and GILLIGAN commit the offence.
D Neither YEUNG nor GILLIGAN commits the offence because ELVIN is not a police officer.

Question 8.6

GLANVILLE is having a bonfire party but does not invite HOCKLEY. HOCKLEY feels insulted and so when GLANVILLE is out, he places a small gas canister at the base of the bonfire believing that when it is lit the canister will explode and put the bonfire out. HOCKLEY believes that this is perfectly safe although there is a very minor chance that the explosion may hurt someone. During the party, the bonfire is lit and five minutes later the canister explodes. The gas canister hits GLANVILLE in the temple, causing him to lose consciousness.

Which of the statements below is true regarding HOCKLEY's liability for an offence of assault?
A HOCKLEY is not liable because for an assault to be committed, force must be applied directly. The placing of the canister in the bonfire is an indirect application of force.
B HOCKLEY is liable for an offence as he foresees the possibility of someone being hurt but nevertheless goes on to take the risk.
C HOCKLEY is not liable because he must actually intend to cause harm to some person when placing the canister in the bonfire.

D HOCKLEY is liable because the risk of the canister exploding and causing harm would have been obvious to any reasonable person.

Question 8.7

CATON steals a car and is pursued by PC STONE who is driving a police livery vehicle. CATON drives into a cul-de-sac and is followed by the officer. CATON realises that there is no way out of the cul-de-sac and that he will be arrested if he does not ram PC STONE's vehicle. Intending to escape and avoid arrest, CATON drives into the officer's car. CATON realises that this may cause an injury to PC STONE. The resulting crash causes multiple cuts to PC STONE's face, requiring 30 stitches. CATON is caught several minutes later.

With regard to assaults under the Offences Against the Person Act 1861, which of the statements below is correct?

A In these circumstances, CATON has 'inflicted' the injury and so the appropriate offence would be one of a s. 20 wounding.

B CATON commits s. 20 wounding, as there was no intent to wound or cause grievous bodily harm.

C CATON's actions were malicious and carried out in order to resist arrest. This means that he commits s. 18 wounding.

D CATON's actions would not provide the evidence required for a successful prosecution under the Offences Against the Person Act.

Question 8.8

BROSTER puts a letter through FELLOWS' front door intending that when FELLOWS reads the letter he will fear immediate unlawful violence. To create that fear, BROSTER has written words in the letter containing numerous threats of unlawful personal violence that will take place a minute or two after FELLOWS reads the letter. FELLOWS reads the letter and as a consequence he believes that he is going to be assaulted.

Would BROSTER's activities constitute an assault?

A No, because FELLOWS cannot fear immediate personal violence.

B Yes, as long as the force or violence apprehended by FELLOWS is a certainty.

C No, words, whether said or written, can never amount to an assault.

D Yes, where the words threatening immediate unlawful force come in the form of a letter, an assault may have been committed.

Question 8.9

STANFORD and HARTELL are neighbours who have had a long-standing dispute over car parking outside their respective houses. One afternoon, STANFORD parks his car directly outside HARTELL's house. HARTELL sees this and grabbing hold of an imitation pistol he runs outside and confronts STANFORD. Intending to make STAN-FORD believe he will be subject to immediate unlawful violence, HARTELL points the imitation pistol at STANFORD and says, 'If you don't move your car, I'll shoot you!' HARTELL believes the threat and moves his car.

Considering the offences of assault and battery only (under s. 39 of the Criminal Justice Act 1988), which of the below comments is true?

A STANFORD's actions would constitute a 'battery'.

B STANFORD does not commit an assault as this is a conditional threat.

C STANFORD has committed an offence of 'assault'.

D STANFORD does not commit an assault as he cannot physically harm HARTELL with an imitation pistol.

Question 8.10

Whether an offence is an assault occasioning actual bodily harm (contrary to section 47 of the Offences Against the Person Act) will be guided by reference to CPS Charging Standards and case law.

With regard to those standards and case law, which of the below statements is correct?

A CPS Charging Standards state that a minor fracture is too serious an injury to be classed as a s. 47 assault.

B A momentary loss of consciousness caused by a kick but without physical injury would not constitute 'actual harm'.

C Harm that is merely 'transient and trifling' is not covered by this offence.

D The cutting of a person's hair against their will could not amount to actual bodily harm as hair above the scalp is no more than dead tissue.

ANSWERS

Answer 8.1

Answer **C** — Answer A is incorrect, as an assault cannot be committed by an omission. When O'HARE threatens to assault GUNNING it is a conditional threat; the assault will not be committed because of the presence of the dog and therefore, GUNNING cannot fear immediate application of force. An assault is committed at point C because the 'indirect' application of force (via the dog), qualifies as an assault.

Investigators' Manual, paras 2.2.4–2.2.4.1   **DV = 5**

Answer 8.2

Answer **C** — In *R* v *Ireland* [1998] AC 147, it was held that telephone calls to a victim, followed by silences, could amount to an assault. This makes answers B and D incorrect. The harm caused in *R* v *Ireland* was psychiatric harm and the offender was charged and convicted of a s. 47 assault. This does not mean that psychiatric harm caused to the victim will limit the charge to a s. 47 assault only; there is nothing to stop an offence of s. 20 assault being committed when the harm is of a psychiatric nature, making answer A incorrect.

Investigators' Manual, paras 2.2.4, 2.2.18   **DV = 5**

Answer 8.3

Answer **B** — A person may consent to the use of force but that does not mean that the person causing the injury will be able to use the defence against a charge relating to assaults, making answer A incorrect. Whether the defence has any merit will often depend on the circumstances and the degree of harm caused. There are several cases that relate to this proposition, the most notable being *R* v *Brown* [1994] 1 AC 212. In this case, the House of Lords followed a policy decision that mirrors answer B. In *R* v *Wilson* (1996) 2 Cr App R 241, the court held that consensual activity between husband and wife is not a matter for criminal investigation although this would depend on the degree of harm caused, making answer C incorrect. The European Court of Human Rights considered the case of *R* v *Brown* (above) and held that it could justifiably be made the subject of criminal investigation on the grounds of 'protection of health' and that investigation and prosecution of such activity did not infringe the Article 8 rights to private life.

Investigators' Manual, paras 2.2.6, 2.2.7   **DV = 7**

Answer 8.4

Answer **B** — Whilst the circumstances described would constitute an offence of obstruct police (contrary to s. 89(2) of the Act) (*Ingleton* v *Dibble* [1972] 1 QB 480) there is no specific power of arrest for the offence, making the arrest unlawful. Therefore PC TERNAN would not be acting in the execution of his duty and as a consequence, CHIPMAN cannot be guilty of an offence of assaulting the officer contrary to s. 89(1) of the Act. This makes answers A and C incorrect. Answer D is incorrect as although the arrest was unlawful, when a prisoner is arrested and brought before a custody officer, that officer is entitled to assume that the arrest has been lawful. Therefore, if the prisoner goes on to assault the custody officer, that assault will nevertheless be an offence under s. 89(1) even if the original arrest turns out to be unlawful (*DPP* v *L* [1999] Crim LR 752).

Investigators' Manual, paras 2.2.13, 2.2.14.   **DV = 6**

Answer 8.5

Answer **A** — This offence applies to arrests made by several groups of people including store detectives, making answer D incorrect. To commit the offence the offender must assault any person knowing that the person assaulted was trying to make or help in an arrest. This knowledge is not present in GILLIGAN's mind making answers B and C incorrect.

Investigators' Manual, para. 2.2.12   **DV = 6**

Answer 8.6

Answer **B** — An assault can be committed by the direct or indirect application of force, making answer A incorrect. The state of mind required for the offence to be complete is that the defendant either intended to cause harm or subjective recklessness as to that consequence, making answer C incorrect. Subjective recklessness involves the belief of the person committing the offence, not the objective view of a reasonable person, making answer D incorrect.

Investigators' Manual, paras 2.2.4, 2.2.5   **DV = 6.5**

Answer 8.7

Answer **C** — Whilst there is no intention to wound, CATON's actions are 'malicious'. Maliciousness means that the defendant must realise that there is a risk of some harm being caused to the victim. The defendant does not need to foresee the degree of harm that is eventually caused, only that his/her behaviour may bring about some harm to the victim. When the harm is caused with *intent to resist or prevent lawful apprehension* (arrest), the s. 18 wounding offence is made out. This makes answers A, B and D incorrect.

Investigators' Manual, paras 2.2.18, 2.2.19   **DV = 5**

Answer 8.8

Answer **D** — Answer A is incorrect as in *R v Ireland* [1998] AC 147, the House of Lords suggested that a threat to cause violence 'in a minute or two' might be enough to qualify as an assault. The force or violence apprehended by the victim does not have to be a 'certainty'. Causing fear of some possible violence can be enough (*R v Ireland*), making answer B incorrect. Words can amount to an assault provided they are accompanied by the required *mens rea*, making answer C incorrect. In *R v Constanza* [1997] 2 Cr App R 492, it was held by the Court of Appeal that where the words threatening immediate unlawful force come in the form of letters, an assault may have been committed.

Investigators' Manual, para. 2.2.4.2   **DV = 7**

Answer 8.9

Answer **C** — A 'battery' is the actual application of force requiring some degree of contact; there has been no such contact so answer A is incorrect. Answer D is incorrect as even though the pistol is an imitation and incapable of firing it is the intention of the defendant coupled with the belief of the victim that is important. These circumstances would constitute an assault (answer C). Answer B is incorrect as this *is not* a conditional threat. A conditional threat would be something like STANFORD approaching HARTELL and pointing the pistol at him and saying, '*If you ever park your car outside my house I'll shoot you!*' The threat in the question is different as it is an immediate threat conditional upon some real circumstance—move your car or else!

Investigators' Manual, para. 2.2.4.1   **DV = 6**

Answer 8.10

Answer **C** — CPS Charging Standards include minor fractures as an injury that would constitute a s. 47 assault, making answer A incorrect. In *T* v *DPP* [2004] EWHC 183 (Admin), the Administrative Court accepted that a momentary loss of consciousness can amount to ABH, making answer B incorrect. In *DPP* v *Smith (Ross Michael)* [2006] 2 All ER 16, it was held that cutting hair amounted to ABH. Harm that is merely 'transient and trifling' is not covered by the offence (*R* v *Donovan* [1934] 2 KB 498).

Investigators' Manual, para. 2.2.17   **DV = 5.5**

9 | Threats to Kill, Child Abduction, Kidnap and False Imprisonment

QUESTIONS

Question 9.1

BALDWIN hates HIGGS as the two have had numerous fights with each other. BALDWIN is drinking in his local pub when he sees ROBERTS, a friend of HIGGS, walk into the pub. BALDWIN approaches ROBERTS and says, 'Next week I'm getting a gun and I'm gonna use it to kill HIGGS'. BALDWIN does not intend ROBERTS to believe the threat will be carried out; he just enjoys intimidating HIGGS's friends. ROBERTS believes BALDWIN and passes the threat onto HIGGS who does not fear the threat at all.

Why has no offence of making a threat to kill (s. 16 of the Offences Against the Person Act 1861) been committed?

A Because BALDWIN has made a threat to kill another person at some time in the future.

B Because the person to whom the threat is directed (HIGGS) does not fear that the threat would be carried out.

C Because the threat has been made to a third party (ROBERTS) rather than the person to whom the threat is directed.

D Because the person making the threat does not do so with the intention that the person receiving it (ROBERTS) would fear it would be carried out.

Question 9.2

HILL has separated from his common-law wife, YEO. There is a 15-year-old child by this relationship and the two have an informal understanding that HILL will have the child on weekends and YEO will have the child during the week. On Tuesday afternoon, YEO comes to your police station to report an offence of child abduction.

She tells you that she has received a telephone call from HILL telling her he has taken the child to Germany and will not be back for two more weeks. HILL stated he had attempted to contact YEO but had been unable to communicate with her. YEO wants HILL arrested and charged with the offence of child abduction (contrary to s. 1 of the Child Abduction Act 1984).

What will you tell her?

A HILL has not committed an offence under this legislation as it only applies to a child under the age of 14.

B HILL has committed the offence but he may be able to avail himself of a defence to the charge in these circumstances.

C HILL has not committed the offence as the child has been taken out of the United Kingdom for less than one month.

D HILL has committed the offence but the consent of the Attorney General is required before a charge of child abduction is brought.

Question 9.3

HAYMAN (aged 16 yrs) and NICHOLL (aged 13 yrs) are in a park when they are approached by EAMES (aged 30 yrs). EAMES tells them that he has just had his bike stolen and asks them if they would help him look for it. This is not true as EAMES's real motive is to attack the boys and sexually assault them at the first opportunity. Both boys willingly agree to EAMES's request and walk towards some nearby bushes where EAMES claims he left the bike. After walking some 30 metres with EAMES, the boys have second thoughts and run off.

Has EAMES committed an offence of Child Abduction (contrary to s. 2 of the Child Abduction Act 1984)?

A Yes, but only in relation to NICHOLL.

B No, because both HAYMAN and NICHOLL consented to go with EAMES.

C Yes, both HAYMAN and NICHOLL are covered by the legislation.

D No, neither of the boys has been removed from the lawful control of any person.

Question 9.4

SMITH is selling her house to GLYNN and the two have verbally agreed a price. Before any contracts are signed, SMITH has her house revalued and discovers that she can obtain another £20,000 should she put it back up for sale. In view of this, SMITH contacts GLYNN to ask for more money. GLYNN is outraged and goes to SMITH's house. SMITH lets GLYNN into her house but when he becomes abusive she demands he leave; he refuses. SMITH then tries to leave the house but GLYNN stops her by telling her that she is not leaving until she signs a contract agreeing to sell at the lower price. SMITH begins to cry and several minutes later GLYNN decides to leave.

Considering the offence of false imprisonment only, which of the statements below is correct?

A The offence is not committed because SMITH has not been physically detained.

B The offence will only be committed if GLYNN intends to restrain SMITH's movements.

C Keeping SMITH in her home for however short a time may amount to false imprisonment.

D Common law states that false imprisonment cannot be committed in the home of the complainant.

Question 9.5

MARSTON is part of a religious commune. UNWIN believes that MARSTON is in danger as the commune will ask MARSTON to turn all her property over to them. UNWIN decides that she will return MARSTON to her parents' home by whatever means are necessary. UNWIN visits the commune and finds MARSTON. She asks MARSTON to walk with her while they discuss her situation and MARSTON agrees. MARSTON refuses to return with UNWIN who then lies to MARSTON stating that MARSTON's mother is seriously ill and that she must come with her. MARSTON agrees and begins walking with UNWIN. Several minutes later, MARSTON asks for proof of her mother's illness from UNWIN who, at this point, physically drags MARSTON along for several metres before she lets her go.

At what point, if at all, does UNWIN first commit the offence of kidnap?

A When UNWIN initially begins walking with MARSTON intending to return her by whatever means necessary.

B When she lies to MARSTON about her mother and MARSTON walks with her for several minutes.

C When UNWIN uses physical force to drag MARSTON for several metres.

D UNWIN does not commit the offence because she has a lawful excuse to carry away MARSTON.

Question 9.6

POTTS and OLDFIELD lived together as common-law husband and wife but the relationship has ended. There were two children by this relationship, ANN (aged 12 yrs) and MARTIN (aged 16 yrs). Both children now live with their mother (OLDFIELD) who has lawful custody of the children. One evening, POTTS visits his children. While OLDFIELD goes out shopping, POTTS persuades the two children to go on holiday with him to Spain for two weeks. The children agree and all three leave for Spain without the consent of OLDFIELD.

Would this constitute an offence of child abduction (contrary to s. 1 of the Child Abduction Act)?

A No, as POTTS has taken the children outside the United Kingdom for less than one month.

B Yes, but only in relation to ANN.

C No, because POTTS is the father of both children.

D Yes, in relation to ANN and MARTIN.

Question 9.7

RICKWOOD works in a high security building where all the doors to the section where he works are controlled electronically. BRADISH approaches the control panel for the door locks and turns it off. This causes all of the doors in RICKWOOD's section of the building to lock shut. BRADISH believes that someone may have been locked in the building as a consequence of his actions but is not sure. As a result, RICKWOOD is locked in his section for 20 minutes until the door locks are released.

Which of the statements below is correct with regard to the offence of false imprisonment?

A RICKWOOD would have to be detained for several hours before a charge of false imprisonment would be appropriate.

B The offence is not committed because BRADISH did not actually intend anyone's freedom to be restrained.

C The fact that BRADISH was reckless as to whether anyone would be locked in means the offence is committed.

D BRADISH will only be found guilty of the offence if a jury consider his actions were reckless.

ANSWERS

Answer 9.1

Answer **D** — The offence of making a threat to kill can only be committed if it can be shown that the threat was made with the *intention* that *the person receiving it* would fear it would be carried out. It is the *intention* of the person who makes the threat that is important in this offence. It is immaterial that the threat to kill is a threat to kill another in the future, making answer A incorrect. It is also immaterial that the person to whom the threat is directed does not believe the threat and that that threat has been made via a third party, making answers B and C incorrect.

Investigators' Manual, para. 2.3   **DV = 7**

Answer 9.2

Answer **B** — This legislation applies to children under the age of 16, making answer A incorrect. A person would not commit an offence if they took a child out of the UK for less than a month *and* they are a person in whose favour there is a residence order in force with respect to the child. In this case there is an informal arrangement, making answer C incorrect. Although HILL commits the offence, it is the consent of the Director of Public Prosecutions that is required before bringing a charge under this legislation. HILL may be able to avail himself of the defence under s. 1(5)(b) of the Act, i.e. that he has taken all reasonable steps to communicate with YEO but has been unable to communicate with her.

Investigators' Manual, paras 2.4.1, 2.4.2   **DV = 6**

Answer 9.3

Answer **A** — The legislation covers children under the age of 16 years, making answer C incorrect. The fact that the boys consented to go with EAMES is irrelevant, making answer B incorrect. The Act talks about the taking or detaining of a child and this includes keeping a child where they are found or inducing the child to remain with the defendant or another person. Effectively, this taking or keeping is complete when the defendant substitutes his or her authority or will for that of the person in lawful control of the child and in this example the substitution takes place when EAMES walks with the boys towards the bushes (*R* v *Leather* (1993) 98 Cr App R 179). Therefore, answer D is incorrect.

Investigators' Manual, para. 2.4.3   **DV = 4**

Answer 9.4

Answer **C** — There is no requirement for the detaining of a person to be carried out by a physical action, just that their movement be restrained; this may be achieved by words alone, making answer A incorrect. The mental element required to commit this offence was stated in *R* v *Rahman* (1985) 81 Cr App R 349 as being 'the unlawful and intentional or reckless restraint of a victim's movement from a particular place' so the offence can be committed recklessly, making answer B incorrect. The 'particular place' can be absolutely anywhere and this includes a victim's own house.

Investigators' Manual, para. 2.5   **DV = 8**

Answer 9.5

Answer **B** — The offence of kidnap is the unlawful taking or carrying away of one person by another by force or fraud (*R* v *D* [1984] AC 778). At point 'A' UNWIN's intentions are to remove MARSTON by any means, however, MARSTON has voluntarily consented to walk with UNWIN and no fraud or force is used. At point 'B' the offence is committed as UNWIN has used a fraud to move MARSTON from one point to another; distance is no object. Although a 'lawful excuse' would provide UNWIN with a defence to the charge, a concern for finances or a moral or spiritual concern would not suffice; there must be a necessity recognised as law (*R* v *Henman* [1987] Crim LR 333, CA), making answer D incorrect.

Investigators' Manual, para. 2.6   **DV = 3**

Answer 9.6

Answer **B** — This offence can be committed by any person listed under s. 2 of the Act who is connected to the child/children. The Act states that a person is connected with a child (at s. 2(b)) in the case of a child whose parents were not married to each other at the time of his birth, if there are reasonable grounds for believing that he is the father of the child, i.e. POTTS. However, just because POTTS is the father of the children does not afford him immunity from this offence, making answer C incorrect. The offence can only be committed in relation to a child under the age of 16 so it cannot be committed in relation to MARTIN, making answer D incorrect. The fact that POTTS has taken the children outside the UK for less than one month is immaterial. The time factor is only relevant if there is a residence order in existence in favour of POTTS (and there is not); what is relevant is that POTTS has taken ANN outside the UK without the consent of OLDFIELD, making answer A incorrect.

Investigators' Manual, para. 2.4.1   **DV = 6**

Answer 9.7

Answer **C** — Detention for however short a period may amount to false imprisonment, making answer A incorrect. The state of mind required for this offence is 'subjective recklessness' making answers B and D incorrect.

Investigators' Manual, para. 2.5   **DV = 5**

10 Public Order and Racially Aggravated Offences

QUESTIONS

Question 10.1

WIDDOWS, WARD and SLEWS visit a nightclub and get extremely drunk. As a result of their drunken behaviour they are thrown out of the club. They decide to get revenge on the doorman of the club and wait for him in a nearby deserted alley. When the doorman leaves the club, WIDDOWS, WARD and SLEWS approach him and tell him that they are going to 'cut his eyes out'. The doorman laughs at all three and has no fear whatsoever for his personal safety. The three continue making threats and are arrested shortly afterwards.

Do WIDDOWS, WARD and SLEWS commit violent disorder?

A Yes, all three men had the required 'common purpose' necessary. If this element were not present in the actions of the three men then no offence of violent disorder would take place.

B No, the Public Order Act 1986 specifically caters for the effects of 'drunkenness' and the three would be able to state their awareness was impaired and use the defence.

C Yes, the fact that the doorman was not frightened of the three men makes no difference. It is not necessary to prove that a person of reasonable firmness was actually caused to fear for their safety.

D No, the doorman would be classed as a person of reasonable firmness and he must fear for his personal safety. As he does not, the offence is incomplete.

Question 10.2

MALKIN has a long-running dispute with his neighbour HOLLYOAKE. After a heated argument one evening MALKIN decides to get revenge on HOLLYOAKE by smashing a greenhouse in HOLLYOAKE's back garden. MALKIN stands in his own back garden and uses a mobile phone to call his neighbour. When HOLLYOAKE answers the phone MALKIN says, 'Look out of your back window'. HOLLYOAKE looks out of the window and as he does so, MALKIN leans over the garden fence separating the two houses and smashes several panes of greenhouse glass with a hammer.

Does MALKIN commit an affray, contrary to s. 3 of the Public Order Act 1986?

A Yes, the threat is accompanied by actions (MALKIN smashed the pane of glass).

B No, HOLLYOAKE is inside a dwelling when the threat is made to him.

C Yes, this offence can be committed in private as well as public places.

D No, affray does not include conduct towards property.

Question 10.3

JEWELL, FAGAN and BREEN are all drinking in a nightclub. JEWELL and FAGAN think it will be funny to lace BREEN's orange juice with a double vodka each time he has a drink in order to get him drunk. After several drinks, JEWELL is drunk and cannot control his behaviour. All three become involved in an argument with a barman resulting in the three men assaulting the barman. The police are called to the nightclub and all three are arrested for, amongst other offences, violent disorder.

Considering the offence of violent disorder only, which of the statements below is correct?

A The fact that BREEN's awareness was impaired by intoxication makes no difference to the proceedings.

B BREEN could claim that his intoxication was not self-induced and if successful he will be acquitted. As a result, JEWELL and FAGAN will be acquitted of the charge of violent disorder.

C BREEN cannot claim that his intoxication was not self-induced as this defence only applies when the behaviour of the defendant was due solely to taking or administrating a substance in the course of medical treatment.

D Even if BREEN were to successfully claim his intoxication was not self-induced and be acquitted, his presence at the scene would be enough for a prosecution against JEWELL and FAGAN to be continued.

Question 10.4

O'MALLEY has been falsely claiming state benefits and is informed by MIRZA that his benefits will be withdrawn. O'MALLEY writes a threatening letter to MIRZA after being told of the action by the Benefits Agency. The police investigate the fraudulent claims by O'MALLEY and four and a half months after his benefits had been withdrawn, the police arrest and charge O'MALLEY for deception-related offences. O'MALLEY blames MIRZA for his situation and writes a second threatening letter to him.

Would O'MALLEY be liable for an offence under ss. 1 and 2 of the Protection from Harassment Act 1997?

A Yes, as on occasions the courts have accepted that two instances of behaviour by the defendant several months apart will suffice.
B No, the courts have held that people in such public service posts are expected to be more robust and therefore less likely to be distressed or frightened by the content of such personal communications.
C Yes, O'MALLEY would be liable for the offence from the moment MIRZA receives the first letter.
D No, as although there has been a course of conduct on two occasions, they are so far apart in time that they would not constitute an offence under this legislation.

Question 10.5

WINDSOR and LOVETT work 30 feet apart in the same factory. WINDSOR approaches LOVETT at 10.00am one morning and states, 'I've never liked your family, I think I'll go and beat your dad up now'. LOVETT fears that WINDSOR will use violence on his father and runs off to warn him, he then returns to work. Two hours later, WINDSOR sends LOVETT a text message on his mobile phone stating, 'I've never liked you, I think I'll beat you up now'. LOVETT runs away from WINDSOR fearing that violence will be used against him. LOVETT reports WINDSOR's behaviour to the police.

Considering the offence of putting people in fear of violence (s. 4 of the Protection from Harassment Act 1997) only, which of the below is true?

A WINDSOR is guilty of the offence because he has caused LOVETT to fear that violence will be used on two occasions.
B For the offence to be complete, the prosecution must show that WINDSOR intended to cause LOVETT to fear that violence will be used.
C WINDSOR is not guilty of the offence because both threats must cause LOVETT to fear that violence will be used against him.
D WINDSOR does not commit the offence because there is a specific requirement that the activity making up the course of conduct be of the same nature.

Question 10.6

YOUNG and SCOTT share a house and both men have strong anti-Muslim feelings. The two men make a banner that says, 'Death to Muslims!' Intending to stir up racial hatred, they display the banner inside the front window of their house so that passing cars and pedestrians can see it.

Considering the offence of using words, behaviour or display of written material under s. 18 of the Public Order Act 1986, which of the statements below is correct?

A No offence is committed because the banner is displayed inside a dwelling house.

B YOUNG and SCOTT commit the offence but could only be prosecuted with the consent of the Director of Public Prosecutions.

C No offence is committed because Muslims are not covered by the legislation.

D YOUNG and SCOTT commit the offence for which there is no defence.

Question 10.7

ASPINALL is unemployed and desperately needs cash. He is given £25 by POWELL to hand out leaflets to members of the public. POWELL promises ASPINALL that if he hands out all the leaflets he will receive a further £25. The leaflets contain material on white supremacy movements and are intended to stir up racial hatred against black people. ASPINALL is aware of the content of the leaflets and their purpose but only wants to distribute them to receive payment from POWELL and begins distributing the leaflets to members of the public.

With regard to s. 19 of the Public Order Act 1986 only, which of the below is correct?

A This offence can only be committed in a public place.

B Although ASPINALL commits the offence, he would be able to claim a defence under s. 19, as he did not intend to stir up racial hatred.

C ASPINALL does not commit the offence because he did not publish the written material.

D ASPINALL commits the offence as having regard to all the circumstances racial hatred is likely to be stirred up.

Question 10.8

OLLERTON and KHAN are neighbours and are in dispute over the boundary between their respective back gardens. One evening, OLLERTON comes home to find that KHAN has erected a fence between the two gardens. OLLERTON loses her temper and begins to break the fence. As OLLERTON is breaking the fence, KHAN comes out into the back garden. Motivated by frustration over the fence rather than racism, OLLERTON says to KHAN, 'How dare you put up a fence you Muslim pig'. KHAN is not upset by OLLERTON's comments, as he is not a Muslim.

Would this offence of criminal damage be 'racially aggravated' under s. 28 of the Crime and Disorder Act 1998?

A Yes, as it is immaterial whether OLLERTON's hostility is also based, to any extent, on any other factor.

B No, because KHAN is not personally upset by the situation.

C Yes, but only because the words uttered were said during the commission of the offence.

D No, because OLLERTON was motivated to utter the words merely by frustration rather than racism.

ANSWERS

Answer 10.1

Answer **C** — Answer A is incorrect as there is no requirement for a 'common purpose' for the offence of violent disorder to be committed. Section 6 of the Public
Order Act 1986 does cater for the effects of drunkenness, but unless the intoxication is as a result of drugs taken in the course of medical treatment or it is not
self-induced, the defendant will be deemed to be aware of his/her activities as if
he/she were sober, making answer B incorrect. The fact that the doorman is not in
fear is irrelevant; the person of reasonable firmness need not be present at the scene
and so answer D is incorrect.

Investigators' Manual, paras 2.7.1.1, 2.7.2   **DV = 6.5**

Answer 10.2

Answer **D** — An affray cannot be committed when the conduct of the defendant
is directed towards property alone. This is specifically mentioned in s. 8 of the Act
where it is stated that 'violence means any violent conduct *except in the context of affray*, it includes violent conduct towards *property* as well as violent conduct towards
persons'.

Investigators' Manual, paras 2.7.1.1, 2.7.3   **DV = 6**

Answer 10.3

Answer **B** — Section 6 of the Public Order Act specifically caters for the effects of
self-induced intoxication. If a person is responsible for becoming intoxicated, they
cannot use that intoxication as a defence to a charge under the Public Order Act
unless they can show that the intoxication was not self-induced, for example by
somebody 'spiking' their drinks or that it was the result of taking a substance in the
course of medical treatment. Intoxication can be as a result of drink, drugs or a combination of the two. This makes answers A and C incorrect. In order to convict on a
charge of violent disorder, you must show that there were three people involved. If
this is not proved then the court must acquit each defendant (*R v McGuigan* [1991]
Crim LR 719). This makes answer D incorrect.

Investigators' Manual, paras 2.7.1.2, 2.7.2   **DV = 8**

Answer 10.4

Answer **A** — The 'course of conduct' that makes a defendant liable for this offence must take place on at least two occasions, making answer C incorrect. In *Lau* v *DPP* [2000] Crim LR 580, the court said that regard should be had to the relative times that the incidents took place and that the further apart in time that they took place, the less likely it was that a court would find that harassment had taken place. However, in *Baron* v *Crown Prosecution Service*, 13 June 2000, unreported, the court held that two instances several months apart will suffice (four and a half months apart as in the question), making answer D incorrect. The court further held that people in public service posts were entitled to the same protection as any other member of the public and that the fact they were employed in such a capacity made no difference to the conduct of the defendant, making answer B incorrect.

Investigators' Manual, para. 2.8.12.1   **DV = 7.5**

Answer 10.5

Answer **C** — The course of conduct may be two distinctly different types of behaviour; there is no requirement that they be similar in nature, making answer D incorrect. The prosecution do not have to show an intention in the mind of the defendant, rather one which is subject to a test of reasonableness against the standards of an ordinary person in possession of the same information as the defendant, making answer B incorrect. The course of conduct has to cause a person to fear that, on at least two occasions, violence will be used against him rather than a member of their family (*Mohammed Ali Caurti* v *DPP* [2002] Crim LR 131), making answer A incorrect. If the fear is not present on both occasions then the offence is not committed.

Investigators' Manual, para. 2.8.14.7   **DV = 3**

Answer 10.6

Answer **C** — Answer D is incorrect because there is a specific defence to this offence if the accused is inside a dwelling and had no reason to believe their activities would be heard or seen by a person outside that or any other dwelling. This means that answer A is incorrect as both men intended the sign to be seen by people in the street. Answer B is incorrect as the offence can only be prosecuted with the consent of the Attorney General (or Solicitor General). Although Muslims are covered by racially aggravated offences under the Crime and Disorder Act 1998, they are a religious group and this area of criminal law was not specifically extended to cover religious groups.

Investigators' Manual, paras 2.8.9–2.8.10.2   **DV = 2**

Answer 10.7

Answer **D** — Section 19 of the Public Order Act 1986 deals with the publishing or distribution of written material with intent to stir up racial hatred. Answer A is incorrect as this offence can be committed in public or in private. Answer B is incorrect as although there is a defence to this offence, it is only available if the person can show that they were unaware of the content of the material and did not suspect and had no reason to suspect that it was threatening, abusive or insulting. Answer C is incorrect as the offence can be committed by distribution to the public or a section of the public as well as by publication to that group.

Investigators' Manual, paras 2.8.9–2.8.11.2   **DV = 6**

Answer 10.8

Answer **A** — Answer B is incorrect as the Administrative Court has held that the victim's own perception of the words used was irrelevant, as was the fact that the victim was not personally upset by the situation (*DPP* v *Woods* [2002] EWHC Admin 85). In the same case it was stated that the fact that the defendant might have been motivated to utter the words merely by frustration rather than racism was also irrelevant, making answer D incorrect. This is in addition to the Act itself, which states at s. 28(3) that it is immaterial whether or not the offender's hostility is also based, to any extent, on any other factor. Answer C is incorrect as a racially aggravated offence can take place *immediately before, at the time of committing an offence or after committing the offence.*

Investigators' Manual, para. 2.8.2   **DV = 4**

11 Criminal Damage

QUESTIONS

Question 11.1

HARDCASTLE assists his wife in her job as a warden of a block of flats for pensioners. HARDCASTLE's wife constantly complains about the poor condition of the fire alarm and worries that if it is not changed the pensioners' lives will be in danger and there might be a large amount of damage caused to the flats if there is a fire. To demonstrate to the owner of the flats that the fire alarm needs changing, HARDCASTLE sets fire to some bedding in one of the flats. Eventually, the fire alarm activates and the fire is put out. HARDCASTLE is arrested for arson.

Would HARDCASTLE be able to claim that he had a lawful excuse to commit criminal damage?

A Yes, because the damage was caused in order to protect the property.

B No, because what has been done by HARDCASTLE is not done in order to protect property.

C Yes, because the damage was caused in order to protect the lives of the pensioners.

D No, because the defence of 'lawful excuse' does not apply to offences of arson.

Question 11.2

WATE is a vicar who wishes to protest against Great Britain's involvement in the invasion and occupation of Iraq. He visits the Houses of Parliament and, as a sign of his disapproval of the occupation, he writes a quotation from the Bible in ink on a pillar outside the main door to the building. He honestly believes what he has done is morally right.

Which of the statements below is correct?

A WATE would have a defence if he claims he had damaged the property as a reasonable means of protecting other property located in Iraq from being damaged by warfare.

B WATE would have a defence if he claimed that he was carrying out God's instructions and therefore had a lawful excuse based on his belief that God was entitled to consent to such damage.

C WATE has not committed criminal damage. It is immaterial whether his beliefs for causing criminal damage were justified or not, what matters is that the beliefs were honestly held.

D WATE is guilty of criminal damage because it has been held that a belief in The Almighty's consent is not a lawful excuse and that such conduct would be too remote from any need to protect property in Iraq.

Question 11.3

DYKE has a long-standing disagreement with MONK over who owns a section of land that lies between their respective houses. One evening, after DYKE has been drinking at his local pub, he decides to get revenge on MONK and walks up the drive of MONK's house intent on damaging MONK's property.

At what point does DYKE first commit an offence of criminal damage?

A As DYKE enters the driveway he stamps on and destroys some flowers that are growing wild at the entrance to the drive.

B DYKE passes a garden shed owned by MONK and, although he knows it will easily be washed off, he smears the word 'Wanker' in mud across the shed.

C DYKE picks up a large container of black paint and pours this over MONK's front lawn.

D DYKE approaches a chicken coop and reaches inside. He picks up a chicken and breaks its legs.

Question 11.4

FALLON is a tramp searching for somewhere to sleep for the night. He breaks into an abandoned detached house and using some old furniture for fuel, sets a fire that quickly burns out of control, destroying part of the house. FALLON only escapes with his life because of the rapid attendance of the fire brigade. Because of the gap between the neighbouring houses there is no likelihood that the fire will spread to any other buildings.

Would FALLON be liable for an offence under s. 1(2) of the Criminal Damage Act 1971?

A Yes, because of FALLON's actions he recklessly endangered his own life.

B No, because FALLON did not intend to endanger his own or any other person's life.

C Yes, what matters is the potential for damage and danger created by FALLON's conduct.

D No, because the fire brigade attended and because of the gap between the houses, there was no actual danger to life.

Question 11.5

MAYHEW breaks off his engagement to CUTHBERT who takes the news badly. CUTHBERT is desperate to rekindle the relationship and phones MAYHEW telling him that unless the two of them get back together, she will steal his car, set it alight and burn herself alive in it. CUTHBERT does not intend to carry out her threat but does intend for MAYHEW to believe her. Unknown to CUTHBERT, MAYHEW has sold his car and so does not actually fear that the threat will be carried out.

Which of the statements below is correct with regard to a threat to destroy or damage property under s. 2 of the Criminal Damage Act 1971?

A CUTHBERT is not guilty of the offence because MAYHEW has sold his car and therefore knows that the threat is incapable of being carried out.

B The offence is not committed because CUTHBERT has not threatened to destroy or damage her own property.

C The offence is not committed because CUTHBERT never intended to carry out her threat.

D CUTHBERT has committed the offence because her intention was to make MAYHEW fear that the threat would be carried out.

Question 11.6

AMBROSE and FARRAR are sacked from a supermarket. Both believe that they have been treated unfairly and intending to cause the supermarket to lose trade they stand outside the supermarket talking loudly about how, before they were sacked, they placed crushed glass inside hundreds of loaves of bread sold by the supermarket. Both men are lying as no food was tampered with. Their actions cause dozens of potential customers to shop elsewhere. DOWN hears the two men and believing what he has heard he phones a TV company telling them the food at the supermarket is contaminated. The news is broadcasted causing the supermarket to close down for two weeks.

Who, if anyone, commits an offence of contamination or interference with goods under s. 38(2) of the Public Order Act 1986?

A DOWN only.

B AMBROSE and FARRAR.

C AMBROSE, FARRAR and DOWN.

D No offence is committed by any of the men.

Question 11.7

FISHER argues with NEGUS and decides that he will take revenge on him by pouring a container of paint stripper over NEGUS's car. FISHER does not have any paint stripper and so visits a garage owned by SMITH and asks if he will provide him with the paint stripper. When SMITH asks why FISHER wants it, FISHER tells him of his plan. SMITH tells FISHER that the paint stripper is at the back of his garage and advises FISHER to wait for a week before he commits the criminal damage so that NEGUS will not suspect that FISHER is responsible. FISHER collects the paint stripper and tells SMITH that he will take his advice.

Considering the offence of having articles with intent to destroy or damage property (s. 3 of the Criminal Damage Act 1971) only, which of the statements below is correct?

A In these circumstances, both SMITH and FISHER would commit the offence.

B Only SMITH commits this offence as FISHER is not the owner of the paint stripper and therefore cannot have custody or control over it.

C Only FISHER commits the offence as he is the only person who actually has physical possession of the paint stripper.

D Neither SMITH nor FISHER commit the offence as the criminal damage will take place at some time in the future.

Question 11.8

REECE is fired from his job as a cleaner at a fast-food outlet. He is extremely annoyed by this and wants revenge. He telephones the manager of the fast-food outlet and lies to her. REECE states that a friend of his has put strong acid in some of the soap dispensers in the male and female toilets at the outlet. REECE intends that the manager will have to shut the fast-food outlet down for several days and lose income as a consequence. The manager does not believe REECE and ignores the threat.

Which of the statements below is correct with regard to the offence of contaminating or interfering with goods (contrary to s. 38(2) of the Public Order Act 1986)?

A REECE commits the offence because he intended to cause an economic loss to the fast-food outlet.

B As no acid has actually been put into the soap dispensers the offence is incomplete.

C REECE would commit the offence but only if the manager actually believed his threat.

D The offence is not committed as REECE has threatened the contamination of manufactured goods rather than foodstuffs.

Question 11.9

PREEDY lives in a caravan and parks it on land belonging to a farmer that backs onto RASHID's garden. RASHID is outraged by PREEDY's presence and is concerned that PREEDY will move his caravan into his garden. To prevent this happening, RASHID digs a trench two feet deep along the land belonging to the farmer. RASHID also paints a slogan across the front of PREEDY's caravan that says, 'LEAVE NOW TRAVELLER SCUM!'.

Considering offences relating to criminal damage only, which of the comments below is correct?

A RASHID would have a lawful excuse for damaging the farmers land if he believed that he had a right in law to commit the damage.

B RASHID only commits criminal damage to PREEDY's caravan, as you cannot damage land.

C RASHID may have a defence to damaging the land if he believes that the farmer would consent to the damage if he knew of the circumstances.

D RASHID commits criminal damage to PREEDY's caravan and, in addition, this offence would be racially aggravated.

ANSWERS

Answer 11.1

Answer **B** — Answer D is incorrect as the defence of lawful excuse may apply to any type or form of criminal damage. Section 5(2) of the Criminal Damage Act 1971 gives the circumstances when a person may have a lawful excuse to damage or destroy property. This must involve an immediate need for the action taken in order to protect the property and also that the means adopted were reasonable having regard to the circumstances. In this question, HARDCASTLE's activities would not fall into either of the last two categories and the defence would fail, making answers A and C incorrect. These were the circumstances in *R v Hunt* (1977) 66 Cr App R 105. In this case the court held that the action taken was in order to draw attention to a defective fire alarm and not done in order to protect property.

Investigators' Manual, paras 2.9.2, 2.9.2.7   **DV = 5**

Answer 11.2

Answer **D** — This question is based on the case of *Blake* v *DPP* [1993] Crim LR 586. Although the two defences under ss. 5(2)(a) and 5(2)(b) both involve the honestly held belief of the defendant, it does not mean that any honestly held belief will suffice, making answer C incorrect. *Blake* protested against Great Britain's involvement in the Gulf war and damaged a pillar outside the Houses of Parliament. His defence was as per answers A and B and the Divisional Court's response was as per answer D.

Investigators' Manual, para. 2.9.2.7   **DV = 8**

Answer 11.3

Answer **B** — Under s. 10 of the Criminal Damage Act 1971, flowers growing wild on any land would not be classed as property making answer A incorrect. The items referred to in options B, C and D would all be classed as property; land can be subject to criminal damage along with wild creatures that are ordinarily kept in captivity or have been reduced into possession (the chickens). There is no requirement that criminal damage be associated with an economic loss. It has been held by the Divisional Court that graffiti smeared in mud, even though it is easily washed off, can amount to criminal damage (*Roe* v *Kingerlee* [1986] Crim LR 735). Therefore the point at which the offence is first committed is at point B.

Investigators' Manual, para. 2.9.2.3   **DV = 7**

Answer 11.4

Answer **C** — The aggravated form of criminal damage can only be committed if the life endangered is someone else's other than the defendants, making answers A and B incorrect. Answer B is further incorrect as the offence can be committed recklessly. Answer D is incorrect, as it does not matter that there was no *actual* danger to life. What is relevant is the *potential danger* to life. This question is based on the circumstances in *R* v *Sangha* [1988] WLR 519 where the court held that had a reasonable bystander been present, they would have seen the possible risk that the fire might cause to the lives of others in the area and found Sangha guilty of the offence.

Investigators' Manual, para. 2.9.3   **DV = 2**

Answer 11.5

Answer **D** — The central element for the commission of this offence is that the defendant *intended* the complainant to fear that the threat would be carried out. That threat can be to destroy or damage property belonging to that or another person or to destroy or damage his/her own property in a way that will endanger the life of that other or a third person, making answer B incorrect. The fact that CUTHBERT never intended to carry out her threat or that the threat is incapable of being carried out makes no difference, making answers A and C incorrect.

Investigators' Manual, para. 2.9.5   **DV = 8**

Answer 11.6

Answer **B** — DOWN's activities are catered for by s. 38(6) of the Act which states that although it is an offence to claim that goods have been interfered with, this will not include a person who in good faith reports or warns that such acts have been or appear to have been committed. This makes answers A and C incorrect. The offence under s. 38 can be committed in a variety of ways, one of those being to claim that goods have been contaminated with the intention of causing economic loss to any person by reason of the goods being shunned, making answer D incorrect.

Investigators' Manual, para. 2.10   **DV = 4**

Answer 11.7

Answer **A** — The offence under s. 3 of the Act is committed when an individual has anything in his custody or control intending without lawful excuse to *use it* or *cause or permit another to use it* to destroy or damage property belonging to another or to destroy or damage his own or another's property in such a way that he knows is likely to endanger the life of some other person. It is not necessary to be the owner of the item in order to commit this offence, making answer B incorrect. Neither is it necessary to actually have physical possession of the item, making answer C incorrect. The fact that the damage is planned for a week's time is immaterial as it is the intention of the parties that is relevant for this offence, making answer D incorrect.

Investigators' Manual, para. 2.9.6.1   **DV = 3**

Answer 11.8

Answer **A** — Answer B is incorrect as the Act caters for the threat of contamination with goods under s. 38(2). Whether the manager believes REECE is immaterial as it is the intention of the person making the threat that is important, making answer C incorrect. Section 38(5) states that 'goods' include substances whether natural or manufactured and whether or not incorporated in or mixed with other goods. This means that soap dispensers would be covered by the Act, making answer D incorrect.

Investigators' Manual, para. 2.10   **DV = 7**

Answer 11.9

Answer **C** — Answer B is incorrect as property for the purposes of the offence of criminal damage (under s. 10 of the 1971 Criminal Damage Act) includes land. Answer A is incorrect as there are two lawful excuses under s. 5(2) of the Act; neither relate to a belief in a right in law to commit damage. Answer D is incorrect as 'travellers', as opposed to traditional gypsies, are not capable of being a racial group so the slogan would not be classed as a racially aggravating feature of the criminal damage.

Investigators' Manual, paras 2.8.6, 2.9.2.5–2.9.2.6   **DV = 3**

12 | Misuse of Drugs

QUESTIONS

Question 12.1

TURVEY has just lost his job and is finding money hard to come by. RANDELL feels sorry for TURVEY and gives him a packet of 10 cigarettes that also contains a small amount of cocaine. TURVEY knows nothing about the cocaine inside the packet of cigarettes. Several hours later, TURVEY is stopped by PC MAIR who discovers the cocaine inside the cigarette packet.

Which of the statements below is correct with regard to TURVEY?

A Provided TURVEY has physical control of the cigarettes and knows of their presence he has 'possession' of the drug.

B The only requirement for 'possession' is that TURVEY had the drug in his physical control.

C To show that TURVEY has 'possession' of the drug you must show that he actually knew that what he possessed was cocaine.

D TURVEY cannot be in 'possession' of the cocaine because he does not know of its existence.

Question 12.2

WILLSON is the landlord of a flat rented out to BOWN. WILLSON is aware of the fact that BOWN is cultivating several cannabis plants in the flat. BOWN goes on holiday and asks MELLING to water his plants until he returns. MELLING has no idea that the 'plants' are cannabis plants and is watering them when the police execute a warrant at the premises.

Apart from BOWN, who, if either, commits the offence of cultivation of cannabis (contrary to s. 6 of the Misuse of Drugs Act 1971)?

A Only WILLSON, as the landlord, commits the offence.

B Only MELLING commits the offence.

C Both WILLSON and MELLING commit the offence.

D Neither WILLSON nor MELLING commit the offence.

Question 12.3

You are taking part in a drugs operation. The subjects of the operation are MENSAH and ROWLES, both well-known drug dealers. MENSAH arrives at the car park of a local pub and begins to deal. Shortly afterwards, ROWLES arrives driving a van. You and your colleagues carry out the operation and MENSAH and ROWLES are detained in the car park. In ROWLES' van is £20,000 worth of heroine. ROWLES states that the heroin belongs to MENSAH and he was only looking after it for £100 while MENSAH dealt the drug.

What offence(s) under the Misuse of Drugs Act 1971 does ROWLES commit?

A Possession of a controlled drug (s. 5(2)) only.

B Supplying a controlled drug (s. 4(3)) only.

C Possession with intent to supply a controlled drug (s. 5(3)) only.

D Possession with intent to supply (s. 5(3)) and supplying a controlled drug (s. 4(3)).

Question 12.4

It is SHANAHAN's birthday and he gets drunk with some friends at a pub. On his way home McFADDEN stops him. SHANAHAN knows McFADDEN is a drug dealer. McFADDEN asks SHANAHAN to drop an envelope at an address and gives SHANA-HAN £100 to deliver it. Because SHANAHAN is drunk he has no reason to suspect the envelope contains drugs and accepts the offer. SHANAHAN is approaching the delivery address when he is arrested for possessing a controlled drug (which was inside the envelope) with intent to supply.

Would SHANAHAN have any defence under s. 28(2) of the Misuse of Drugs Act 1971?

A Yes, in these circumstances SHANAHAN's 'reason to suspect' was impaired by his drunken condition and because the 'reason to suspect' is judged subjectively he will be able to use a defence.

B No, the fact that SHANAHAN was drunk is irrelevant. He knew McFADDEN was a drug dealer and should suspect that the envelope contains drugs because of the large reward for delivering it.

C Yes, SHANAHAN could state that he neither knew nor suspected that the envelope contained a controlled drug and that he neither knew nor suspected that he was supplying it to another.
D No, this section only provides a defence to the offence of unlawful possession of a controlled drug.

Question 12.5

DC BAUGH is working undercover in an area well known for the sale and distribution of controlled drugs. She is approached by CREIGHTON who is considering robbing DC BAUGH. To find out if DC BAUGH has any money and is worth robbing, CREIGHTON offers to supply some cocaine to her for £200. CREIGHTON does not have any cocaine and has no intention of supplying DC BAUGH with the drug.

Which of the statements below is correct?
A CREIGHTON commits an offence of supplying a controlled drug to DC BAUGH.
B No offence is committed by CREIGHTON, as he did not possess the cocaine to make good on his offer to DC BAUGH.
C CREIGHTON is not guilty of an offence, as he had no intention of supplying the drug to DC BAUGH.
D As CREIGHTON made his offer to an undercover police officer, he can claim that the offer to supply was not a 'real' offer.

Question 12.6

MOSTAFA is convicted of an offence of supplying a controlled drug (contrary to s. 4(3) of the Misuse of Drugs Act 1971) and is sentenced to 5 years' imprisonment for the offence.

Considering the law with regard to travel restriction orders (under the Criminal Justice and Police Act 2001), which of the statements below is correct?
A This offence of supplying a controlled drug is not covered by the legislation in relation to travel restriction orders.
B The minimum period for such an order is 4 years.
C MOSTAFA must surrender his UK passport as part of the order.
D If an order was made then MOSTAFA may apply to the court that made the restriction order to have it revoked or suspended.

Question 12.7

GRAPNELL is subject to a travel restriction order under the Criminal Justice and Police Act 2001. A rival gang of drug dealers kidnaps him outside his home address in London. The gang drive GRAPNELL to Scotland and then take him to Northern Ireland. From Northern Ireland the gang take GRAPNELL to France.

At what stage, if at all, does GRAPNELL commit an offence of contravening the travel restriction order?

A When he enters Scotland.

B When he enters Northern Ireland.

C When he enters France.

D The offence is not committed.

Question 12.8

One of the main practical effects of being able to identify the classification of a controlled drug is determine the mode of trial and sentencing powers of the court.

Which of the below drugs would be classified as Class B?

A Heroin.

B 'Magic mushrooms' (containing psilocin).

C 'Crystal meth' (methylamphetamine).

D Ketamine.

Question 12.9

CUTLER and HAVELIN are both drug addicts who use heroin on a regular basis. They obtain some heroin and HAVELIN obtains two items, a tourniquet and a hypodermic syringe, to assist in the administration of the drug. HAVELIN offers to supply both articles to CUTLER so that he can administer the drug to himself.

With which, if any, of the two items would HAVELIN commit the offence of supplying articles for administering or preparing controlled drugs (contrary to s. 9A of the Misuse of Drugs Act 1971)?

A The tourniquet only.

B The hypodermic syringe only.

C The tourniquet and the hypodermic syringe.

D Neither of the two items.

Question 12.10

MIRZA owns a café that is managed by NORTHALL. The café is regularly frequented by a group of teenagers who smoke cannabis inside the café. NORTHALL is fully aware that the teenagers use controlled drugs in the café but does not know what drug they use and as the teenagers are such good customers he decides to ignore their activities. MIRZA has no idea that the teenagers even use the café let alone smoke cannabis on the premises.

With regard to the offence of being the occupier or manager of premises and permitting drug use (contrary to s. 8 of the Misuse of Drugs Act 1971), which of the below statements is correct?

A Neither MIRZA nor NORTHALL would commit the offence because smoking cannabis or cannabis resin is not covered by this particular piece of legislation.

B The fact that MIRZA does not know the teenagers smoke drugs in the café is immaterial; this is an offence of strict liability and as the café owner he commits the offence.

C NORTHALL commits the offence but would only be found guilty if the prosecution could show that he knew what type of drugs were being used by the teenagers.

D MIRZA does not commit the offence because he does not know that the teenagers are smoking cannabis in his café.

Question 12.11

Section 1 of the Anti-social Behaviour Act 2003 provides a power to close premises if certain conditions are met in relation to drugs and disorder.

Who can issue a closure notice in respect of such premises?

A Any police officer.
B A police officer not below the rank of Inspector.
C A police officer not below the rank of Superintendent.
D A Magistrates' Court.

Question 12.12

A closure notice (under s. 1 of the Anti-social Behaviour Act 2003) has been issued in respect of 180 Bayliss Avenue after several incidents of serious disorder took place there due to the use of the premises to smoke 'crack' cocaine.

With regard to the issue of a closure order in respect of 180 Bayliss Avenue, which of the following statements is true?

A The application for a closure order must be heard by a magistrates' court not later than 24 hours after the notice has been served.

B A magistrates' court can adjourn any hearing regarding the closure order for a period of not more than 14 days.

C If a closure order is made it will not exceed a period of one month.

D Closure orders can be extended but not beyond a total of three months.

Question 12.13

DC PHILLIPS (in plain clothes) has been taking a witness statement and is walking back to her car when she sees BOND and FARMER acting suspiciously. BOND is talking to FARMER who is sitting in a car and smoking. DC PHILLIPS approaches the two and as she does so she smells what she thinks is cannabis being smoked. She suspects that the two men are committing offences contrary to the Misuse of Drugs Act 1971 and that she will find drugs on their persons and in the car.

With regard to the power of entry, search and seizure under s. 23 of the Misuse of Drugs Act 1971, which of the following comments is correct?

A DC PHILLIPS cannot exercise powers under s. 23 unless she is in uniform.

B DC PHILLIPS can search both BOND and FARMER and also search the car FARMER is sitting in

C The power cannot be exercised unless DC PHILLIPS reasonably believes that offences contrary to the Act are being committed.

D DC PHILLIPS can search BOND and FARMER but not FARMER's car.

ANSWERS

Answer 12.1

Answer **A** — This question does not ask if TURVEY has committed an offence, merely if he satisfies what the law requires for 'possession' of the drug. In order to be in possession of anything, the common law requires physical control of the object plus knowledge that it contains something, making answers B and C incorrect. The fact that TURVEY does not know of the existence of the cocaine within the cigarette packet may afford him a defence to a charge of possession but he still 'possesses' the drug, making answer D incorrect.

Investigators' Manual, paras 2.11.5–2.11.5.5 **DV = 3**

Answer 12.2

Answer **B** — Although WILLSON knows of the existence of the cannabis plants, this does not mean that he commits the offence. For the offence to be committed you must show some element of attention to the plant by the defendant, making answers A and C incorrect. The element of attention could be watering the plant. In proving the offence it is only necessary to show that the plant is of the genus *Cannabis* and that the defendant cultivated it; it is not necessary to show that the defendant knew it to be a cannabis plant (*R v Champ* (1981) 73 Cr App R 367), making answer D incorrect.

Investigators' Manual, para. 2.11.8.7 **DV = 2**

Answer 12.3

Answer **C** — This question is as per the circumstances in *R v Maginnis* [1987] AC 303. It has been held that a person holding a controlled drug belonging to another for a short while and then handing it back does not 'supply'. However, the situation differs when the person holding the drug does so for some reward or benefits from the activity in some way. In *Maginnis*, the court held that the defendant would have been 'supplying' the drug had he returned it to the drug trafficker who had left a packet of cannabis resin in Maginnis' car. As the drug had not been returned to the trafficker, Maginnis was in possession with intent to supply, as per answer C.

Investigators' Manual, para. 2.11.8.3 **DV = 4**

Answer 12.4

Answer **B** — Section 28 provides a defence for several offences under the act, one of those being possession with intent to supply, making answer D incorrect. The fact that SHANAHAN knew McFADDEN as a drugs dealer and was paid a large amount of money to deliver the envelope would negate any defence he may attempt to raise as he should have 'reason to suspect' the envelope contained drugs in theses circumstances, making answer C incorrect. The 'reason to suspect' is judged objectively (*R* v *Young* [1984] 1 WLR 654) so where a 'reason to suspect' is not apparent because the defendant is too intoxicated to see it, the defence will not apply, making answer A incorrect.

Investigators' Manual, paras 2.11.7.2–2.11.7.3   **DV = 4**

Answer 12.5

Answer **A** — The offence under s. 4(3) states that it is an offence to supply or offer to supply a controlled drug. The offence is complete when the offer is made. It is irrelevant whether or not the defendant actually has the means to meet the offer or even intends to carry it out (*R* v *Goodard* [1992] Crim LR 588), making answers B and C incorrect. If the offer was made to an undercover police officer the offence is still committed (*R* v *Kray*, 10 November 1998, unreported).

Investigators' Manual, paras 2.11.8.2, 2.11.8.3   **DV = 3.5**

Answer 12.6

Answer **D** — The offences that are covered by travel restriction orders include the supply of controlled drugs, making answer A incorrect. Answer B is incorrect as the minimum period for such an order is 2 years (s. 33(3)). Answer C is incorrect as an offender *may* be required to surrender his/her UK passport as part of the order.

Investigators' Manual, para. 2.11.9.3   **DV = 7**

Answer 12.7

Answer **C** — The offence is committed when the person subject to the order leaves the UK. It is immaterial that GRAPNELL has been kidnapped, as the conduct of the defendant does not have to be voluntary.

Investigators' Manual, para 2.11.9.3   **DV = 3**

Answer 12.8

Answer **D** — Answers A, B and C are all Class A drugs; Ketamine is a Class B drug.

Investigators' Manual, para. 2.1.4   **DV = 3.5**

Answer 12.9

Answer **A** — Hypodermic syringes, or parts of them, are not covered by this offence (s. 9A(2)), making answers B and C incorrect. The tourniquet would be covered as this offence deals with 'articles' used in the administration or preparation of drugs to 'himself or another', making answer D incorrect.

Investigators' Manual, para. 2.11.8.8   **DV = 2**

Answer 12.10

Answer **D** — Cannabis and cannabis resin are covered by this offence (s. 8(d)), making answer A incorrect. This offence can only be committed if the occupier or person concerned in the management of the premises *knowingly* permits the use of drugs in the prescribed manner. This is not an offence of strict liability and so answer B is also incorrect. It is not necessary to show that the defendant knew exactly what drugs were being produced, supplied etc.; only that they were 'controlled drugs' (*R v Bett* [1999] 1 All ER 600), making answer C incorrect.

Investigators' Manual, para. 2.11.8.10   **DV = 5**

Answer 12.11

Answer **C** — Section 1 of the Act states that this section applies to premises if a police officer not below the rank of *Superintendent* believes that the conditions have been met.

Investigators' Manual, para. 2.11.8.11   **DV = 3.5**

Answer 12.12

Answer **B** — An application for the closure order must be heard by a magistrates' court not later than *48* hours after the notice has been served, making answer A incorrect. Answers C and D are incorrect as closure orders can last a maximum of *three* months and can be extended up to a total of *six* months.

Investigators' Manual, para. 2.11.8.12   **DV = 3**

Answer 12.13

Answer **B** — The power under s. 23 is exercisable by a constable who does not have to be in uniform and who has *reasonable grounds to suspect* that a person is in possession of a controlled drug in contravention of the Act, making answers A and C incorrect. Answer D is incorrect as the Act provides the power to search and detain persons and any vehicle or vessel in which the constable suspects that the drug may be found.

Investigators' Manual, para. 2.11.9.1   **DV = 6.5**

13 | Firearms and Gun Crime

Question 13.1

NIELSEN is the owner of a slaughterhouse and is licensed under s. 10 of the Firearms Act 1968 to possess slaughtering instruments. One of the instruments that he keeps for this purpose is a hand-held electric 'stun gun'. The 'stun gun' develops a fault and is beyond repair but rather than throw it away, NIELSEN takes the broken 'stun gun' to his home address. He intends to keep it in a display cabinet to show his friends the sort of instruments he uses at work.

Considering only the offence of possessing a prohibited weapon contrary to s. 5 of the Firearms Act 1968, which of the following statements is true?

A NIELSEN commits the offence as the 'stun gun' is a prohibited weapon and he has it in his possession away from his place of work.

B No offence is committed because NIELSEN is a licensed slaughterer and s. 10 of the Act allows him to possess the 'stun gun'.

C As NIELSEN only intends to keep the 'stun gun' as a display item the offence would not be committed.

D NIELSEN cannot commit this offence because an electric 'stun gun' is only a prohibited weapon as long as it can discharge an electric current.

Question 13.2

CALVER buys an antique vase from LAVERICK for £15,000 and although LAVERICK has asked for the money several times, CALVER has always refused to pay it. LAVERICK goes to CALVER's home address and demands payment. The two have an argument during which CALVER tells LAVERICK that he will never pay him. LAVERICK puts his hands behind his back an onto an imitation 9 mm Beretta pistol. He tells CALVER that he has a gun and that if CALVER does not pay him he will be shot and killed.

Why is no offence under s. 16 of the Firearms Act 1968 committed?

A No offence is committed because LAVERICK has not actually endangered CAL-VER's life.

B No offence is committed because the threat is a conditional one.

C No offence is committed because the threat is made with an imitation firearm.

D No offence is committed because the firearm was never produced or shown to CALVER.

Question 13.3

PC SHANKS carries out a s. 1 PACE search on YOUNIS who has been found tres-passing in a building. In the course of the search, PC SHANKS finds a loaded air-pistol in YOUNIS's back pocket. She seizes the air-pistol and arrests YOUNIS for an offence under s. 20(1) of the Firearms Act 1968 (trespassing with a firearm in a building). YOUNIS struggles with the officer and punches her in the face attempt-ing to prevent PC SHANKS from making the arrest. YOUNIS manages to take hold of the loaded air-pistol and points it at the officer, telling her to leave him alone. YOUNIS then strikes PC SHANKS in the face with the butt of the pistol.

At what stage, if at all, does YOUNIS commit an offence under s. 17 of the Fire-arms Act (using a firearm to resist arrest)?

A When he initially struggles with PC SHANKS and punches her in the face.

B When he takes hold of the air-pistol and points it at PC SHANKS.

C When he strikes PC SHANKS in the face with the butt of the pistol.

D The offence under s. 17 of the Act is not committed.

Question 13.4

WHITHAM assaults GORMLEY, breaking GORMLEY's wrist during the attack. GORM-LEY reports the assault to DC BUTTERS who visits WHITHAM's home address two days after the original assault. WHITHAM invites the officer into his house and into the lounge where DC BUTTERS arrests WHITHAM for a s. 20 wounding. As the arrest is made, DC BUTTERS sees an imitation Magnum 44 on a lounge table.

Is WHITHAM liable for an offence of possessing a firearm while being arrested for a Schedule 1 offence?

A No, because a s. 20 wounding is not a Schedule 1 offence.

B Yes, but only if WHITHAM is found guilty of the s. 20 assault.

C No, as WHITHAM must actually have the weapon in his physical possession.

D Yes, it is immaterial that the weapon is an imitation firearm.

Question 13.5

You arrest CHU for an offence of robbery and he is later sentenced to a term of imprisonment for 3 years.

When would CHU be able to legally possess a firearm without committing an offence under s. 21 of the Firearms Act 1968?

A CHU must not have a firearm in his possession at any time before the end of a 3-year period beginning on the date of his release.

B CHU must not have a firearm in his possession at any time before the end of a 5-year period beginning on the date of his release.

C CHU must not have a firearm in his possession at any time before the end of a 7-year period beginning from the date of his release.

D CHU must not, at any time, have a firearm in his possession.

Question 13.6

JOHNSON is homeless and looking for somewhere to stay for the night. He decides to break into a garage (realising that he will be a trespasser in the process) for shelter. Once inside the garage he searches for something to sleep on and finds an imitation Magnum 44 firearm. He puts the firearm in his rucksack. Due to the noise JOHNSON made when breaking into the garage the police are called and PC COXHILL detains JOHNSON inside the garage.

With regard to the offence of trespassing with a firearm in a building (contrary to s. 20(1) of the Firearms Act 1968) which of the statements below is true?

A JOHNSON would commit an offence but as the weapon is an imitation firearm it is not an arrestable offence.

B JOHNSON would not commit the offence, as he did not enter the garage with the imitation firearm in his possession.

C PC COXHILL could arrest JOHNSON in these circumstances.

D The offence is not committed because the Magnum 44 is an imitation firearm.

Question 13.7

MILLER discovers that PALFREY has been having an affair with his wife. He finds PALFREY drinking in a pub and approaches him. MILLER is holding several fingers inside his jacket and points them at PALFREY saying, 'Stand still or I'll blow you away'. MILLER intends PALFREY to believe he has a firearm. PALFREY believes MILLER and stands still. MILLER picks up a glass from the bar, breaks it and pushes it into PALFREY's neck intending to and actually causing grievous bodily harm to PALFREY.

Is MILLER guilty of possessing a firearm while committing a Schedule 1 offence (contrary to s. 17(2) of the Firearms Act 1968)?

A No, Schedule 1 does not extend to causing grievous bodily harm with intent.

B Yes, the offence can be committed when in possession of an imitation firearm and MILLER's fingers would represent an imitation firearm.

C No, MILLER must be in possession of a firearm as opposed to an imitation firearm.

D Yes, as long as MILLER is subsequently convicted of the offence of causing grievous bodily harm with intent.

Question 13.8

KING and HUNSTONE are both released from prison on the same day. KING had been sentenced to 4 years' imprisonment for an offence of robbery and HUNSTONE had been sentenced to 12 months' imprisonment for an offence of burglary.

According to s. 21 of the Firearms Act 1968, when, if ever, can KING and HUNSTONE lawfully possess a firearm?

A KING and HUNSTONE can never lawfully possess a firearm.

B KING can never lawfully possess a firearm; HUNSTONE can lawfully possess a firearm five years after his release.

C KING can lawfully possess a firearm five years after his release; HUNSTONE can lawfully possess a firearm three years after his release.

D KING can lawfully possess a firearm three years after his release; HUNSTONE can lawfully possess a firearm one year after his release.

Question 13.9

Sections 22 to 24 of the Firearms Act 1968 create a number of offences relating to the possession of firearms by people of a certain age.

In which of the below circumstances has an offence been committed under those sections?

A NOVAK is 18 years old and is in possession of an air weapon together with ammunition for the weapon.

B STANLEY is 16 years old and is in possession of an air weapon under the supervision of his 22-year-old brother. ✓

C KARIM is 14 years old and is in possession of an assembled shotgun which is securely covered so that it cannot be fired. ✓

D DONOVAN is 13 years old and in possession of a section 1 firearm under the supervision of his 35-year-old father.

ANSWERS

Answer 13.1

Answer **A** — Answer D is incorrect as an electric 'stun gun' has been held to be a prohibited weapon as it discharges an electrical current (*Flack* v *Baldry* [1988] 1 WLR 393) and it continues to be a prohibited weapon even if it is not working (*R* v *Brown, The Times*, 27 March 1992). The test as to whether a weapon is prohibited or not is purely objective and is not affected by the intentions of the defendant (*R* v *Law* [1999] Crim LR 837), making answer C incorrect. Although s. 10 of the Act allows licensed slaughterers to possess such items, this is only applicable when the weapon is possessed in any slaughterhouse or knackers' yard in which the person is employed and if this condition is not met, then the exemption will not apply. This makes answer B incorrect.

Investigators' Manual, paras 2.12.4.1, 2.12.4.2, 2.12.5.4   **DV = 7.5**

Answer 13.2

Answer **C** — The intention does not have to be an immediate one and it may be conditional (*R* v *Bentham* [1973] QB 357), making answer B incorrect. There is no need for the firearm to be produced or shown to another, making answer D incorrect. This is an offence of intent and it is not required that the life of another be endangered, only that the intent to do so exists, making answer A incorrect. The offence cannot be committed using an imitation firearm.

Investigators' Manual, para. 2.12.8.1   **DV = 6**

Answer 13.3

Answer **D** — It is an offence for a person to make any use whatsoever of a firearm or imitation firearm with intent to resist or prevent the *lawful* arrest or detention of himself or another. However, whilst the offence of trespassing with a firearm (under s. 20(1) of the Firearms Act 1968) is an arrestable offence, this is not the case if the weapon concerned is an imitation firearm or an air weapon; it is a summary only offence. The effect of this is that the arrest of YOUNIS is unlawful making it impossible for him to commit the offence of resisting arrest under s. 17 of the Act.

Investigators' Manual, paras 2.12.8.3, 2.12.8.6   **DV = 2**

Answer 13.4

Answer **D** — Section 20 assaults are covered by Schedule 1 to the Act, making answer A incorrect. There is no need for the defendant to be subsequently convicted of the Schedule 1 offence. All that is needed is to prove that he/she had the weapon in his/her possession at the time of his/her arrest for the offence (*R* v *Nelson (Damien)* [2000] 3 WLR 300), making answer B incorrect. With regard to possession, you need to prove that the person was in possession of the firearm but not that they actually had it with them (*R* v *North* [2001] Crim LR 746), making answer C incorrect.

Investigators' Manual, para. 2.12.8.4   **DV = 6**

Answer 13.5

Answer **D** — A person who has been sentenced to custody for life or to preventive detention, imprisonment, corrective training, youth custody or detention in a young offender institution for 3 years or more must not, at any time, have a firearm or ammunition in his/her possession.

Investigators' Manual, para. 2.12.9   **DV = 2**

Answer 13.6

Answer **A** — Answer D is incorrect as the offence can be committed if the defendant is in possession of a firearm *or an imitation firearm.* Answer C is incorrect as the offence is an arrestable offence *unless* the firearm is an imitation firearm or an air weapon. Answer B is incorrect as there is no requirement that the defendant had the firearm/imitation firearm with him/her when entering the building.

Investigators' Manual, para. 2.12.8.5   **DV = 4**

Answer 13.7

Answer **A** — Answer B is incorrect as although the offence can be committed with an imitation firearm, 'fingers' have been held not to constitute an imitation firearm (*R* v *Bentham* [2005] 1 WLR 1057). Answer C is therefore incorrect as the offence can be committed with an imitation firearm. Answer D is incorrect as there is no need for the defendant to be subsequently convicted of the Schedule 1 offence (*R* v *Nelson (Damien)* [2000] 3 WLR 300).

Investigators' Manual, para. 2.12.4.7, 2.12.8.4   **DV = 6**

Answer 13.8

Answer **B** — A person sentenced to 3+ years' imprisonment can never lawfully possess a firearm; a person sentenced to 3+ months' imprisonment *but less than three years*, can possess a firearm five years after the date of their release.

Investigators' Manual, para. 2.12.9   **DV = 5.5**

Answer 13.9

Answer **D** — NOVAK is not covered by the age restrictions as they end when a person reaches the age of 17, meaning answer A is not an offence. A person under 17 may possess an air weapon and ammunition if they are under the supervision of another who is at least 21 years old, meaning answer B is not an offence. Answer C is not an offence as a person under the age of 15 may be in possession of an assembled shotgun if it is securely covered so that it cannot be fired. Answer D is an offence as a person under 14 must not have a section 1 firearm in their possession in any circumstances.

Investigators' Manual, para. 2.12.9.2   **DV = 5.5**

PART THREE

Sexual Offences

14 | The Sexual Offences Act 2003, Rape and Sexual Assault

QUESTIONS

Question 14.1

WRIGHT works with LAKER and during an office party he suggests to LAKER that they have sex together; LAKER refuses. This annoys WRIGHT and later on he follows LAKER into the female toilets. WRIGHT demands that LAKER talk with him in one of the toilet cubicles and once inside, WRIGHT locks the door. WRIGHT demands to know why LAKER refused to have sex with him and when LAKER begins to cry, WRIGHT tells her he would be happy if she took part in oral sex with him. LAKER asks to be let out of the cubicle but WRIGHT refuses. LAKER realises that WRIGHT will not let her out, so agrees to have oral sex with him and allows WRIGHT to put his penis in her mouth.

Considering the offence of rape only (contrary to s. 1 of the Sexual Offences Act 2003), which of the statements below is correct?

A No offence of rape has been committed because LAKER consented to the act of oral sex.

B Rape can only be committed if WRIGHT penetrates the vagina or anus of LAKER.

C WRIGHT commits rape, as LAKER was unlawfully detained at the time of the relevant act.

D WRIGHT has not committed rape because he has not used violence or caused LAKER to believe immediate violence would be used against her.

Question 14.2

DUPONT approaches THOMPSON in the street. He shows her a photograph of her 3-year-old son and says, 'Me and my mate have been watching you and your boy, my mate's watching him now. Unless you do as I say, my mate will hurt your kid.'

THOMPSON believes that her son is in immediate danger and that DUPONT's associate will harm him. DUPONT demands that THOMPSON follow him into a nearby alleyway where he puts his fingers into DUPONT's vagina. DUPONT does not have a friend watching THOMPSON's child, who is in no actual danger at the time of the act.

Has DUPONT committed an offence of rape?

A Yes, because at the time of the relevant act he has caused THOMPSON to believe that immediate violence would be used against another person.

B No, because he did not use violence against THOMPSON or cause her to believe that immediate violence would be used against her.

C Yes, because he has intentionally deceived THOMPSON into taking part in the relevant act.

D No, because intentionally penetrating THOMPSON's vagina with his fingers is not the *actus reus* of rape.

Question 14.3

SALHAN goes to a house party but because she is taking medication she only drinks orange juice. Her friend, CROSS, thinks it will be funny to spike SALHAN's drinks and without SALHAN's knowledge adds several vodkas to SALHAN's orange juice causing SALHAN to become disorientated and drowsy. SALHAN goes to a bedroom in the house and lies down to get some rest. ALLEN walks into the room and seeing SALHAN on the bed he suggests that they have sexual intercourse. ALLEN has no idea that SALHAN is suffering from the combined effects of the medication and the vodka. SALHAN agrees and the two have sexual intercourse. The next day, SALHAN realises what has happened and accuses ALLEN of rape.

Which of the statements below is true?

A ALLEN is not guilty of rape, as he did not know that SALHAN had had her drinks spiked.

B The offence could only be committed if ALLEN was the person who had spiked SALHAN's drinks.

C ALLEN is guilty of rape, as at the time the sexual intercourse took place, a substance had been administered to SALHAN that was capable of causing her to be stupefied.

D Administering a substance capable of causing the complainant to be stupefied or overpowered would not constitute an offence of rape.

Question 14.4

ALLDAY and MASSEY (both males) have consensual anal intercourse. Immediately after the act, ALLDAY feels extremely guilty and begs MASSEY not to tell either of their wives what they have done. MASSEY punches ALLDAY in the face and tells him he will do what he likes. MASSEY then demands that ALLDAY place his penis in MASSEY's mouth. Under the threat of violence, ALLDAY does so. Several minutes later, MASSEY demands anal intercourse. ALLDAY refuses but MASSEY tells him that he will tell their wives of their activities and as a result, ALLDAY allows MASSEY to have anal sexual intercourse with him.

At what stage, if at all, is the offence of rape committed?
A When MASSEY punches ALLDAY in the face immediately after the act of anal sexual intercourse.
B When ALLDAY is forced to put his penis into MASSEY's mouth.
C When ALLDAY is forced to allow MASSEY to have anal sexual intercourse for a second time.
D The offence of rape is not committed.

Question 14.5

HARRISON has recently had gender reassignment surgery where the penis was re-moved and replaced with a surgically constructed vagina. HARRISON attends a party and flirts with DARVEL suggesting that the two of them should have sexual in-tercourse to which DARVEL agrees. The two go to a bedroom and begin to have sexual intercourse (penis to surgically constructed vagina). Several minutes into the act, HARRISON feels sick and asks DARVEL to stop. DARVEL takes no notice of HAR-RISON and continues to have sexual intercourse with HARRISON for several minutes despite HARRISON's protests. DARVEL then penetrates HARRISON's anus with his penis against HARRISON's wishes.

Which of the statements below is correct?
A A surgically constructed vagina would not be classed as part of the body for the purposes of rape.
B DARVEL commits rape when, after HARRISON asks him to stop, he continues to penetrate HARRISON's surgically constructed vagina.
C No offence of rape is committed because HARRISON initially consented to sexual intercourse with DARVEL.
D DARVEL only commits rape when he penetrates HARRISON's anus.

Question 14.6

CLAY goes to a party held at PIKE's house. During the evening of the party he goes into the bathroom where he sees WEBSTER lying on the floor having passed out from drinking too much. CLAY locks the bathroom door and removes all of WEBSTER's clothes. CLAY lies next to WEBSTER and kisses her, putting his tongue into WEBSTER's mouth in the process. Several minutes later he places his tongue into WEBSTER's vagina. CLAY then puts his penis inside WEBSTER's mouth before he puts a finger into WEBSTER's vagina.

At what point does CLAY commit an offence of assault by penetration (contrary to s. 2 of the Sexual Offences Act 2003)?

A When he puts his tongue into WEBSTER's mouth.
B When he puts his tongue into WEBSTER's vagina.
C When he puts his penis into WEBSTER's mouth.
D When he puts his finger into WEBSTER's vagina.

Question 14.7

HUNN and her common-law husband, DARROW, kidnap POOLE in a bid to extort a cash ransom from POOLE's husband. The two blindfold and handcuff POOLE and keep her in a basement flat for several days before the ransom is paid. During this time POOLE is subject to abuse by HUNN and DARROW. HUNN forces a candle into POOLE's vagina and while HUNN carries out this act, DARROW pushes a candle into POOLE's anus.

Considering the offence of assault by penetration (s. 2 of the Sexual Offences Act 2003) only, which of the statements below is correct?

A Only DARROW is guilty of this offence as it can only be committed by a male.
B Only DARROW commits the offence as assault by penetration only relates to the penetration of the vagina.
C Both HUNN and DARROW commit the offence.
D Neither HUNN nor DARROW commits the offence because POOLE was not penetrated with a part of the body.

Question 14.8

KELMSLEY has a fetish for handbags. He obtains sexual pleasure from rubbing his penis against handbags held by females whilst he is a passenger on a busy commuter train. One morning he approaches PIGRAM (a passenger on the train) and intending to obtain sexual gratification he takes out his penis and rubs it against PIGRAM's handbag. KELMSLEY is fully aware that PIGRAM would not consent to this activity.

Does KELMSLEY commit an offence of sexual assault (s. 3 of the Sexual Offences Act 2003)?

A Yes, because he is aware that PIGRAM would not have consented to the activity.

B No, because he has not touched a sexual organ or orifice.

C Yes, because his conduct was intentional rather than accidental.

D No, because he has not touched another person.

Question 14.9

LAND is arrested on suspicion of a triple murder. She tells DC MOULT, the female arresting officer, that she has hidden a knife inside her vagina and the police will never get hold of it. She tells DC MOULT that at the first opportunity she will use the knife to kill a police officer in the custody area. As a result, Inspector FOWLER authorises an intimate search of LAND to recover the knife. Because of the urgency of the situation, the intimate search takes place at the police station. LAND does not consent to the search and, against LAND's wishes, DC MOULT inserts her finger into LAND's vagina and recovers the knife.

Which of the statements below is correct?

A DC MOULT commits an offence of rape (contrary to s. 1 of the Sexual Offences Act 2003).

B DC MOULT commits an offence of assault by penetration (contrary to s. 2 of the Sexual Offences Act 2003).

C DC MOULT commits an offence of sexual assault (contrary to s. 3 of the Sexual Offences Act 2003).

D DC MOULT commits no offence in these circumstances.

Question 14.10

SPENCER is standing at a bus stop directly behind TUCKETT who is holding an umbrella in his hand. TUCKETT is aware that SPENCER is relatively close to him and deliberately moves his umbrella so that the tip moves between SPENCER's legs and touches her vagina through her trousers. TUCKETT obtains sexual gratification from the act.

Considering only s. 3 of the Sexual Offences Act 2003, which of the statements below is correct?

A TUCKETT commits the offence because 'touching' includes touching with anything, in this case the umbrella.

B The offence has not been committed because TUCKETT must touch SPENCER with a part of his body.

C For the offence to be committed, the touching must amount to penetration.

D As the touching was carried out through SPENCER's trousers, the offence is incomplete.

Question 14.11

YARDLEY, MAJOR and LOCKHART (all females) are drinking together at LOCKHART's house. YARDLEY and LOCKHART take off all their clothes and begin to kiss and touch each other while MAJOR watches. LOCKHART asks MAJOR to kiss YARDLEY's breasts, to which MAJOR refuses. LOCKHART tells MAJOR that unless she does as she demands she will be assaulted. Because of the threat and against her will, MAJOR does as LOCKHART demands. YARDLEY consents to the act.

What is LOCKHART's liability in relation to the offence of causing a person to engage in sexual activity without consent (s. 4 of the Sexual Offences Act 2003)?

A LOCKHART does not commit the offence, as it must involve penetration.

B Because YARDLEY consented to the act, LOCKHART does not commit the offence.

C LOCKHART has committed the offence in these circumstances.

D As LOCKHART is a female, she cannot commit this offence.

Question 14.12

NAZIR and BOSWELL are walking down an alleyway when DEVILLE approaches them. DEVILLE produces a handgun and demands that BOSWELL kneel on the ground while NAZIR places his penis in BOSWELL's mouth. Fearing that they will be harmed NAZIR and BOSWELL do as they have been told to.

Considering these circumstances in light of s. 4 of the Sexual offences Act 2003 only, which of the statements below is correct?

A This offence is punishable with a maximum sentence of 5 years' imprisonment.

B This offence is punishable with a maximum sentence of 10 years' imprisonment.

C This offence is punishable with a maximum sentence of 15 years' imprisonment.

D This offence is punishable with a maximum sentence of life imprisonment.

Question 14.13

Section 75 of the Sexual Offences Act 2003 has created evidential presumptions about consent. If it is proved that the defendant did a relevant act and that any of the circumstances in s. 75(2) existed and the defendant knew they existed, the complainant will be taken not to have consented and the defendant will be taken not to have reasonably believed that the complainant consented.

Which of the circumstances below would not form part of a presumption made under s. 75(2) of the Act?

A The complainant was and the defendant was not unlawfully detained at the time of the relevant act.

B The complainant was asleep or otherwise unconscious at the time of the relevant act.

C Because of the complainant's physical disability, the complainant would not have been able at the time of the relevant act, to communicate to the defendant whether the complainant consented.

D The complainant was intentionally deceived as to the nature or purpose of the relevant act.

Question 14.14

ABLITT is in a nightclub where he begins talking to RICHARDS who is an actress. ABLITT tells RICHARDS that he is only in the country for a week after which he will fly out to America where he will be directing a film starring a major Hollywood actor; this is a lie as ABLITT is in fact a plumber. ABLITT tells RICHARDS that he can get her a part in the film but he will only do so if she has sexual intercourse with him. To further her acting career, RICHARDS goes to ABLITT's house where she has sexual intercourse with him.

What effect will s. 76 of the Sexual Offences Act 2003 have on ABLITT's actions?

A As ABLITT has deceived RICHARDS regarding the nature of the act, RICHARDS will be presumed not to consent to it.

B RICHARDS will be presumed not to have consented to the act as ABLITT has intentionally deceived her by impersonating a film director.

C It will have no effect as ABLITT has not impersonated a person known personally to RICHARDS.

D It will have no effect as this section relates to the use of violence to obtain consent from the victim.

Question 14.15

CHANNON (aged 35 yrs) kidnaps ILIFF (aged 12 yrs) and forces ILIFF to have sexual intercourse with him (penis to vagina). CHANNON is later arrested for an offence of rape (s. 1 of the Sexual Offences Act 2003).

Which of the statements below is correct?

A The prosecution will have to prove intentional penetration alone.

B The prosecution will have to prove the child's age alone.

C The prosecution will have to prove intentional penetration and the child's age.

D The prosecution will have to prove intentional penetration, the child's age and the fact that ILIFF did not consent to the act.

Question 14.16

SHARPE kidnaps YOUNG and locks her in the basement of his house for several days. During this time SHARPE compels YOUNG to put a vibrator into her mouth. SHARPE tells his friend, HEMMING, about YOUNG and invites HEMMING to watch him abuse her. HEMMING enters the basement and watches YOUNG being abused. HEMMING asks YOUNG if she will have sexual intercourse with him. YOUNG does not reply so HEMMING has sexual intercourse with her (penis to vagina).

Which of the statements below is correct with regard to the Sexual Offences Act 2003?

A HEMMING commits the offence of rape (contrary to s. 1 of the Sexual Offences Act 2003).

B Both SHARPE and HEMMING commit the offence of rape (contrary to s. 1 of the Sexual Offences Act 2003).

C SHARPE commits the offence of assault by penetration (contrary to s. 2 of the Sexual Offences Act 2003).

D Both SHARPE and HEMMING commit the offence of assault by penetration (contrary to s. 2 of the Sexual Offences Act 2003).

Question 14.17

VENNER is having sexual intercourse with STANE. During the act, VENNER gets carried away and puts his fingers into STANE's mouth. Although no force was used by VENNER, the act was done without STANE's consent.

What offence does VENNER commit?

A Rape (contrary to s. 1 of the Sexual Offences Act 2003).

B Assault by penetration (contrary to s. 2 of the Sexual Offences Act 2003).

C Sexual assault by touching (contrary to s. 3 of the Sexual Offences Act 2003).

D Causing a person to engage in sexual activity without consent (contrary to s. 4 of the Sexual Offences Act 2003).

Question 14.18

LAMBERT (aged 15 yrs) is the victim of an offence of sexual activity with a child (contrary to s. 9 of the Sexual Offences Act 2003). She speaks to DC SALK (the officer in the case), as she is concerned that her identity will be disclosed during the forthcoming trial.

What advice should DC SALK offer?

A LAMBERT is entitled to anonymity throughout her lifetime.

B Only rape victims are entitled to anonymity.

C LAMBERT's identity will be protected until she is 18 years old.

D Anonymity is only provided to victims where violence has formed part of the offence.

ANSWERS

Answer 14.1

Answer **C** — Rape can be committed if a male penetrates the vagina, anus or mouth of his victim, making answer B incorrect. Although the use or threat to use violence would negate consent (s. 72(2)(a) and (b)), this is not the only way that a complainant can be deemed to have refused consent to the relevant act, making answer D incorrect. Consent will only be true consent if the person agrees by choice and has the freedom and capacity to make that choice. Under s. 75(2)(c) of the Act, the complainant is taken not to have consented to the relevant act if the complainant was, and the defendant was not, unlawfully detained at the time of the relevant act, making answer A incorrect.

Investigators' Manual, paras 3.3, 3.3.3   **DV = 7**

Answer 14.2

Answer **D** — Although answer A is correct insofar as the consent obtained from THOMPSON is not true consent as it is obtained by threatening immediate violence against another person, the *actus reus* of rape is the penetration of the vagina, anus or mouth of another person with the penis, making this answer incorrect. Answer B is incorrect as had DUPONT used violence, this would still not be rape. The deception in rape must be as to the nature or purpose of the relevant act, not the circumstances leading up to the act, making answer C incorrect.

Investigators' Manual, paras 3.3, 3.3.3   **DV = 6**

Answer 14.3

Answer **A** — Answer D is incorrect as these circumstances are catered for in s. 75(2)(f) of the Act. *Any person* can administer or cause the substance to be taken, making answer B incorrect. Under s. 75 (evidential presumptions about consent), it must be proved that the defendant (i) did the relevant act, (ii) that any of the circumstances specified in subsection (2) existed, and (iii) that the defendant *knew* that those circumstances existed. In these circumstances, ALLEN does not know that SALHAN has had her drinks spiked and therefore is not guilty of the offence of rape, making answer C incorrect.

Investigators' Manual, paras 3.3, 3.3.3   **DV = 6.5**

Answer 14.4

Answer **C** — Violence must be used or threatened immediately before or at the time of the relevant act. The first act of anal sexual intercourse was consensual and the violence took place after the act, making answer A incorrect. Answer B is incorrect as rape is committed when the defendant intentionally penetrates the vagina, anus or mouth of the complainant with his penis and is not committed when the defendant forces the complainant to penetrate his mouth with their penis. The offence is committed at point C as at this point MASSEY is penetrating the anus of ALLDAY (who does not consent to the penetration) and MASSEY reasonably believes that he does not consent, making answer D incorrect in the process.

Investigators' Manual, paras 3.3, 3.3.3   **DV = 4.5**

Answer 14.5

Answer **B** — Answer A is incorrect as s. 79(3) of the Act states that references to the body include references to a part surgically constructed (in particular, through gender reassignment surgery). Answer C is incorrect because although HARRISON initially agreed to sexual intercourse with DARVEL, s. 79(2) of the Act states that penetration is a continuing act from entry to withdrawal so that where a person consents at the time of entry to penetration, but then withdraws consent and the penetration continues, the person penetrating is guilty of rape. This section makes answer D incorrect, as the offence of rape is complete when HARRISON continues penetration of DARVEL's vagina.

Investigators' Manual, paras 3.3, 3.3.1   **DV = 5**

Answer 14.6

Answer **B** — The offence under s. 2 of the Act is committed when a person intentionally penetrates the vagina or anus of another person with a part of his body or anything else. The offence is not committed by penetration of the mouth of the victim making answers A and C incorrect. The offence is committed at point B as at this point, CLAY penetrates WEBSTER's vagina with his tongue (a part of his body), making answer D incorrect.

Investigators' Manual, para. 3.4.1   **DV = 5**

Answer 14.7

Answer **C** — This offence can be committed by a male or female against a male or female, making answer A incorrect. The offence is committed when the vagina or anus of the victim is penetrated by the offender, making answer B incorrect. The penetration can be with a part of his/her body or anything else, making answer D incorrect.

Investigators' Manual, para. 3.4.1   **DV = 8**

Answer 14.8

Answer **D** — Options A, B and C are all relevant to the offence of Sexual Assault. For the offence to be complete, the defendant must reasonably believe that the victim does not consent to the touching. The part of the body touched does not have to be a sexual organ or orifice and the conduct of the defendant must be intentional rather than accidental. However, the offence of sexual assault is only committed when the defendant intentionally touches another person and would be incomplete when an inanimate object, such as a handbag, is the subject of the assault.

Investigators' Manual, paras 3.2.2, 3.4.2   **DV = 5**

Answer 14.9

Answer **D** — Rape can only be committed by a male, making answer A incorrect. An intimate search carried out in these circumstances is legal and so the central issue in relation to these circumstances is whether the activity is 'sexual'. Section 78 of the Act defines the word 'sexual' so that it excludes medical procedures and intimate searches where (in this case) LAND does not consent to the penetration and DC MOULT does not reasonably believe that LAND consents. As the activity would not be considered 'sexual', answers B and C are incorrect.

Investigators' Manual, paras 3.2.1.1–3.4.2   **DV = 3**

Answer 14.10

Answer **A** — A sexual assault under s. 3 of the Act is committed when a person intentionally touches another person, the touching is sexual and the victim does not consent to the touching and the offender does not reasonably believe that the victim consents. Section 79(8) defines 'touching' for the purposes of the act as including touching with (a) any part of the body, (b) with anything else or (c) through anything and in particular includes touching amounting to penetration. The definition of 'touching' therefore includes the use of the umbrella to commit the offence as it falls under s. 79(8)(b) of the Act, making answers B, C and D incorrect.

Investigators' Manual, paras 3.2.2, 3.4.2   **DV = 8**

Answer 14.11

Answer **C** — Answer A is incorrect as the offence involves any activity that is 'sexual' as opposed to acts involving penetration only. The fact that YARDLEY consented to the act is immaterial as MAJOR (the victim) did not consent, making answer B incorrect. Answer D is incorrect as this offence can be committed by a male or female.

Investigators' Manual, para. 3.4.3   **DV = 7**

Answer 14.12

Answer **D** — The sentencing provisions of this offence make it punishable with life imprisonment. These circumstances arise when the offence involves penetration, in particular: of the victim's anus or vagina, *of the victim's mouth with a penis* (BOSWELL), of any other person's anus or vagina with a part of the victim's body or *of any person's mouth by the victim's penis* (NAZIR).

Investigators' Manual, para. 3.4.3   **DV = 5**

Answer 14.13

Answer **D** — Remember that this questions asks you, *'Which of these is a lie?'* Answers A, B and C are all correct. Answer D is incorrect as this is a conclusive presumption about consent under s. 76 of the Act.

Investigators' Manual, paras 3.3.3, 3.3.4   **DV = 2**

Answer 14.14

Answer **C** — This section of the Act relates to the use of some form of deception in order to obtain consent from the victim and not the use of violence to obtain consent (covered by s. 75 of the Act), making answer D incorrect. Answer A is incorrect as RICHARDS has not been deceived into the act by a misrepresentation as to the nature of the act, RICHARDS knew that what she was doing was sexual intercourse.

Answer B is incorrect as the person impersonated must be known *personally* to the victim.

Investigators' Manual, para. 3.3.4   **DV = 2**

Answer 14.15

Answer **C** — If the victim of the offence is under 13, the prosecution simply have to prove intentional penetration and the child's age. No issue of 'consent' arises.

Investigators' Manual, para. 3.3   **DV = 4.5**

Answer 14.16

Answer **A** — Rape can only be committed by a male intentionally penetrating the vagina, anus or mouth of the victim with his penis. This makes answer B incorrect. Assault by penetration does not include penetration of the victim's mouth, making answers C and D incorrect. Where the complainant was, and the defendant was not, unlawfully detained at the time of the relevant act and the defendant knew that fact existed, it will be presumed that the victim did not consent.

Investigators' Manual, paras 3.3, 3.3.3   **DV = 7.5**

Answer 14.17

Answer **D** — Rape can only be committed using the penis, making answer A incorrect. Assault by penetration can only be committed by penetrating the anus or vagina and not the mouth, making answer B incorrect. Sexual touching does not relate to penetration, making answer C incorrect.

Investigators' Manual, paras 3.3, 3.4.1, 3.4.2, 3.4.3   **DV = 6**

Answer 14.18

Answer **A** — Under the Sexual Offences (Amendment) Acts 1976 and 1992, victims of most sexual offences, including rape and indecency with children, are entitled to anonymity throughout their lifetime.

Investigators' Manual, para. 3.1.3   **DV = 4.5**

15 | Child Sex Offences

QUESTIONS

Question 15.1

STEADMAN (aged 17 yrs) is approached by KEANE (aged 14 yrs). KEANE has a 'crush' on STEADMAN and she asks STEADMAN if he will have sexual intercourse with her. STEADMAN refuses but states that he will take part in oral sex with KEANE. The two meet a few hours later when STEADMAN places his penis into KEANE's mouth.

In relation to s. 9 of the Sexual Offences Act 2003 (sexual activity with a child), which of the statements below is correct?

A No offence is committed by STEADMAN as he is under 18 years of age.

B No offence is committed by STEADMAN as KEANE has consented to the act.

C No offence is committed by STEADMAN as KEANE is over 13 years of age.

D No offence is committed by STEADMAN as the sexual activity does not involve penetration of the vagina or the anus.

Question 15.2

CASE and her boyfriend PRIZEMAN (both aged 25 yrs) are babysitting SHIPMAN (aged 12 yrs). CASE and PRIZEMAN are watching television in the downstairs lounge when PRIZEMAN sees SHIPMAN looking through an open doorway into the lounge and watching the television. CASE is unaware of the presence of SHIPMAN. PRIZE-MAN undresses CASE and begins to have sexual intercourse with her. He intends that SHIPMAN should see the act and wishes to obtain sexual gratification from that fact. Unknown to PRIZEMAN, who believes SHIPMAN is watching, SHIPMAN has in fact returned to her bedroom on the first floor and does not see PRIZEMAN undress CASE and have sexual intercourse with her.

Is PRIZEMAN guilty of an offence of engaging in sexual activity in the presence of a child (contrary to s. 11 of the Sexual Offences Act 2003)?

A Yes, even though SHIPMAN is not present PRIZEMAN intended the act to be viewed by her.
B No, because SHIPMAN is not present or in a place where she can observe the act.
C Yes, because PRIZEMAN believes that SHIPMAN is watching the sexual activity.
D No, because CASE was never aware of SHIPMAN's presence.

Question 15.3

An offence under s. 11 of the Sexual Offences Act 2003 is committed when a person engages in sexual activity in the presence of a child.

Which of the statements below is correct with regard to this offence?
A The person committing this offence must be at least 16 years old.
B The activity need not be carried out in order to obtain sexual gratification.
C There must be a person under 16 years old present or in a place from which the defendant can be observed.
D It is necessary to show that the child was aware of the activity.

Question 15.4

LANDEN (aged 20 yrs) approaches EIFION (aged 12 yrs) in a park. LANDEN persuades EIFION to accompany him back to his house where LANDEN plays a DVD to EIFION that contains animated cartoon images of sexual activity. LANDEN obtains sexual gratification from this activity.

Has LANDEN committed an offence under s. 12 of the Sexual Offences Act 2003 (causing a child to watch a sexual act)?
A Yes, the images that EIFION sees can be images of imaginary persons so an animated cartoon image would be covered by the offence.
B No, the sexual act must be performed by LANDEN.
C Yes, but only because EIFION is under 13 years of age; if he were over 13, then the offence would not be committed.
D No, the image must be that of a 'person' engaged in sexual activity and not of a cartoon.

Question 15.5

HUGHES (aged 45 yrs) holds a barbeque at his house and invites a large number of guests and their children. Several hours after the barbeque has started, HUGHES goes into his house and into his study where he turns on his computer and goes on to the Internet. While he is on the Internet he visits several pornographic sites that show pictures of adults taking part in explicit sexual activity. HUGHES has left the door to his study open because he believes all of his guests are outside and nobody will see what he is doing. HUGHES's purpose when he is looking at the pictures is to obtain sexual gratification. Unknown to HUGHES, FORREST (aged 15 yrs) is looking at the same pictures because HUGHES has left the door to his study open.

Considering the offence of causing a child to watch a sexual act (contrary to s. 12 of the Sexual Offences Act 2003), which of the below is correct?

A As there are children at the party HUGHES would know of the likelihood of a child seeing the images and therefore commits an offence.

B As HUGHES has acted for the purposes of sexual gratification, the offence is complete.

C HUGHES does not commit the offence as still images are not included in this section of the legislation.

D HUGHES does not commit an offence under this section as he must intentionally cause another person to watch the activity.

Question 15.6

If a child or young person under the age of 18 years does anything that would be an offence under ss. 9 to 12 of the Sexual Offences Act 2003, s. 13 of the Act makes that activity an offence.

What is the purpose of this section of the Act?

A The purpose of this section is to provide a lower penalty of 1 year's imprisonment where the offender is aged under 18 years.

B The purpose of this section is to provide a lower penalty of 3 years' imprisonment where the offender is aged under 18 years.

C The purpose of this section is to provide a lower penalty of 5 years' imprisonment where the offender is aged under 18 years.

D The purpose of this section is to provide a lower penalty of 7 years' imprisonment where the offender is aged under 18 years.

Question 15.7

DEVILLE has been on holiday to Thailand on several occasions. During his holidays he had sexual intercourse with girls under 13 years old. He tells his friend, HALL-BROOK, about his holiday experiences. HALLBROOK asks DEVILLE if he will arrange flights, hotel accommodation and personal contacts for him so that he can visit Thailand for the same reason. HALLBROOK tells DEVILLE that he has never done anything like this before and so when he goes to Thailand he may not actually have sexual intercourse with girls under the age of 13. DEVILLE makes the necessary arrangements for HALLBROOK in the belief that HALLBROOK will have sexual intercourse with girls under 13 once he arrives in Thailand.

With regard to s. 14 of the Sexual Offences Act 2003 (arranging or facilitating the commission of a child sex offence), which of the statements below is true?

A DEVILLE does not commit the offence as he has arranged for the activities to take place outside the UK.

B DEVILLE commits the offence as he believes that HALLBROOK will have sexual intercourse with girls under 13 years of age.

C DEVILLE will commit the offence if HALLBROOK actually has sexual intercourse with girls under the age of 13; if he does not then DEVILLE does not commit the offence.

D DEVILLE does not commit the offence as he only believes rather than intends that HALLBROOK will have sexual intercourse with girls under the age of 13.

Question 15.8

EVERLY is a predatory paedophile and wishes to rape a girl under the age of 13 (contrary to s. 5 of the Sexual Offences Act 2003). He befriends CLAMP (a girl aged 9 yrs) using an Internet 'chat room' and arranges to meet her outside her school the next day in order to commit the offence. Unknown to EVERLY, CLAMP is not a 9-year-old child but is in fact a police officer using the Internet to track and arrest paedophiles.

Why is no offence of arranging or facilitating the commission of a child sex offence (contrary to s. 14 of the Sexual Offences Act 2003) committed by EVERLY?

A Because this offence is only committed when a person arranges or facilitates something that he intends another person to do or believes that another person will do.

B Because rape of a child under 13 (contrary to s. 5 of the Sexual Offences Act 2003) is not an offence that is covered by this section.

C Because the offence could never be committed. The person that EVERLY had arranged to meet is a police officer and not a 9-year-old child.

D Because the arrangements were made using the Internet and not face to face.

Question 15.9

BALLARD (aged 20 yrs) attends his cousin's 18th birthday party. During the evening of the party he speaks to GALBRAITH who tells BALLARD that she is only 14 years old. GALBRAITH tells BALLARD that she would like to see a tennis match at Wimbledon but cannot afford a ticket. BALLARD asks GALBRAITH to meet him in a week's time as he has a contact at Wimbledon and can obtain tickets for free; GALBRAITH agrees. One week later, BALLARD travels to meet GALBRAITH as he has obtained a ticket for Wimbledon for her. However, on the journey to meet her, BALLARD decides to sexually assault GALBRAITH after their meeting and travels to meet her with that intent.

With regard to the offence of meeting a child following sexual grooming (s. 15 of the Sexual Offences Act 2003) which of the statements below is correct?

A The offence is not committed as BALLARD did not intend to sexually assault GALBRAITH when they first met.
B BALLARD commits the offence as he is travelling to meet GALBRAITH with the intention to commit a relevant offence.
C BALLARD will only commit the offence when he actually meets with GALBRAITH.
D BALLARD does not commit the offence as he has not met or communicated with GALBRAITH on at least two earlier occasions.

Question 15.10

HARVEY (aged 45 yrs) is on holiday in Cyprus. He goes to an Internet café where he communicates with PREECE in an Internet 'chat room'. PREECE tells HARVEY that she is 15 years old and lives in the USA. During the course of his holiday, HARVEY communicates with PREECE on another five occasions during which the two exchange home addresses. In their last communication, PREECE tells HARVEY that she would like to have sexual intercourse with him if she ever visited the UK, an offer that HARVEY accepts. HARVEY returns home to the UK and one week after his return, PREECE pays a surprise visit to HARVEY's home address. PREECE tells HARVEY that she would like to make good on her promise and have sexual intercourse with him.

Has HARVEY committed an offence contrary to s. 15 of the Sexual Offences Act 2003 (meeting a child following sexual grooming)?

A No, because the original communications took place in Cyprus and not in the UK.
B Yes, because HARVEY accepted the offer of sexual intercourse from PREECE.
C No, because this was not an intentional meeting on HARVEY's part.
D Yes, because the communications can take place in any part of the world.

Question 15.11

SHARRAT (aged 36 yrs) has a son (aged 2 yrs). While SHARRAT's wife is out working, SHARRAT enters his son's nursery and puts his penis inside his son's mouth.

> In relation to s. 25 of the Sexual Offences Act 2003 (sexual activity with a child family member), which of the below is correct?

A SHARRAT is not liable for this offence as it does not include penetration of the victim's mouth.

B SHARRAT has committed the offence and because his victim is under 16 years of age the punishment is life imprisonment.

C SHARRAT has committed the offence which is triable on indictment and punishable with 14 years' imprisonment.

D SHARRAT has committed the offence which is triable either way and punishable with 5 years' imprisonment.

Question 15.12

POWELL (aged 26 yrs) drives to a family wedding reception where he speaks to his first cousin, IMBER (aged 17 yrs). IMBER has lived in Australia all her life and this is the first time the two have ever met. The two talk to each other all night and as the evening draws to a close, IMBER tells POWELL that she wants to have sexual intercourse with him. The two go outside the wedding venue, get into POWELL's car and have sexual intercourse (penis to vagina).

> Considering ss. 25 and 27 of the Sexual Offences Act 2003, has POWELL committed an offence?

A No, because a first cousin is not a relevant family relationship.

B Yes, because IMBER is under 18 years of age.

C No, because IMBER is over 16 years of age.

D Yes, sexual intercourse with a first cousin would constitute an offence.

Question 15.13

Under s. 25 of the Sexual Offences Act 2003 (sexual activity with a child family member), the prosecution will have to prove that defendant 'touched' the victim and that the touching was 'sexual'. However, other evidence must be proved in order for a defendant to be found guilty of such an offence.

Which of the below is correct with regard to the other evidence?

A The age of the victim must be proved and the defendant will have an evidential burden to discharge in that regard.

B The existence of the relevant family relationship between the defendant and the victim and the age of the victim must be proved and the defendant will have an evidential burden to discharge in that regard.

C The existence of the relevant family relationship between the defendant and the victim must be proved and the prosecution will have an evidential burden to discharge in that regard.

D The age of the victim must be proved and the prosecution will have an evidential burden to discharge in that regard.

Question 15.14

JARVIS (aged 15 yrs) is the half-brother of LYONS (aged 15 yrs). The two attend the same school and go on a school trip to Wales where they share a tent. One evening, LYONS takes off all of his clothes and approaches JARVIS, suggesting that they should have anal sexual intercourse together. JARVIS is offended and flatly refuses.

With regard to ss. 25, 26 and 27 of the Sexual Offences Act 2003, which of the statements below is correct?

A LYONS does not commit an offence under either section as a half-brother is not a relevant family relationship (s. 27 of the Act).

B LYONS is guilty of an offence of sexual activity with a child member (s. 25 of the Act)

C LYONS does not commit an offence under either section as he is under 18 years of age.

D LYONS is guilty of an offence of inciting sexual activity with a child member (s. 26 of the Act).

Question 15.15

RENTON (aged 25 yrs) visits his old foster parent, STRAKER. While visiting STRAKER, RENTON is introduced to THAWLEY (aged 16 yrs) who has been living with STRAKER for the past two years. Prior to this meeting, RENTON and THAWLEY have never met each other. RENTON and THAWLEY get on extremely well and begin to see each other on a regular basis as boyfriend and girlfriend. One month after their initial meeting, RENTON and THAWLEY have consensual sexual intercourse.

Has RENTON committed an offence contrary to s. 25 of the Sexual Offences Act 2003?

A Yes, as RENTON and THAWLEY have the same foster parent.

B No, because sexual intercourse between the two is consensual.

C Yes, because THAWLEY is under 18 years of age.

D No, because RENTON and THAWLEY have never lived in the same household.

Question 15.16

WOOD (aged 17 yrs) and PERCIVAL (aged 17 yrs) have been going out together for six months and have had sexual intercourse on a number of occasions. Their respective parents have met each other several times and they begin a relationship together that leads to their marriage. This results in both parents, WOOD and PERCIVAL moving into the same house.

If WOOD and PERCIVAL now have sexual intercourse, which of the below will be true with regard to s. 25 of the Sexual Offences Act 2003 (sexual activity with a child family member)?

A WOOD and PERCIVAL are now stepsister and stepbrother and they cannot have sexual intercourse without committing an offence.

B The only way that WOOD and PERCIVAL would not commit an offence would be if they were lawfully married at the time.

C WOOD and PERCIVAL will not commit an offence as their sexual relationship pre-dates the newly created family relationship.

D WOOD and PERCIVAL are both under the age of 18 and cannot commit the offence.

Question 15.17

MUXLOW (aged 15 yrs) has sexual intercourse (penis to vagina) with KILLEN (aged 57 yrs) who is MUXLOW's grandmother.

Considering only the offence of sex with an adult relative (contrary to s. 64 of the Sexual Offences Act 2003), who, if anyone, is guilty of the offence?

A MUXLOW only.

B KILLEN only.

C MUXLOW and KILLEN.

D Neither MUXLOW nor KILLEN commit the offence.

Question 15.18

HASTINGS (aged 18 yrs) and BRISTOW (aged 18 yrs) are stepbrother and stepsister and have both lived within the same house for 12 years. HASTINGS and BRISTOW are staying at a friend's house when HASTINGS asks BRISTOW if she will have oral sex with him. BRISTOW consents and HASTINGS puts his penis into BRISTOW's mouth.

Would this activity constitute an offence of sex with an adult relative (contrary to s. 64 of the Sexual Offences Act 2003)?

A No, the relationship of stepbrother and stepsister are excluded from this offence.

B Yes, s. 64 of the Act includes the relationship of stepbrother and stepsister.

C No, this section does not cover the act of penetration of the mouth with the penis.

D Yes, as they have both lived in the same household for 12 years.

Question 15.19

ARCHER (aged 25 yrs) meets BARNARD (aged 23 yrs) in a bar. The two go on to a nightclub together and then go back to ARCHER's home address. ARCHER masturbates BARNARD's penis before putting her forefinger into BARNARD's anus. The two then have consensual sexual intercourse (penis to vagina). Unknown to either ARCHER or BARNARD they are in fact brother and sister.

At what point, if at all, does the offence of sex with an adult relative (s. 64 of the Sexual Offences Act 2003) take place?

A When ARCHER masturbates BARNARD.

B When ARCHER puts her forefinger into BARNARD's anus.

C When ARCHER and BARNARD have consensual sexual intercourse.

D The offence under s. 64 is not committed in these circumstances.

Question 15.20

CANNON (aged 19 yrs) has consensual anal intercourse with DARROCH (aged 40 yrs) who is CANNON's uncle. This is an offence contrary to s. 64 of the Sexual Offences Act 2003 (sex with an adult relative).

If the two men were to be prosecuted for this offence, what is the maximum sentence that can be imposed on them?

A The maximum sentence for this offence is 2 years' imprisonment.

B The maximum sentence for this offence is 3 years' imprisonment.

C The maximum sentence for this offence is 4 years' imprisonment.

D The maximum sentence for this offence is 5 years' imprisonment.

Question 15.21

GATRELL (aged 21 yrs) is living with his partner HADLOW (aged 17 yrs) in an enduring family relationship. GATRELL takes a dozen photographs of HADLOW taking
part in simulated sex acts with INGLEY (aged 25 yrs). HADLOW and INGLEY are both
naked in the photographs and both consent to the photographs being taken by
GATRELL. GATRELL wishes to keep the photographs for his own pleasure and does
not intend to distribute them in any way.

With regard to the taking of indecent photographs (contrary to s. 1 of the Protection of Children Act 1978 (as amended by s. 45 of the Sexual Offences Act
2003)), has GATRELL committed an offence?

A Yes, as the photographs show a person other than GATRELL and HADLOW.

B No, because GATRELL and HADLOW were living together in an enduring family
relationship.

C Yes, because indecent photographs of a child under 18 years of age cannot be
taken in any circumstances.

D No, because HADLOW consented to the photographs being taken and she is over
16 years of age.

Question 15.22

JOHNSON (aged 20 yrs) takes indecent photographs of LAWFORD (aged 16 yrs).
At the time the photographs are taken by JOHNSON, all the requirements of s. 45
of the Sexual Offences Act 2003 (providing a defence to the taking of indecent
photographs) are satisfied so that the actual taking of the photographs is not in
itself illegal.

Considering only s. 1 of the Protection of Children Act 1978 (indecent photographs of children), at what stage, if at all, would JOHNSON commit an offence?

A When he has the indecent photographs in his possession to view them for his
own personal pleasure.

B When he has the indecent photographs in his possession with a view to showing
them to his friend, MANNING (aged 23 yrs).

C When he has the indecent photographs in his possession and shows them to his
friend, NEWPORT (aged 23 yrs).

D JOHNSON does not commit an offence in these circumstances.

Question 15.23

ROLFE is a local councillor who is running an anti-child pornography campaign. Because of ROLFE's campaign, PARNELL (a paedophile) decides to send ROLFE a large number of indecent photographs of children in order to offend him. PARNELL contacts OXLEY, a delivery van driver, to deliver a parcel containing hundreds of indecent photographs of children under the age of 10 to ROLFE's home address. OXLEY (unaware of the contents) collects the parcel from PARNELL and places it on the front seat of his van and sets off. Several miles later, OXLEY has to brake sharply to avoid an accident and the parcel slips off the front seat and hits the dashboard of his van. In the process, the packaging is damaged and OXLEY sees the contents. OXLEY needs the money for delivering the parcel and so continues to his destination where he delivers the parcel to ROLFE. The photographs outrage ROLFE and, believing he has a legitimate reason to show the photographs, he shows them to a local newspaper editor as evidence to highlight his anti-child pornography campaign.

Who has committed an offence contrary to s. 1 of the Protection of Children Act 1978?

A PARNELL only.

B PARNELL and OXLEY.

C PARNELL and ROLFE.

D PARNELL, OXLEY and ROLFE.

Question 15.24

Section 1 of the Protection of Children Act 1978 and s. 160 of the Criminal Justice Act 1988 both deal with indecent photographs and 'pseudo-photographs' of children. These images can be obtained, in many cases, via the use of the Internet. There has been a significant amount of authoritative case law in this area that investigators ought to be aware of when gathering evidence of these offences.

With regard to the authoritative case law, which of the statements below is correct?

A 'Making' a pseudo-photograph does not include voluntarily browsing through indecent images of children on and from the Internet.

B Evidence showing how a computer had been used to access paedophile news groups, chat-lines and websites would not be relevant to a case relating to the creation of an indecent image of a child.

C An image consisting of two parts of two different photographs taped together (the naked body of a woman taped to the head of a child) would not be a 'pseudo-photograph'.

D Downloading images from the Internet will not amount to 'making' a photograph.

Question 15.25

SANDBROOK (aged 25 yrs) has several indecent photographs of TAFANO (aged 14 yrs) posted through his front door. SANDBROOK had not made any prior request for these photographs to be delivered. SANDBROOK opens the envelope containing the photographs and having examined them he leaves them on a shelf in his flat. Six months later, SANDBROOK's flat is raided by the police and the photographs of TAFANO are discovered. SANDBROOK states that he has not shown or distributed the photographs of TAFANO to anyone else nor did he intend to do so.

With regard to s. 160 of the Criminal Justice Act 1988, which of the statements below is correct?

A SANDBROOK does not commit the offence as the photographs are of a child aged over 13 yrs of age.

B SANDBROOK has committed the offence but would have a defence because the photographs were sent to him without any prior request.

C As SANDBROOK has not shown or distributed the photographs to anyone else, he has not committed an offence under this Act.

D SANDBROOK has committed the offence, which is punishable with up to 5 years' imprisonment.

ANSWERS

Answer 15.1

Answer **A** — The offence under s. 9 of the Act can only be committed where the defendant is aged 18 years or over. Answer B is incorrect as whether KEANE consented to the act or not is irrelevant. Answer C is incorrect as this offence applies to a person aged under 16 years of age. Answer D is incorrect as this section covers the sexual activity that takes place between the two.

Investigators' Manual, para. 3.5.1   **DV = 4**

Answer 15.2

Answer **B** — This offence is committed if a person aged 18 or over (A) engages in sexual activity, for the purpose of obtaining sexual gratification and the activity is engaged in *when another person is present or is in a place from which (A) can be observed*. The fact that PRIZEMAN intended SHIPMAN to view the act (answer A) or the fact that he believed her to be watching the activity (answer C) are both immaterial if SHIPMAN is not present or in a place from which PRIZEMAN can be observed. Answer D is incorrect, as the fact that CASE was unaware of SHIPMAN's presence would not preclude PRIZEMAN committing the offence if SHIPMAN was present when the activity took place.

Investigators' Manual, para. 3.5.2   **DV = 3**

Answer 15.3

Answer **C** — Answer A is incorrect as the person committing this offence must be at least 18 years old. Answer B is incorrect as not only must the activity carried out be 'sexual', but also it must be carried out in order to obtain sexual gratification. Answer D is incorrect as it is not necessary to show that the child was in fact aware of the activity in every case.

Investigators' Manual, para. 3.5.2   **DV = 4**

Answer 15.4

Answer **A** — This offence relates to causing a child to watch a third person engage in sexual activity or to look at an image of any person engaging in an activity.

Answer B is incorrect on that basis. Answer C is incorrect because the offence can be committed against a child aged under 16 years of age. Answer D is incorrect as s. 79(5) of the Act states that an 'image' includes images of an imaginary person and, as such, animated cartoon images would be covered by the legislation.

Investigators' Manual, para. 3.5.3   **DV = 7**

Answer 15.5

Answer **D** — The offence of causing a child to watch a sexual act under s. 12 of the Act must be committed *intentionally*. Answer A is incorrect as although there might be a chance that children would see the images, unless HUGHES has carried out the activity with the intention that a child will observe it then the offence is not committed. Answer B is incorrect as although HUGHES has carried out the act for the purposes of sexual gratification, the sexual gratification aspect of the offence is incomplete. Sexual gratification for the purposes of this section must be gained by watching the child watching the activity of a third person or an image and not by watching an image for oneself. Answer C is incorrect as the term 'image' includes a moving or a still image.

Investigators' Manual, para. 3.5.3   **DV = 8**

Answer 15.6

Answer **C** — The purpose of s. 13 of the Sexual Offences Act 2003 is to provide a lower penalty of 5 years' imprisonment where the offender is aged under 18 years.

Investigators' Manual, para. 3.5.1   **DV = 4**

Answer 15.7

Answer **B** — The offence of arranging or facilitating the commission of a child sex offence can be committed if the arranging or facilitating is for an offence to be committed in any part of the world, making answer A incorrect. Answer C is incorrect as the offence is complete whether or not the sexual activity takes place. Answer D is incorrect as the offence is complete if the defendant arranges or facilitates something that he intends to do, intends another person to do, *or believes that another person will do.*

Investigators' Manual, para. 3.5.4   **DV = 7.5**

Answer 15.8

Answer **B** — A person can only commit an offence under s. 14 of the Act if he arranges or facilitates an offence that would be an offence under ss. 9 to 13 of the Act. The offence under s. 14 of the Act can be committed if the defendant arranges or facilitates something *that he intends to do,* as well as arranging or facilitating the acts of others, making answer A incorrect. Answer C is incorrect as this offence is complete whether sexual activity takes place or not. Whether the person contacted is a police officer makes no difference as it is the arranging or facilitating that is the crux of the offence. Answer D is incorrect as there are no limitations as to the nature or type of contact. The arrangements or facilitation can be made by any means whatsoever, the Internet being a prime example.

Investigators' Manual, para. 3.5.4   **DV = 2**

Answer 15.9

Answer **D** — Answer A is incorrect as the intentions of the defendant at the time of the first meeting with a potential victim are immaterial; it is the defendant's intentions at the time of either meeting with or travelling to meet the victim after two previous communications or meetings that is relevant. Answer B is incorrect because BALLARD has not met or communicated with GALBRAITH on two previous occasions. Answer C is incorrect as the offence can be committed when travelling to meet the victim with the requisite intent.

Investigators' Manual, para. 3.5.4   **DV = 3**

Answer 15.10

Answer **C** — The meetings or communication, for the purposes of this section, can have taken place in any part of the world (s. 15(2)), making answer A incorrect. Answer D is incorrect as for HARVEY to trigger an offence under this section he must either take part in an *intentional* meeting with PREECE or travel with the intention of meeting PREECE. As PREECE has travelled to HARVEY and the meeting was without the knowledge of HARVEY, i.e. a surprise visit, HARVEY does not commit the offence. Answer B is incorrect as the fact that HARVEY accepted an offer for sexual intercourse via the Internet would not make HARVEY criminally responsible under this section.

Investigators' Manual, para. 3.5.4   **DV = 3**

Answer 15.11

Answer **C** — Answer A is incorrect as the *actus reus* of this offence includes penetration of the victim's mouth with the defendant's penis. Answer B is incorrect as the law makes no distinction in sentence with regard to the age of the victim. Answer D is incorrect as when the offence involves penetration, it is indictable only and the maximum sentence is 14 years' imprisonment.

Investigators' Manual, para. 3.5.5   **DV = 4**

Answer 15.12

Answer **A** — The relevant age with regard to s. 25 of the Act is that the victim is under 18 years of age, making answer C incorrect. Sexual intercourse with a relative who is under 18 would constitute an offence under this section as long as the relationship between the parties is a relevant family relationship as stated in s. 27 of the Act. First cousins are not included in the list of relevant family relationships making answers B and D incorrect.

Investigators' Manual, para. 3.5.5   **DV = 4**

Answer 15.13

Answer **B** — Apart from 'touching' and 'sexual', there are two further elements that must be proved in relation to s. 25 of the Act. The first is the existence of the relevant family relationship (making answers A, C and D incorrect) and the second is the age of the victim. In addition, answers C and D are incorrect in respect of both the relationship and the age of the victim, the *defendant* will have an evidential burden to discharge in that regard (s. 25(2) and (3)).

Investigators' Manual, para. 3.5.5   **DV = 7.5**

Answer 15.14

Answer **D** — Answer A is incorrect as the relationship of half-brother is covered by s. 27 of the Act. Answer B is incorrect as LYONS has not actually touched JARVIS and so the offence under s. 25 is incomplete. Answer C is incorrect as a person under 18 years of age can commit this offence but the maximum penalty is less in such circumstances.

Investigators' Manual, para. 3.5.5   **DV = 5**

Answer 15.15

Answer **D** — This question revolves around the issue of whether there is a relevant family relationship between RENTON and THAWLEY. Section 27 of the Act defines core family relationships and also provides additional categories where a relationship will be deemed to exist. One of those categories is when the defendant and the victim *live or have lived* in the same household and they have the same parent or foster parent. Although RENTON and THAWLEY have the same foster parent (STRAKER) they do not live and never have lived in the same household. In other words, there is no family relationship between the two. This fact makes answers A and C incorrect. Answer B is incorrect as whether the sexual intercourse was consensual or not is immaterial for the purposes of an offence under s. 25 of the Act.

Investigators' Manual, para. 3.5.5   **DV = 3**

Answer 15.16

Answer **C** — Section 29 of the Act caters for sexual relationships which pre-date family relationships. A person is not liable for a familial child sex offence under s. 25 where a lawful sexual relationship existed between the parties immediately before the onset of the circumstances giving rise to the familial relationship. Although WOOD and PERCIVAL are now stepsister and stepbrother they do not commit the offence because of s. 29, making answer A incorrect. A further exception (under s. 28 of the Act) relates to marriage exceptions, however, this is not the only exception and therefore answer B is incorrect. Answer D is incorrect as persons under the age of 18 can commit this offence.

Investigators' Manual, para. 3.5.5   **DV = 8**

Answer 15.17

Answer **B** — Both parties can commit this offence if one relative (who is 16 or over) intentionally penetrates the vagina or anus of another relative (aged 18 or over) with anything, or penetrates their mouth with his penis. Therefore, as MUXLOW is only 15 years old he cannot commit the offence making answers A and C incorrect. This offence replaces the former offence of incest and widens the relatives who can be held responsible for the offence. This now includes grandparent and grandchild making answer D incorrect.

Investigators' Manual, para. 3.5.6   **DV = 5.5**

Answer 15.18

Answer **A** — Answer B is incorrect as the relationship of stepbrother and stepsister is not included in the term 'relationship' for the purposes of s. 64 of the Act. Answer C is incorrect as penetration of the mouth with the penis is part of the *actus reus* of this offence. Answer D is incorrect, as the fact that the two have lived in the same household for 12 years has no bearing on an offence under this section.

Investigators' Manual, para. 3.5.6   **DV = 3**

Answer 15.19

Answer **D** — Although ARCHER and BARNARD are brother and sister and are there-fore 'relatives' for the purposes of s. 64 of the Act, the offence under s. 64 can only be committed when the relative knows (or could reasonably be expected to know) that he/she is related to the other. If this knowledge is not present then the offence cannot be committed, making answers A, B and C incorrect. If the two were know-ingly related then the offence would take place at point B as masturbation is not included in the *actus reus* of the offence.

Investigators' Manual, para. 3.5.6   **DV = 7**

Answer 15.20

Answer **A** — The offence under s. 64 of the Act is triable either way and is punish-able by up to 2 years' imprisonment, making answers B, C and D incorrect.

Investigators' Manual, para. 3.5.6   **DV = 5**

Answer 15.21

Answer **A** — Section 1(1)(a) of the Protection of Children Act 1978 makes it an offence for a person to take, or permit to be taken or to make, any indecent photo-graph or pseudo-photograph of a child. Section 45 of the Sexual Offences Act 2003 amends the Protection of Children Act so that where photographs are concerned a person will be considered a 'child' if they are 16 or 17 years of age. However, photo-graphs taken and used within an established relationship will not be criminalised if: (i) the defendant proves that the photograph in question was of a child aged 16 or over and at the time of the taking or making, he and the child were married or living together as partners in an enduring family relationship; and (ii) the child consented to the photograph being taken or the defendant reasonably believed that the child consented; and (iii) the photograph must not be one that shows a person other than the child and the defendant. If *any* of these conditions is not satisfied then the prosecution need only prove the offence as set out in s. 1(1)(a) of the 1978 Act. Answers B and D are incorrect as they only form part of the potential defence available to GATRELL. In addition, answer D is incorrect as it asserts that taking photographs of a child over the age of 16 is permissible with the consent of the child. Answer C is incorrect as the above defence exists if all three elements are present.

Investigators' Manual, para. 3.5.7   **DV = 2.5**

Answer 15.22

Answer **D** — If all the requirements of s. 45 of the Sexual Offences Act 2003 are met this will mean that at the time the photographs were taken (i) LAWFORD was at least 16 years of age and JOHNSON and LAWFORD were either married or living together in an enduring family relationship; and (ii) there is enough evidence to show that LAWFORD consented to the photograph being taken; and (iii) the photograph does not show any other person other than the child and the defendant. The activities at points A, B and C are all offences under s. 1 of the Protection of Children Act 1978 but will not be if s. 45 of the Sexual Offences Act 2003 is satisfied. Therefore, answers A, B and C are all incorrect as JOHNSON will not commit an offence in these circumstances.

Investigators' Manual, para. 3.5.7   **DV = 3**

Answer 15.23

Answer **B** — Under s. 1(1)(b) of the Act it is an offence to distribute or show indecent photographs or pseudo-photographs. PARNELL is guilty of this offence by sending the package containing the indecent photographs, via OXLEY, to ROLFE. Answers A and C are incorrect as OXLEY is also guilty of this offence. It would be a defence for a person charged with such an offence under s. 1(4)(b) of the Act to prove that he had not himself seen the photographs or pseudo-photographs and did not know, nor had any cause to suspect, them to be indecent. OXLEY would have been able to avail himself of this defence up until the point when he realised what the contents of the package were. Answer D (and also answer C again) is incorrect as ROLFE does not commit the offence. Although ROLFE has shown the photographs to another person he would have a defence under s. 1(4)(b) of the Act which states that he will have a defence if he had a legitimate reason for distributing or showing the photographs or pseudo-photographs.

Investigators' Manual, para. 3.5.7   **DV = 2**

Answer 15.24

Answer **C** — Answer A is incorrect as 'making' a pseudo-photograph *does* include voluntarily browsing through indecent images of children on and from the Internet (*R v Smith and Jayson* [2002] EWCA Crim 683). Answer B is incorrect as evidence showing how a computer had been used to access paedophile news groups, chat-lines and web sites *would* be relevant to a case relating to the creation of an indecent image of a child (*R v Mould* [2001] 2 Crim App R(s) 8). Answer D is incorrect as downloading images from the Internet *will* amount to 'making' a photograph (*R v Bowden* [2000] 2 WLR 1083). Answer C is correct as stated in *Goodland* v *DPP* [2000] 1 WLR 1427.

Investigators' Manual, para. 3.5.7   **DV = 2**

Answer 15.25

Answer **D** — Answer A is incorrect as a 'child' is a person under the age of 18 years of age at the material time. Answer B is incorrect as although the photographs were sent to SANDBROOK without any prior request being made by him for such material (the first part of the defence under s. 160(2)(c)), he has kept them for an unreasonable time thereby defeating the defence. Answer C is incorrect as showing or distributing the indecent photographs relates to an offence under s. 1 of the Protection of Children Act 1978 and not to the offence of possessing indecent photographs under this Act.

Investigators' Manual, para. 3.5.7   **DV = 4.5**

16 | Protection of Children

QUESTIONS

Question 16.1

DC WELL receives information that PORT has physically abused her children and visits PORT who lets the officer into her house. DC WELL speaks to JANE PORT (aged 16 yrs) and ALEX PORT (aged 12 yrs). JANE PORT has several cuts and bruises to her face; ALEX PORT shows no signs of being physically abused. JANE PORT tells the officer that her mother is responsible for her injuries and that this is not the first time she has been assaulted by her. ALEX PORT tells the officer that he has heard his mother beating his sister and it frightens him and he cannot eat as a result. Because of what he has seen and heard, DC WELL is considering taking both children into 'Police Protection' (under s. 46 of the Children Act 1989).

Which of the statements below is correct?

A DC WELL can take ALEX PORT into 'Police Protection' but cannot take JANE PORT into 'Police Protection' because she is not a 'child' for the purposes of the Act.

B DC WELL can take JANE PORT into 'Police Protection' if he has reasonable cause to believe that she will suffer significant harm and ALEX PORT because of any impairment he may suffer from hearing his sister being ill-treated.

C DC WELL can take JANE PORT into 'Police Protection' but cannot take ALEX PORT into 'Police Protection' because he has not suffered any physical abuse.

D DC WELL cannot take either of the children into police protection in these circumstances.

Question 16.2

DC HAMBLING has taken JEPHCOTT into 'Police Protection' (under s. 46 of the Children Act 1989).

What is the maximum period that JEPHCOTT can spend in 'Police Protection'?

A 24 hours.

B 48 hours.

C 72 hours.

D 96 hours.

Question 16.3

MILBURN (aged 13 yrs) is subject to an emergency protection order and is in the care of his social worker, PRINCE. MILBURN's stepfather, HOLT, rings MILBURN on his mobile phone and tells him that life would be far better for him if he ran away from PRINCE's care and came back to his family. HOLT tells MILBURN that if he does run away from PRINCE he will take him to Disneyland in Florida.

Has HOLT committed an offence of acting in contravention of a protection order (contrary to s. 49 of the Children Act 1989)?

A Yes, he has induced and incited MILBURN to run away from a responsible person.

B No, this offence can only be committed by taking MILBURN away from the responsible person.

C Yes, but only if MILBURN actually runs away from the responsible person.

D No, this offence relates to children who are in care or in police protection and not to those subject to an emergency protection order.

Question 16.4

JUDSON leaves FOXLEY, her common-law husband, after their relationship breaks down and takes their 3-year-old child with her. FOXLEY contacts DC BANHAM and reports the child's absence. DC BANHAM later locates JUDSON who is staying in a women's refuge with her 3-year-old child. At the request of JUDSON, DC BANHAM tells FOXLEY that the child is safe but refuses to tell him where the child is. FOXLEY hires a solicitor and *ex parte* (i.e. without telling the police) applies for an order from the County Court under s. 33 of the Family Law Act 1986, requiring the police to disclose the information.

Considering the law with regard to the disclosure of a child's whereabouts, which of the below is correct?

A If FOXLEY obtains such an order then DC BANHAM will have to provide him with details of the child's whereabouts.

B An order under s. 33 in respect of the police will be made without their presence (*ex parte*) in all cases.

C If FOXLEY's application is successful then DC BANHAM will have to tell FOXLEY's solicitor of the child's whereabouts.

D It has been held that only in exceptional circumstances will the police be asked to divulge the whereabouts of a child under a s. 33 order.

ANSWERS

Answer 16.1

Answer **B** — Section 46 of the Act states that where a constable has reasonable cause to believe that a child would otherwise be likely to suffer significant harm, he may remove the child to suitable accommodation. Answer A is incorrect as a 'child' is someone who is under 18 years old (s. 105). Answer C is incorrect as the definition of 'harm' is very broad and includes forms of ill-treatment that are not 'physical'. It also covers the impairment of health (physical or mental) and also physical, intellectual, emotional, social or behavioural development. The definition also extends to impairment suffered from seeing or hearing the ill-treatment of *any other person*. Answer D is incorrect for the above reasons.

Investigators' Manual, para. 3.6.6   **DV = 6.5**

Answer 16.2

Answer **C** — The longest period that a child can spend in 'Police Protection' is 72 hours (s. 46(6)).

Investigators' Manual, para. 3.3.6   **DV = 4**

Answer 16.3

Answer **A** — Answer D is incorrect as s. 49(2) states that this offence applies to a child who is in care, subject of an emergency protection order or in police protection (s. 46). A 'responsible person' is any person who at the time has care of the child by virtue of a care order, an emergency protection order or by s. 46 of the Act, i.e. PRINCE. The offence can be committed by (a) taking a child to whom this section applies away from a responsible person, or (b) keeping such a child away from a responsible person, or (c) inducing, assisting or inciting such a child to run away from or stay away from the responsible person. Therefore, answers B and C are incorrect.

Investigators' Manual, para. 3.6.8   **DV = 7.5**

Answer 16.4

Answer **D** — This question relates to the circumstances in *S* v *S (Chief Constable of West Yorkshire Intervening)* [1999] 1 All ER 281. In this case, Butler-Sloss LJ stated that an order under s. 33 provides for the information to be disclosed to the court and not to any other party or his/her solicitor, making answers A and C incorrect. She also stated that an order made under s. 33 should not normally be made in respect of the police without their being present, making answer B incorrect.

Investigators' Manual, para. 3.6.9   **DV = 7**

17 | Preparatory Offences

QUESTIONS

Question 17.1

FEARING applies for a job as a lifeguard at his local swimming pool. Part of his prospective duties will include giving swimming lessons to children between the ages of 5 and 12 years old. FEARING's ulterior motive is to gain employment at the swimming pool and then take indecent photographs of the children (contrary to s. 1 of the Protection of Children Act 1978). To help him get the job, he forges several certificates that state he has passed examinations as a lifeguard. As a result, FEARING is given the job as a lifeguard.

Considering the offence of committing a criminal offence with intent to commit a sexual offence (s. 62 of the Sexual Offences Act 2003), which of the below is right?

A FEARING does not commit the offence as taking indecent photographs of children under s. 1 of the Protection of Children Act 1978 is not a 'relevant sexual offence'.

B This offence can only be committed if the criminal offence is one of kidnapping or false imprisonment, therefore, FEARING has not committed the offence.

C Until FEARING commits a sexual assault on one of the children he cannot be arrested for committing this offence.

D FEARING has initially committed an offence of obtaining a pecuniary advantage by deception (s. 16 of the Theft Act 1968) and therefore commits this offence.

Question 17.2

HALLAM's car breaks down in a country lane late one night. Rather than risk getting lost, she decides to sleep in her car and seek assistance in the morning. Several hours later, MILLENSTED walks past HALLAM's car and sees her sleeping inside. He decides to sexually touch HALLAM (an activity that would constitute an offence under s. 3 of the Sexual Offences Act 2003). MILLENSTED smashes the front window of the car and crawls inside. HALLAM, who is woken by the noise, manages to open one of the car doors and gets away from MILLENSTED.

With regard to the offence of trespass with intent to commit a sexual offence (s. 63 of the Sexual Offences Act 2003) which of the statements below is correct?

A The only intention that would make MILLENSTED guilty of this offence would be an intention to rape HALLAM.

B MILLENSTED has not committed the offence as a car would not be classed as a structure or part of a structure for the purposes of this offence.

C MILLENSTED has committed the offence as the term 'premises' for the purpose of s. 62 will include a vehicle.

D As HALLAM escaped before MILLENSTED committed the relevant sexual offence, he does not commit the offence.

Question 17.3

DIX decides that he is going to break into a house owned by AVERLEY. His intention is to commit an offence of rape (contrary to s. 1 of the Sexual Offences Act 2003) against AVERLEY and so he equips himself with a rope to tie her up with, condoms to minimise any DNA evidence he may leave and a bayonet to threaten her with. When DIX arrives at AVERLEY's house he sees her next-door neighbour, LAMBURN, leaving for an evening out. DIX decides that he will break into LAMBURN's house first and steal anything of value before he breaks into AVERLEY's house to rape her. He breaks into LAMBURN's house and steals property before breaking into AVERLEY's house.

At what point, if at all, does DIX commit an offence of trespass with intent to commit a sexual offence (contrary to s. 63 of the Sexual Offences Act 2003)?

A When he decides to break into AVERLEY's house and equips himself with the rope, condoms and bayonet.

B When he breaks into LAMBURN's house.

C When he breaks into AVERLEY's house.

D As rape is an offence that is specifically catered for by s. 10 of the Theft Act 1968, DIX does not commit the offence.

Question 17.4

JORDAN commits an offence of administering a substance with intent (contrary to s. 61 of the Sexual Offences Act 2003).

Which of the below is correct with regard to this offence?

A This offence carries a maximum sentence of 2 years' imprisonment.

B This offence carries a maximum sentence of 3 years' imprisonment.

C This offence carries a maximum sentence of 10 years' imprisonment.

D This offence carries a maximum sentence of 15 years' imprisonment.

Question 17.5

PEACH is drinking in a bar with McMANUS and WRIGHT. PEACH decides that he wants to have sexual intercourse with WRIGHT but knows that she is married and will never consent. He mentions this to McMANUS and gives McMANUS some Rohypnol (a 'date-rape' drug) to place in WRIGHT's drink. When WRIGHT is not looking, McMANUS puts the drug into WRIGHT's lager, intending to stupefy WRIGHT so as to enable PEACH to have sexual intercourse with her. WRIGHT drinks her drugged lager and quickly becomes ill. Before anything else happens, one of WRIGHT's friend's appears and takes her home.

Which of the statements below is correct with regard to the offence of administering a substance with intent (contrary to s. 61 of the Sexual Offences Act 2003)?

A McMANUS has not committed the offence because he did not administer the drug with the intention of engaging in sexual activity with WRIGHT.

B No offence has been committed in these circumstances because no sexual activity took place.

C Only McMANUS has committed the offence in these circumstances.

D PEACH and McMANUS commit the offence in these circumstances.

ANSWERS

Answer 17.1

Answer **A** — Section 62 of the Sexual Offences Act 2003 states that a person commits an offence under this section if he commits any offence with the intention of committing a relevant sexual offence. There are no restrictions on the nature or type of offence committed as long as it can be shown that there was an intention, when committing the original offence, to commit a relevant sexual offence. This makes answer B incorrect. Answer C is incorrect as the offence under s. 62 is committed when the first offence is committed with the required intention. Answer D is incorrect as although FEARING has committed an offence, taking photographs of children (contrary to s. 1 of the Protection of Children Act 1978) is not a 'relevant offence' for the purposes of s. 62. A 'relevant offence' means a sexual offence under Part 1 of the Sexual Offences Act 2003.

Investigators' Manual, para. 3.7.1   **DV = 2**

Answer 17.2

Answer **C** — Answer A is incorrect as HALLAM intends to commit a 'relevant sexual offence' (i.e. an offence under Part 1 of the Sexual Offences Act 2003). Answer D is incorrect as this is an offence of intention rather than consequence, therefore, there is no need to prove that the substantive sexual offence took place. The term 'premises' for the purposes of this offence is far wider than that which relates to burglary under the Theft Act 1968. Section 63(2) of the Sexual Offences Act 2003 defines 'premises' as including a structure or part of a structure and this will include a tent, a vehicle or vessel or other temporary or movable structure. This makes answer B incorrect.

Investigators' Manual, para. 3.7.2   **DV = 6**

Answer 17.3

Answer **C** — Answer A is incorrect as at this stage, DIX has not trespassed on any premises even though he has the intention of doing so. Answer D is incorrect as although s. 10 of the Theft Act 1968 caters for offenders entering premises in such circumstances and with this intent, it does not mean that an offender intending rape does not commit this offence. Rape is still a relevant sexual offence. Answer B is incorrect as the defendant must intend to commit the relevant sexual offence on the premises where he/she is a trespasser. Unless DIX intends to commit a relevant sexual offence in LAMBURN's house he does not commit the offence (although he would be guilty of aggravated burglary at this stage).

Investigators' Manual, para. 3.7.2   **DV = 5**

Answer 17.4

Answer **C** — This offence is punishable with a maximum sentence of 10 years' imprisonment (under s. 4 of the Sexual Offences Act 1956 the equivalent offence carried a term of 2 years' imprisonment and had no specific power of arrest).

Investigators' Manual, para. 3.7.3   **DV = 5**

Answer 17.5

Answer **D** — Section 61(1) of the Act states that a person is guilty of an offence if he administers a substance to, or causes a substance to be taken by, another person (B), knowing that (B) does not consent and with the intention of stupefying or overpowering (B) so as to enable *any person* to engage in sexual activity that involves (B). Answer A is incorrect as it does not matter that McMANUS is not the person who will engage in sexual activity if he is administering the substance. Answer B is incorrect as the fact that sexual activity did not take place is immaterial if the substance is administered with that intent. 'Administering' or 'causing to be taken by' cover a broad range of conduct and would include a set of circumstances where PEACH persuades McMANUS to administer a drug to WRIGHT so that PEACH could have sex with WRIGHT, making answer C incorrect.

Investigators' Manual, para. 3.7.3   **DV = 6.5**

Evidence

PART FOUR

Evidence

18 | Presumptions, State of Mind, Criminal Conduct and Bail

QUESTIONS

Question 18.1

DC McSHANE arrests LAVERICK for an offence of witness intimidation. During the course of the arrest, LAVERICK assaults DC McSHANE. LAVERICK is charged with both offences but pleads 'not guilty' to the charge of assaulting a police officer and the case goes to trial.

Which of the statements below is correct?

A Evidence that DC McSHANE was acting in the capacity of a police officer is an irrebuttable presumption of law.

B Evidence that DC McSHANE was acting in the capacity of a police officer is a rebuttable presumption of regularity.

C Evidence that DC McSHANE was acting in the capacity of a police officer is a presumption of fact.

D Evidence that DC McSHANE was acting in the capacity of a police officer is a presumption of intention.

Question 18.2

STEWARD has been charged with an offence of handling stolen goods. The prosecution wish to use s. 27(3) of the Theft Act 1968 to show STEWARD's previous misconduct. STEWARD has a previous conviction for handling stolen goods that is 8 years old and a previous conviction for theft that is 4 years old.

Which of the following statements is true?

A Provided that 7 days' notice in writing has been given to STEWARD of the intention to prove the convictions, both convictions would be admissible.

B Provided that 3 days' notice in writing has been given to STEWARD of the intention to prove the conviction, the handling stolen goods conviction would be admissible.

C Provided that 7 days' notice in writing has been given to STEWARD of the intention to prove the conviction, the theft conviction would be admissible.

D Provided that 3 days' notice in writing has been given to STEWARD of the intention to prove the conviction, both convictions would be admissible.

Question 18.3

LLOYD is involved in an argument with GOUGH at a bowling alley. LLOYD picks up a 14 lb bowling ball and throws it at GOUGH, intending to cause him an injury. GOUGH ducks and the bowling ball hits DOOGAN, causing her an injury. The ball then drops onto a table smashing several glasses in the process.

Considering the doctrine of transferred malice, which of the statements below is correct?

A LLOYD would only be liable for the injury to DOOGAN.

B LLOYD would only be liable for the damage to the glasses.

C LLOYD would be liable for the injury to DOOGAN and the damage to the glasses.

D LLOYD would not be liable for the injury to DOOGAN or the damage to the glasses.

Question 18.4

When considering *mens rea*, offences may fall into the categories of specific and basic intent. The distinction between such offences is important when considering defences.

Which of the offences below would be an offence of basic intent?

A An offence of wounding or inflicting grievous bodily harm (contrary to s. 18 of the Offences Against the Person Act 1861).

B An offence of blackmail (contrary to s. 21 of the Theft Act 1968).

C An offence of contaminating goods (contrary to s. 38 of the Public Order Act 1986).

D An offence of burglary (contrary to s. 9(1)(b) of the Theft Act 1968).

Question 18.5

RAKIC is a 24-year-old man with the mental capacity of a 7-year-old child. He picks up a stone in his back garden and throws it over a fence into his neighbour's back garden, breaking the glass of a greenhouse window. RAKIC is spoken to by a police officer and tells the officer he was only 'having a laugh' and did not stop to think of what damage might be caused by the stone.

Considering the doctrine of 'recklessness', which of the below is correct?

A RAKIC would be liable for the damage and the fact that he has the mental age of a 7-year-old is immaterial.

B RAKIC could be prosecuted for the offence as his state of mind would constitute 'objective' recklessness.

C As RAKIC has failed to consider an obvious risk his actions would be considered reckless.

D As RAKIC was unaware that the risk existed or would exist he would not be reckless.

Question 18.6

MASTERS is evicted from her home and moves in with her next-door neighbour OXFORD. The two are unrelated. OXFORD is housebound and extremely ill and needs constant attention otherwise she will die. MASTERS tells OXFORD that she will look after her and that OXFORD can dismiss the full-time nurse OXFORD has employed to perform this duty; OXFORD agrees. MASTERS looks after OXFORD for 6 months but then becomes bored by the constant care OXFORD requires. MASTERS totally ignores OXFORD for over 4 days and as a result, OXFORD dies.

Would MASTERS be criminally liable for her omission to act?

A No, MASTERS is under no duty to act under a statute, a public office or under the terms of a contract.

B Yes, MASTERS has taken it upon herself to carry out a duty and has then failed to do so.

C No, MASTERS must have some sort of relationship with OXFORD such as a parent with a child.

D Yes, MASTERS has created a dangerous situation and has taken no action to counteract the danger she created.

Question 18.7

WEST assaults LAY by pushing her through a glass window. This causes several deep cuts to LAY's wrists. LAY manages to escape and seek medical attention at a hospital where she is left waiting for some 4 hours before being told that her injuries are not life threatening as long as she has a blood transfusion. LAY is a Jehovah's

Witness and refuses to have the transfusion because of her religious beliefs. As a result of her refusal to have the transfusion, LAY dies from the injuries. Apart from the initial waiting period, hospital staff carried out their duties carefully.

Which of the below is correct with regard to WEST's criminal liability?

A WEST is liable for LAY's death, as defendants must take their victims as they find them. LAY's refusal to have the blood transfusion on religious grounds would not affect WEST's liability.

B WEST is not liable for LAY's death as her refusal to have a blood transfusion breaks the causal link between the assault and LAY's death.

C WEST would not be liable for LAY's death because the negligent treatment LAY received on her arrival at the hospital would be classed as an 'intervening act' breaking the causal link.

D WEST is liable for the death of LAY as under no circumstances could negligent medical treatment ever break the chain of causation from WEST's assault to LAY's death.

Question 18.8

BULL is homeless and breaks into an abandoned house looking for shelter. He goes upstairs into the back bedroom and lies down on a mattress. BULL lights a cigarette and then falls asleep. He wakes up several minutes later to find that the mattress is on fire. BULL does not put out the fire; instead he gets up and goes into another room and goes to sleep. The mattress continues to burn, causing serious damage to the bedroom. The only reason BULL survives is because of the rapid attendance of the fire brigade.

Which of the comments below is correct regarding BULL's criminal liability?

A BULL is not liable as a defendant can only be punished for his/her positive conduct; an omission cannot be punished by criminal law.

B BULL is liable for the criminal damage as he has created a dangerous situation and has a duty to act.

C Unless BULL is under a duty to act under a statute, a contract or because of a public office, he will not be liable for an omission to act.

D BULL is not liable, as criminal law will only punish an omission if the defendant has taken it upon him/herself to carry out a duty and then fails to do so.

Question 18.9

During an argument in a pub, McCLEOD attacks RUMLEY causing him serious brain damage. RUMLEY is already suffering from a serious stomach ulcer when McLEOD attacks him. RUMLEY is taken to hospital but the brain damage caused in the assault prevents doctors from operating on the stomach ulcer that eventually ruptures and kills RUMLEY.

What is McCLEOD's criminal liability in these circumstances?

A McCLEOD will not be liable for the death of RUMLEY as it is the lack of medical treatment that is the cause of RUMLEY's death.

B McCLEOD has no liability for the death of RUMLEY as the ultimate and actual cause of death was an untreated ulcer.

C McCLEOD would be liable for manslaughter, as his criminal conduct has made a significant contribution to RUMLEY's death.

D McCLEOD would not be liable for RUMLEY's death, as the ruptured ulcer would be viewed as an intervening act.

Question 18.10

PYE agrees to accompany his friend BASRAN to an isolated farm where BASRAN intends to steal the car owner's car. PYE is fully aware of BASRAN's intention and has agreed to act as a 'look out' while BASRAN steals the car. PALFREY, the owner of the car, confronts them as BASRAN is breaking into the car. Unexpectedly, BASRAN produces a knife and stabs PALFREY causing her a serious injury. PYE had no idea that BASRAN was carrying a knife and only accompanied BASRAN in order to steal the car.

Considering the law relating to principles and accessories, would PYE be liable with regard to the wounding against PALFREY?

A PYE is an accessory present at the scene of a crime when it is committed. His presence may amount to encouragement that would support a charge of aiding, abetting, counselling or procuring the wounding offence.

B PYE is an accessory who has helped in the commission of an offence. A court will treat him in the same way as the principle offender (BASRAN) for the wounding of PALFREY.

C PYE did not physically assist BASRAN in the wounding of PALFREY. Unless this element forms part of the offence, PYE can never be liable as an accessory to the wounding offence.

D Although PYE and BASRAN are part of a joint enterprise, BASRAN has gone beyond what had been agreed. As such, PYE could not be held liable for the consequences of such an 'unauthorised' act by BASRAN.

Question 18.11

LOVETT has a previous conviction for attempted rape for which he served 3 years' imprisonment. LOVETT is arrested and charged in connection with a s. 18 wounding.

Considering the bail restrictions under s. 25 of the Criminal Justice and Public Order Act 1994, which of the statements below is correct?

A This section only applies to defendants who have a previous conviction for murder, attempted murder or manslaughter and would not affect the granting of bail for LOVETT.

B A previous conviction for attempted rape is covered by this section, as is the charge of s. 18 wounding; bail should only be granted to LOVETT if there are exceptional circumstances which justify it.

C This section only applies to defendants if they have previously been convicted by or before a court in the UK of culpable homicide and so LOVETT's previous conviction will not affect the granting of bail.

D Although LOVETT's previous conviction for attempted rape is relevant, a s. 18 wounding is not and so will not alter the decision to grant bail.

Question 18.12

DC WRAGG arrests SYMONS for 3 robberies and tells the custody officer that SYMONS has carried out the offences with PARTINGTON who has yet to be arrested. The custody officer asks for SYMONS' name and address to which SYMONS replies, 'I'll never say'. DC WRAGG tells the custody officer that SYMONS has failed to answer bail on two previous occasions. Several hours later SYMONS is charged with the offences of robbery although DC WRAGG still has some further enquiries to make regarding the offences. The issue of bail is now being considered.

For which one of the reasons below could bail be refused to SYMONS?

A SYMONS has failed to comply with s. 38(1) PACE as he has refused to provide his name and address.

B If released, SYMONS will interfere with the administration of justice, as the police have still to arrest PARTINGTON.

C There is a risk that SYMONS will abscond and this is evidenced by his previous failure to answer bail.

D SYMONS will interfere with the administration of justice because there are still further enquiries to make regarding the offences.

Question 18.13

You are the officer in charge of a case involving MOUNTFORD. You arrested MOUNTFORD for a deception related offence and charged him at your police station. MOUNTFORD was bailed to appear at your local magistrates' court and the custody officer at the time of his charging, PS GLEDHILL, granted bail on the condition that MOUNTFORD would report to your police station on a daily basis at 6.00pm. MOUNTFORD contacts you and asks if it is possible for his bail conditions to be modified as he has injured his leg and will have difficulty getting to the police station every day at the appointed time.

What will you tell MOUNTFORD?

A MOUNTFORD should make the request to any custody officer at your police station.

B Once bail conditions have been imposed, only a magistrates' court can alter them.

C Only PS GLEDHILL can alter the bail conditions.

D MOUNTFORD can make his request to any custody officer serving at any police station in your force.

Question 18.14

BOON is arrested for burglary. The custody officer decides to give him bail on the condition that he obtains a surety to secure his surrender to custody. BOON suggests that his cousin, MAGEE, will stand as a surety. MAGEE is contacted by the police for this purpose.

Which of the statements below is true?

A MAGEE would have a liability if BOON committed any further offences or interfered with witnesses whilst on bail.

B MAGEE cannot be a surety for BOON because they are related to each other.

C The normal consequence for MAGEE if BOON does not answer bail is that MAGEE would be required to forfeit the entire sum in which he stood surety.

D In order for MAGEE to forfeit the sum in which he stood surety, it would be necessary to prove that he had some involvement in BOON's non-appearance.

Question 18.15

You have arrested MILBURN (aged 13 yrs) on suspicion of burglary. During interview, MILBURN tells you that he has committed at least 30 other burglaries and wants to confess to them. You are considering charging MILBURN with the burglary that he has been arrested for and requesting a remand in police custody under s. 128 of the Magistrates' Courts Act 1980 with a view to interviewing MILBURN for the other 30 offences.

Will such a request be successful?

A Yes, the court can remand MILBURN into local authority accommodation for a period not exceeding 3 days.

B No, such a remand can only be given if MILBURN has attained the age of 15 and the offences are of a violent or sexual nature.

C Yes, MILBURN may be remanded to police custody for a period not exceeding 24 hours.

D No, such a remand may only be sought if its purpose is to make enquiries into the offence for which MILBURN has been charged.

Question 18.16

Sergeant ANDERSON is acting as a custody officer and is considering granting bail to FRAZER. It appears necessary to impose bail conditions on FRAZER in order to prevent him from failing to surrender to custody and to prevent him committing an offence whilst on bail.

Which of the conditions below would Sergeant ANDERSON be unable to impose on FRAZER?

A A requirement that FRAZER resides in a bail hostel or probation hostel.

B A requirement that FRAZER surrenders his passport.

C A requirement restricting FRAZER from entering a certain area or building or to go within a specified distance of a specified address.

D A requirement that FRAZER provides a surety or security.

Question 18.17

PATSTOW has been convicted of burglary on several occasions. She has been charged with another offence of burglary and the case has gone to trial. During the trial, PATSTOW's barrister attacks the character of the main prosecution witness.

When PATSTOW gives evidence, can the prosecution cross-examine her about her previous convictions?

A No, because PATSTOW's barrister rather than PATSTOW herself was the person who attacked the character of the prosecution witness.

B Yes, because the nature of PATSTOW's defence is to involve imputations on the character of a witness for the prosecution.

C No, not unless PATSTOW or her barrister have introduced evidence of PATSTOW's good character.

D Yes, but only because the nature of the charge is the same as that leading to her previous convictions.

ANSWERS

Answer 18.1

Answer **B** — It is presumed that where evidence shows that a person acted in a public or official capacity, in the absence of contrary evidence, that the person was regularly and properly appointed. A typical example of this is on a charge of assaulting a police officer in the course of his/her duty. Evidence that the police officer acted in that capacity is sufficient proof of his/her appointment (*R* v *Gordon* (1789) 1 Leach 515; and see *Cooper* v *Rowlands* [1971] RTR 291). This presumption is a presumption of regularity falling under the heading of rebuttable presumptions of law.

Investigators' Manual, para. 4.1.2   **DV = 2**

Answer 18.2

Answer **C** — Seven days' notice in writing must be given to the defendant that the prosecution intend to prove previous convictions, making answers B and D incorrect. The defendant's previous convictions can be for theft or handling stolen goods, however, the conviction for the offence must be in the 5 years preceding the date of the offence charged. Therefore the handling conviction would not be admissible, making answer A incorrect.

Investigators' Manual, para. 4.1.3   **DV = 3**

Answer 18.3

Answer **A** — The doctrine of transferred malice only operates if the crime remains the same. In *R* v *Latimer* (1886) 17 QBD 359, the defendant lashed out with his belt at one person but missed, striking a third party instead. As it was proved that the defendant had the required *mens rea* when he swung the belt, the court held that the same *mens rea* could support a charge of wounding against any other victim injured by the same act. Therefore, LLOYD is liable for the assault on DOOGAN, making answers B and D incorrect. If the nature of the offence changes, then the doctrine will not operate. LLOYD's *mens rea* to injure will not transfer into the *mens rea* for an offence of criminal damage, making answer C incorrect.

Investigators' Manual, para. 1.12.2.3   **DV = 6.5**

Answer 18.4

Answer **D** — A crime of 'specific' intent is only committed where the defendant is shown to have had a particular intention to bring about a specific consequence at the time of the criminal act. Answers A, B and C are examples of such offences. Answer D (burglary 9(1)(b)) simply requires proof that the person entered the building/part of a building as a trespasser and that he/she went on to commit one of the prohibited acts and, as such, this is an offence of basic intent.

Investigators' Manual, paras 4.2.3.1, 4.2.3.2   **DV = 4**

Answer 18.5

Answer **D** — Since the case of *R* v *G & R* [2003] 3 WLR 1060, the test of objective recklessness has all but disappeared and has been replaced with a subjective risk. RAKIC needs to be aware that a risk existed and as he does not, he is not reckless.

Investigators' Manual, para. 4.2.4.2   **DV = 7.5**

Answer 18.6

Answer **B** — Criminal liability usually arises as a result of a defendant's action. However, in some cases a defendant can be criminally liable because of an omission or a failure to act. The section on omissions gives specific examples of when such a liability may arise, one of those being when a defendant has taken it upon himself/herself to carry out a duty and then fails to do so (*R* v *Stone* [1977] QB 354). Although answers A, C and D all relate to criminal liability via omissions, they are still incorrect. MASTERS is liable for her actions making answers A and C incorrect. Answer D is incorrect as the creation of a dangerous situation involves the doing of some act and then a failure to prevent the harm in question occurring. MASTERS has not 'done' an act.

Investigators' Manual, para. 4.3.3   **DV = 5.5**

Answer 18.7

Answer **A** — This question relates to the 'but for' test applied to the principles surrounding the causation. The simple way to deal with this question is to ask, 'But for WEST's actions, would LAY have died?' The answer is 'No'. The next step is to ask if there has been an intervening act that breaks the chain of causation. Again the answer is 'No'. Defendants must take their victims as they find them, so refusing a blood transfusion on religious grounds will not break the chain of causation (*R v Blaue* [1975] 1 WLR 1411), making answer B incorrect. Negligent treatment has to be grossly negligent to break the chain of causation, making answer C incorrect. Answer D is incorrect because although negligent medical treatment will not normally break the chain of causation, there are exceptions where this has been the case (*R v Jordan* (1956) 40 Cr App R 152).

Investigators' Manual, paras 4.3.4, 4.3.5   **DV = 7**

Answer 18.8

Answer **B** — Criminal conduct is generally associated with the actions of the defendant, however, there are certain circumstances where an omission will attract criminal liability, making answer A incorrect. Such a duty can arise from a number of circumstances including where the defendant is under a duty to act under a statute (answer C), where the defendant has taken it upon him/herself to carry out a duty and then fails to do so (answer D), where the defendant is in a parental relationship with a child or young person or where the defendant creates a situation of danger (answer B and based on the case of *R v Miller* [1983] 2 AC 161). This makes answers C and D incorrect.

Investigators' Manual, para. 4.3.3   **DV = 5.5**

Answer 18.9

Answer **C** — There must be a causal link (or chain of causation) between the act of the defendant and the consequences; this is generally called the 'but for' test, e.g. if McCLEOD had not assaulted RUMLEY would he have died? The answer must be 'no'. If the assault had not taken place then the ulcer could have been operated on and RUMLEY may have lived. This question is based on the circumstances in the case of *R v McKechnie* [1992] Crim LR 194, where the court held that the defendant's actions had made a significant contribution to the victim's death (answer C). Answer A is incorrect as the lack of medical treatment was caused by McCLEOD's assault. Answer B is incorrect as although the ulcer is the *actual* cause of death, it ruptured because of a lack of medical treatment which could not be given because of the brain damage caused by the assault. Answer D is incorrect as the ruptured ulcer is not an intervening act.

Investigators' Manual, paras 4.3.4, 4.3.5   **DV = 6**

Answer 18.10

Answer **D** — Whether an accessory will be liable for the actions of the principle offender will depend on the nature and extent of the offence that was initially agreed to and contemplated by the accessory. The offence agreed to in this scenario was the theft of a car; this is entirely different to the wounding that BASRAN commits. In these circumstances, PYE will not be liable because BASRAN has gone 'beyond what has been tacitly agreed as part of the common enterprise, (*R* v *Anderson* [1966] 2 QB 110). In addition, there need be no physical assistance by the accessory to attract liability.

Investigators' Manual, paras 4.3.6–4.3.6.2   **DV = 7**

Answer 18.11

Answer **D** — Section 25 of the Criminal Justice and Public Order Act 1994 states that bail will only be granted to a defendant who is affected by it in the most exceptional circumstances. A defendant will be subject to this section if he/she has a previous conviction for murder, attempted murder, manslaughter, rape or attempted rape, this makes answers A and C incorrect. LOVETT's previous conviction for attempted rape is, therefore, relevant. However, the defendant must not only have a previous conviction for one of the stated offences but also be charged with one of those offences. LOVETT is charged with a s. 18 wounding which is not covered by the legislation, this makes answer B incorrect.

Investigators' Manual, para. 4.4.5   **DV = 8**

Answer 18.12

Answer **C** — The fact that SYMONS refuses to give his name and address does not satisfy the grounds on which bail can be refused under s. 38 PACE; this is only so if the name and address *cannot be ascertained*, making answer A incorrect. Although refusing bail on the grounds that the defendant will interfere with the administration of justice is a reason for refusing bail, this ground would not apply for the purposes of the police making further enquiries or where other suspects are still to be arrested, making answers B and D incorrect.

Investigators' Manual, paras 4.4.6–4.4.6.7   **DV = 3**

Answer 18.13

Answer **A** — Section 3A of the Bail Act 1976 applies to bail granted by a custody officer and amends s. 3 of the Act. Section 3A(4) states that where a custody officer has granted bail in criminal proceedings *he or another* custody officer serving *at the same police station* may, at the request of the person to whom it was granted, vary the conditions of bail and in doing so he may impose conditions or more onerous conditions.

Investigators' Manual, para. 4.4.7.2   **DV = 7**

Answer 18.14

Answer **C** — A surety has no responsibility or liability should the defendant commit further offences or interfere with witnesses whilst on bail, making answer A incorrect. The decision as to whether a surety is suitable or not rests with the custody officer. The fact that there is a relationship between the two is a consideration but not a bar, making answer B incorrect. It is not necessary to prove that the surety has any involvement in the defendant's non-appearance (*R* v *Warwick Crown Court, ex parte Smalley* [1987] 1 WLR 237), making answer D incorrect.

Investigators' Manual, para. 4.4.7.5   **DV = 8**

Answer 18.15

Answer **C** — Section 128 of the Magistrates' Courts Act 1980 provides that a magistrates' court may remand a person to *police custody* for a period not exceeding 3 days (*24 hours for a person under 17*) for the purposes of enquiries into other offences (*other than the offence for which he/she appears before a court*).

Investigators' Manual, para. 4.4.15   **DV = 6.5**

Answer 18.16

Answer **A** — Section 3A of the Bail Act 1976 applies to bail granted specifically by a custody officer. Section 3A(5) provides for the occasions when a custody officer can consider imposing bail conditions. Answers B, C and D are all conditions that can be imposed. However, there is no authority under s. 3A to bail a defendant to a bail hostel or a probation hostel as this has been omitted from this part of the Act.

Investigators' Manual, paras 4.4.7.1, 4.4.7.2   **DV = 7**

Answer 18.17

Answer **B** — If the defence (either the defendant or his/her representative) attacks the prosecution witness's character then the prosecution can ask questions about the character of the accused including his/her previous convictions.

Investigators' Manual, para. 4.1.3.3 **DV = 3**

19 PACE Codes of Practice, Identification and Interviews

QUESTIONS

Question 19.1

DC MANLER arrests DAWSON for an offence of theft. Due to the circumstances surrounding the arrest, DC MANLER takes DAWSON to a non-designated police station where DC ROBERTS (who is not involved in the investigation) performs the role of custody officer.

As the 'acting custody officer', who, if anyone, should DC ROBERTS inform of these circumstances?

A There is no requirement for DC ROBERTS to inform anyone of the circumstances.
B The custody officer at a designated police station.
C An officer of the rank of Inspector or above at a designated police station.
D An officer of the rank of Superintendent or above at a designated police station.

Question 19.2

DC JOPLIN has arrested FARROW for an offence of aggravated burglary. In the custody block, FARROW requests that he be allowed to telephone his girlfriend, ROWE. ROWE lives with FARROW and DC JOPLIN is concerned that if ROWE speaks to FARROW, she will dispose of any property relating to the aggravated burglary before he searches the home address of FARROW.

In these circumstances, can FARROW be prevented from making the telephone call to ROWE?

A Yes, with the authorisation of an officer of the rank of Superintendent or above.
B No, this right cannot be withheld in any circumstances.
C Yes, if an officer of the rank of Inspector or above authorises it.
D No, because FARROW has not been arrested for a drug trafficking offence.

Question 19.3

MULLAN is in custody for an offence of kidnapping and requests that TURNER (a solicitor friend of MULLAN) represents him whilst he is in police custody. DC SAUL is in charge of the investigation and is concerned that if MULLAN is allowed to use TURNER as a solicitor, TURNER will, inadvertently or otherwise, act in a way that will interfere with evidence connected to the kidnapping.

Which of the statements below is correct?

A DC SAUL should seek a Superintendent's authority to deny MULLAN access to legal advice from TURNER.

B MULLAN should be allowed to speak with TURNER, but to ensure that TURNER acts ethically, his consultations with MULLAN can be monitored by a police officer.

C Once the decision to deny MULLAN his legal advice has been taken, the authorisation applies to all solicitors or legal advisers and lasts up to a maximum of 36 hours.

D MULLAN cannot be denied access to legal advice from TURNER in these circumstances.

Question 19.4

WHORWOOD has been arrested for burglary and has requested the services of a solicitor, a fact that has been recorded on the custody record. Before the custody officer has had a chance to contact WHORWOOD's nominated solicitor, she changes her mind and states that she does not want or need a solicitor.

What course of action should be taken to deal with this situation?

A The custody officer should enquire as to WHORWOOD's change of mind and record the fact that WHORWOOD wishes to proceed without a solicitor on the custody record.

B An officer of Inspector rank or above should enquire as to WHORWOOD's reasons for her change of mind and WHORWOOD should agree to be interviewed without a solicitor in writing or on tape.

C When WHORWOOD is interviewed she should be asked to explain her reasons for her change of mind on tape and state the fact that she is willing to be interviewed without the presence of her solicitor.

D The solicitor should be contacted regardless of her change of mind. If WHORWOOD informs the solicitor that she wishes to continue without his/her presence, this should be recorded on the custody record.

Question 19.5

PARRISH voluntarily attends at a police station in your force area to be dealt with for an offence of theft; he arrives at the police station at 10.00 hrs and is arrested at 10.15 hrs. You have circulated PARRISH as wanted for an offence of rape and you are informed of his detention. You travel to the police station where PARRISH is detained and arrest him for the offence at 13.00 hrs. At no stage has PARRISH been questioned in relation to the offence of rape. You escort PARRISH back to your police station and arrive at 14.00 hrs.

From what time will PARRISH's 'relevant time' be calculated?

A 10.00 hrs.
B 10.15 hrs.
C 13.00 hrs.
D 14.00 hrs.

Question 19.6

TI PERRIN (a trainee investigator) approaches his tutor, DC WALTERS, in the custody block. TI PERRIN asks several questions in relation to the audio-recording of interviews with suspects at a police station. DC WALTERS gives the responses below to TI PERRIN.

Which one is **WRONG**?

A An interview for a matter that can only be tried summarily must be audio-recorded.
B The whole of an interview should be recorded and this includes the taking and reading back of any statement.
C The custody officer can authorise an interviewing officer not to audio record an interview if it is clear from the outset that no prosecution will ensue.
D A decision not to audio record an interview for any reason may be the subject of comment in court and the custody officer should be prepared to justify that decision.

Question 19.7

DYTHAM is arrested for murder and has been in custody for 20 hours. DS KNIBBS, the officer in charge of the case, considers that the investigating and interviewing officers need more time to carry out their enquiries and realises that this will take more than the 24-hour basic period of detention. DS KNIBBS believes that it is unlikely that more than 36 hours will be needed to conclude matters.

Who will approve the 12-hour extension required by DS KNIBBS?

A The custody officer.

B An officer of the rank of Inspector or above.

C An officer of the rank of Superintendent or above.

D A Magistrates' Court.

Question 19.8

SALISBURY is looking out of her bedroom window when she sees COX attempting to break into her neighbour's house. SALISBURY watches COX for a continuous period of five minutes and then telephones the police to tell them what she has seen. SALISBURY describes the approximate age of COX and the clothes he is wearing. The police arrive and COX is arrested. In interview, COX disputes being the person responsible for the offence but does not request an identification parade.

Considering the law with regard to identification, which of the statements below is correct?

A A suspect's failure to request an identification parade means that the police may proceed without one.

B This would not be classed as an identification within the terms of the Codes of Practice as SALISBURY has only described the clothing and approximate age of COX.

C The Codes of Practice are clear; where a witness is available and the suspect disputes being the person responsible for the offence, an identification procedure shall be held.

D Following the decision in R v Forbes, if the police are in possession of sufficient evidence to justify an arrest of a suspect and any identification is disputed then an identification procedure should be held.

Question 19.9

WARDALE has been arrested for an offence of s. 20 wounding by DC HERRIOT. During the course of the taped interview, WARDALE replied 'No comment' to all the questions put to him apart from the question 'Who was responsible for the assault?' to which WARDALE replied, 'It wasn't me'. WARDALE is charged with the offence and after the custody officer charges and cautions him, WARDALE replies, 'I can tell you who committed the assault if you want me to'.

Could WARDALE be interviewed about his comments?

A No, a detainee may not be interviewed about an offence after they have been charged with it, or informed they would be prosecuted for it.

B Yes, to clear up an ambiguity in a previous answer or statement.

C No, this can only be done to prevent or minimise harm or loss to some other person, or the public.

D Yes, as long as WARDALE agrees in writing to be re-interviewed regarding his comments.

Question 19.10

MURPHY (aged 15 yrs) is arrested for burglary. Due to problems with MURPHY's family, SERCOMBE (a responsible adult aged over 18 yrs) is called out to act as the appropriate adult during MURPHY's interview. MURPHY requests that he be allowed to consult a solicitor and HEMSTOCK (a solicitor) attends the police station. MURPHY asks for a consultation with HEMSTOCK but demands that SERCOMBE be excluded from the consultation.

Which of the statements below is correct?

A SERCOMBE will not be excluded as otherwise she cannot advise and assist MURPHY in her role as an appropriate adult.

B If SERCOMBE were related to MURPHY she could not be excluded but as she has no relationship with MURPHY, she can be excluded.

C The solicitor, HEMSTOCK, will make the decision as to whether SERCOMBE will be allowed into the consultation or not.

D If MURPHY wishes to have a private consultation with HEMSTOCK without SERCOMBE being present, he must be permitted to do so.

Question 19.11

PITCHER commits a robbery and is filmed on a town centre CCTV system carrying out the offence. DC THORPE wishes to trace witnesses to the offence and obtains a still image from the CCTV and places this in the local paper. MAYBURY recognises PITCHER from the still image and contacts DC THORPE who subsequently arrests PITCHER.

Considering Code D of the Codes of Practice, which of the statements below is correct?

A There is no requirement for PITCHER or his solicitor to view the material released to the media before any identification procedure is carried out.

B As MAYBURY has recognised PITCHER from a still image placed in a newspaper she would not be allowed to take part in any further identification procedures.

C DC THORPE may keep a copy of the material released to the media for the purposes of recognising or tracing the suspect.

D The fact that MAYBURY identified PITCHER from a still image in a newspaper would not stop her taking part in any further identification procedures.

Question 19.12

You have arrested TRAVIS on suspicion of committing 30 'bogus official' type burglaries. Descriptions of the offender have been obtained for every incident and there is a reasonable chance that each victim would be able to identify the offender. During her interview, TRAVIS denies any involvement in the offences. TRAVIS states that she will stand on an identification parade to prove her innocence.

What action will you take?

A As TRAVIS disputes her involvement there is an identification issue. In these circumstances you must arrange an identification parade in the first instance.

B As there is an identification issue, you must initially offer TRAVIS the choice between taking part in a video identification or standing on an identification parade.

C You should initially offer a video identification to TRAVIS.

D As the officer in the case you may choose freely between a video identification and an identification parade.

Question 19.13

CHURCH is involved in large-scale crowd violence at a football match during which he takes part in a violent disorder. The incident is caught on CCTV film. As well as the CCTV film of the incident, an E-fit is released to the public to identify CHURCH who is recognised from the E-fit by DRAPER. As a result, CHURCH is later arrested, charged and bailed for the offence. On his release, CHURCH makes a series of threatening telephone calls to DRAPER who tape records the threats.

Considering the law relating to photographs, images and sound, which of the statements below is **INCORRECT**?

A Expert evidence may be admitted to interpret the images on film.

B An E-fit of CHURCH would not be treated as a 'visual statement'.

C A police officer familiar with the CCTV of the crowd violence may be allowed to assist the court in interpreting and explaining events shown within the film.

D DRAPER would not be allowed to give evidence identifying CHURCH's voice.

Question 19.14

GROUCOTT admits to an offence of theft and is cautioned. At the time of her caution she had an injury to her left hand that meant no fingerprints relating to that hand could be taken.

Considering s. 27 of the Police and Criminal Evidence Act 1984, which of the statements below is correct?

A GROUCOTT may be required to attend a police station within six months of her caution in order for fingerprints to be taken.

B Section 27 of the Act is only applicable if the person has been convicted of a recordable offence.

C Should GROUCOTT fail to comply with a requirement under s. 27, she can be arrested without warrant.

D GROUCOTT may be required to attend the police station within seven days of her caution in order to take fingerprints.

Question 19.15

You are investigating a s. 20 wounding where the blood of the offender has been found on the clothing of the victim. You strongly suspect that HARPER is responsible for the offence but you have no direct evidence to implicate him. A colleague suggests obtaining an intimate sample (of blood) for DNA analysis from HARPER for elimination purposes.

Is this possible?

A Yes, with an Inspector's authorisation and the consent of HARPER.

B No, an intimate sample can only be obtained from HARPER if he was in police detention.

C Yes, with a Superintendent's authorisation and the consent of HARPER.

D No, because this is not an indictable offence.

Question 19.16

JENKINS (aged 15 yrs) has stolen several bottles of concentrated acid from his school chemistry laboratory and has hidden them in an unknown location on the school premises. The principal of the school has detained JENKINS and contacted the police to deal with the matter. PC McATEER attends the school and is concerned that if the acid is not located immediately it will lead to physical harm to other people. PC McATEER wishes to interview JENKINS regarding the location of the stolen acid and believes that contacting JENKINS's parents would cause an unreasonable delay in the circumstances.

Which of the statements below is correct?

A The principal cannot act as an appropriate adult because JENKINS is suspected of an offence against his educational establishment.

B Under no circumstances can PC McATEER interview JENKINS at his place of education.

C Regardless of the circumstances, JENKINS's parents must be notified of the interview and be present when the interview is carried out.

D If waiting for JENKINS's parents to attend would cause an unreasonable delay, the principal can act as an appropriate adult.

Question 19.17

At 10.00 am DC HEATHCOCK arrests DEBNEY (aged 15 yrs) for an offence of supplying a controlled drug (contrary to s. 4(3) of the Misuse of Drugs Act 1971). DEBNEY arrives at a police station at 11.00 am and as well as his father he requests that his friend, GRUNDY, be informed of his arrest. DC HEATHCOCK is concerned that if GRUNDY is contacted it will lead to interference with evidence relating to the offence.

With regard to DEBNEY's right to have someone informed (s. 56 of the Police and Criminal Evidence Act 1984), which of the comments below is right?

A This right cannot be delayed in any circumstances.

B In these circumstances, DEBNEY's right can be delayed and this delay can continue until 11.00 pm the following day.

C An officer of the rank of Superintendent or above may authorise this delay.

D DEBNEY's rights can be delayed with the authority of an Inspector but cannot be delayed after 10.00 pm the following day.

Question 19.18

DC BUTLIN is interviewing FLATMAN in relation to the kidnapping of his ex-wife. Before the kidnapping took place, FLATMAN told HARLOWE (a civilian witness) that he had considered kidnapping his ex-wife to teach her a lesson after she retained possession of their marital home in the divorce settlement between them. HARLOWE has provided DC BUTLIN with a witness statement to this effect.

Considering the Codes of Practice in relation to significant statements, what action should DC BUTLIN take with regard to FLATMAN's comment to HARLOWE?

A DC BUTLIN should introduce the comment made to HARLOWE at the start of the interview after caution, as it is a significant statement.

B DC BUTLIN may introduce the comment made to HARLOWE at any time during the interview, as unless the comment is a direct admission of guilt it is not a significant statement.

C DC BUTLIN may introduce the comment made to HARLOWE at any time during the course of the interview even though the comment is a significant statement.

D DC BUTLIN may introduce the comment made to HARLOWE at any time during the course of the interview, as it would not be classed as a significant statement.

Question 19.19

DCs CHURCHLEY and RAY are conducting an audio-recorded interview with HOLLAND for an offence of robbery. Also present in the interview is HOLLAND's solicitor, MASPERO. Thirty minutes after the interview has started, HOLLAND asks for a short 2-minute break in the interview while he gathers his thoughts. During the short break, DCs CHURCHLEY and RAY will remain in the interview room with HOLLAND and MASPERO.

Considering Code E of the Codes of Practice, what action should the interviewing officers take?

A The Codes of Practice do not allow for short breaks to be taken. The officers should stop the tapes and vacate the interview room. ⁄

B The officers should remove the tapes from the audio recorder and follow the procedures as if the interview had been concluded.

C As this is only a short break, the officers may turn off the audio recorder and when the interview recommences, continue the interview on the same tapes.

D The officers should leave the tape machine running for the duration of the short break and then continue the interview on the same tapes.

Question 19.20

Section 118 of the Police and Criminal Evidence Act 1984 defines the meaning of 'police detention'.

In which of the circumstances below would the named person not be classed as being in 'police detention'?

A OGDEN is arrested at a police station after attending voluntarily at the station.

B DUNKLEY is arrested by PC WEST and is sitting with the officer in a police livery vehicle waiting to go into a custody block.

C PELHAM is being escorted from the scene of her arrest to a police station by HALSETT (a designated escort officer).

D KHAN is in court after being charged with burglary and is in the charge of PC WYATT.

Question 19.21

DC BAKER arrests ZAFAR for an offence of theft and takes him to a designated police station. On arrival it becomes apparent that there is no custody officer readily available to deal with ZAFAR. PC CHARLES is allocated to perform the role of custody officer and begins to deal with ZAFAR in the custody block. Several minutes later Sergeant EDEN telephones PC CHARLES to see how he is doing. Sergeant EDEN is supervising a road check one mile away from the designated police station.

Considering the law with regard to the provision of custody officers, which of the statements below is correct?

A A constable can only perform the role of custody officer at a non-designated police station.

B PC CHARLES cannot perform the role of custody officer as an officer of at least the rank of Sergeant must perform it.

C As a Sergeant was not readily available then PC CHARLES can perform the role of custody officer.

D Sergeant EDEN would be considered available to carry out the role of custody officer and allowing PC CHARLES to continue in the role would be unlawful.

Question 19.22

DC MOHAMMED arrests WALSH in connection with an offence of aggravated burglary. When WALSH arrives at a police station he indicates that he wishes to have a solicitor to represent him. Due to the circumstances surrounding the offence, DC MOHAMMED wants to take non-intimate samples for evidential purposes from WALSH and also carry out an urgent interview without a solicitor being present (under the provisions of Code C, para. 6.6). WALSH tells DC MOHAMMED that he will not consent to the taking of the non-intimate samples or answer questions in any interview.

Which of the statements below is correct in these circumstances?

A As WALSH has requested a solicitor, any evidence gained from such an interview will be inadmissible because no solicitor was present.

B If WALSH refuses to answer any questions during the course of the urgent interview it may lead to a court drawing an inference from that failure.

C DC MOHAMMED can take non-intimate samples without consent even if WALSH has not consulted his solicitor.

D If an officer of the rank of Inspector or above authorises it, an urgent interview can take place.

Question 19.23

BAXTER has been detained under the Terrorism Act 2000.

When should BAXTER's first review of detention take place?

A As soon as reasonably practicable after his arrest.

B 6 hours after his arrest.

C 12 hours after his arrest.

D 24 hours after his arrest.

Question 19.24

Section 62 of the Police and Criminal Evidence Act 1984 sets out police powers to take intimate samples.

Which of the comments below is **INCORRECT** with regard to that power?

A An intimate sample can be taken by a police officer.

B Intimate samples can be obtained from a suspect who is not in police detention.

C Where an intimate sample is taken from a child under 14 years of age, the only consent required is that of his/her parents or guardian.

D An intimate sample can only be obtained with the consent of the suspect and this consent can be given orally.

ANSWERS

Answer 19.1

Answer **C** — Section 36(9) of the Police and Criminal Evidence Act 1984 states that where an officer performs the duties of a custody officer in the circumstances described in the question, that officer shall inform an officer who (a) is attached to a designated police station, and (b) is of at least the rank of Inspector, that he has done so.

Investigators' Manual, para. 4.5.5   **DV = 7**

Answer 19.2

Answer **C** — Code C, para. 5.6 states that the detained person shall, on request, be given writing materials and/or be allowed to telephone one person for a reasonable time. This privilege may be denied or delayed if an officer of the rank of Inspector or above considers sending the letter or making the telephone call may result in any of the consequences set out in Annex B, paras 1 and 2 of Code C (making answer B incorrect). One of those consequences is that the Inspector believes the exercise of the right will hinder the recovery of property obtained in consequence of the commission of such an offence.

Investigators' Manual, para. 4.5.6.2   **DV = 8**

Answer 19.3

Answer **A** — If an authorising officer, of Superintendent rank or above, considers that access to a solicitor will interfere with evidence relating to a serious arrestable offence, then access to that solicitor may be delayed, making answer D incorrect. This authorisation to delay access is not a 'blanket' authorisation to deny access to *all* legal advisers and in the example given in the question, the authorising officer should consider offering the detained person access to another solicitor on the Duty Solicitor scheme, making answer C incorrect. The consultation with a solicitor must be in private (Code C, para. 6.1). In *Brennan* v *United Kingdom* (2001) 34 EHRR 507, the court held that a suspect's right to communicate confidentially with a solicitor, 'is part of the basic requirements of a fair trial'. The court found that there had been a breach of Article 6(3)(c) because a police officer had been present during a suspect's first interview with his solicitor, making answer B incorrect.

Investigators' Manual, para. 4.5.6.6   **DV = 6**

Answer 19.4

Answer **B** — Paragraph 6.6(d) of Code C deals with the situation where the detainee changes their mind about wanting legal advice. In these circumstances, the interview may be started or continued without delay provided that the detainee agrees to do so (in writing or on tape) and an officer of the rank of Inspector or above has enquired about the detainee's reasons for their change of mind and gives authority for the interview to proceed.

Investigators' Manual, para. 4.5.6.6   **DV = 7.5**

Answer 19.5

Answer **B** — Section 41(2)(c) of the Police and Criminal Evidence Act states that in the case of a person who attends voluntarily at a police station or accompanies a constable to a police station without having been arrested, and is arrested, the 'relevant time' will begin at the time of his/her arrest. In situations where a person is arrested at one police station and has been circulated as wanted by another police station in the same force area, the detention clock for the second offence (in this case for the offence of rape) starts at the same time as for the original offence for which they were arrested.

Investigators' Manual, para. 4.5.6.8   **DV = 4**

Answer 19.6

Answer **A** — Note that the *wrong* response is required. Answers B, C and D are all correct statements relating to the audio-recording of interviews. Answer A is an incorrect statement as summary only offences are not required to be tape-recorded by Code E.

Investigators' Manual, para. 4.7.9.1   **DV = 6.5**

Answer 19.7

Answer **C** — Section 42(1) of the Police and Criminal Evidence Act 1984 permits an officer of Superintendent rank or above to authorise detention beyond 24 hours and up to a maximum of 36 hours. The offence investigated must be an indictable offence and the senior officer must be satisfied that there is not sufficient evidence to charge, that the investigation is being conducted diligently and expeditiously and that the person's detention is necessary to secure or preserve evidence relating to the offence or to obtain such evidence by questioning that person.

Investigators' Manual, para. 4.5.7.4   **DV = 8**

Answer 19.8

Answer **B** — Answer A is incorrect as a suspect's failure to request an identification parade does not mean the police may proceed without one (*R* v *Graham* [1994] Crim LR 262). Answer C is incorrect as (under Code D, para. 3.12) an identification procedure does not need to be held if it is not practicable or would serve no useful purpose in proving or disproving whether the suspect committed the offence. Answer D is incorrect as the exceptions that apply for answer C also apply to decisions when considering *R* v *Forbes*. This question is based on the case of *D* v *DPP* (1998) *The Times*, 7 August 1998, where it was held that an identification had not been made (as per answer B). An identification parade would have served no useful purpose since the clothing would have changed and those persons used for the parade would have been the same approximate age.

Investigators' Manual, para. 4.6.4.3   **DV = 3.5**

Answer 19.9

Answer **B** — Answer A is incorrect as Code C, para. 16.5 details the occasions when it is permissible to re-interview a suspect after they have been charged or informed they will be prosecuted for an offence. There is no requirement for the suspect to agree in writing to this taking place, making answer D incorrect. The re-interviewing of a suspect can take place if it is necessary to (i) prevent or minimise harm or loss to some other person or the public or (ii) to clear up an ambiguity in a previous answer or statement or (iii) in the interests of justice for the detainee to have put to them, and have an opportunity to comment on, information concerning the offence which has come to light since they were charged or informed they might be prosecuted. The reasons for re-interviewing could be any one of the above, making answer C incorrect.

Investigators' Manual, para. 4.7.7   **DV = 2**

Answer 19.10

Answer **D** — The right to have a private consultation with a solicitor also applies to juveniles (Code C, Note 1E). If a juvenile wishes to have a private consultation without the presence of an appropriate adult, they must be permitted to do so.

Investigators' Manual, para. 4.5.6.6 **DV = 7.5**

Answer 19.11

Answer **D** — Code D, paras 3.28 and 3.29 govern identification when the media has been used. When a broadcast or publication is made, a copy of the relevant material released to the media for the purposes of recognising or tracing the suspect must be kept, making answer C incorrect. The suspect or their solicitor must be allowed to view the material released to the media prior to any identification procedure, provided it is practicable and would not unreasonably delay the investigation, making answer A incorrect. The fact that MAYBURY has recognised PITCHER would not preclude her participation in any future identification procedure. However, each witness will be asked, after they have taken part, whether they have seen any broadcast or published films or photographs relating to the offence and any description of the suspect and their replies shall be recorded.

Investigators' Manual, paras 4.6.4.2, 4.6.4.9 **DV = 7.5**

Answer 19.12

Answer **C** — The circumstances of this question would mean that an identification procedure would be held (Code D, para. 3.21). Under Code D, para. 3.14, where an identification procedure is to be held, the suspect shall initially be offered a video identification.

Investigators' Manual, paras 4.6.4.2, 4.6.4.7 **DV = 2**

Answer 19.13

Answer **D** — Be aware of the use of the word *incorrect* in the question. Expert evidence may be admitted to interpret images on film (*R v Stockwell* (1993) 97 Cr App R 260), making answer A correct. In *R v Cook* [1987] 1 All ER 1049, the Court of Appeal decided that E-fits and other witness-generated images would not be classed as 'visual statements', making answer B correct. Police officers who are familiar with a particular film clip (e.g. crowd violence at a football match) may be allowed to assist the court in interpreting and explaining events shown within it (*R* v *Clare and Peach* (1995) 2 Cr App Rep 333), making answer C correct. Generally, a witness (DRAPER) may give evidence identifying the defendant's voice (*R* v *Robb* (1991) 93 Cr App R 161).

Investigators' Manual, paras 4.6.4.11   **DV = 2**

Answer 19.14

Answer **C** — Section 27 of the Police and Criminal Evidence Act 1984 provides that a person may be required to attend a police station to have his/her fingerprints taken if he/she has been convicted of a recordable offence, cautioned in respect of a recordable offence (and admitted the offence), or warned or reprimanded under s.65 of the Crime and Disorder Act 1998 for a recordable offence *and* the fingerprints do not constitute a full set or are not of sufficient quality to allow satisfactory analysis, comparison or matching, making answer B incorrect. The requirement should be made within one month of the conviction, caution, warning or reprimand, making answers A and D incorrect. The person should be given at least 7 days within which to attend, this 7-day period need not fall within the month allowed for making the requirement. Should a person fail to comply with the requirement, they may be arrested without warrant (Code D, para. 4.4).

Investigators' Manual, para. 4.6.5.2   **DV = 3**

Answer 19.15

Answer **A** — The Criminal Justice and Police Act 2001, s. 80(1) changed the authorisation level required to obtain an intimate sample from Superintendent to Inspector, making answer C incorrect. Section 62(2)(a) of the Police and Criminal Evidence Act 1984 states that the type of offence for which an intimate sample may be taken need only be a recordable offence and not an indictable offence, making answer D incorrect. Note 6C of Code D recognises that an intimate sample may be taken from a person not in police detention, for the purposes of elimination, providing his/her consent is given, making answer B incorrect.

Investigators' Manual, para. 4.6.8   **DV = 5**

Answer 19.16

Answer **A** — Code C, para. 11.16 states that a juvenile can be interviewed at his/her place of education in exceptional circumstances and with the agreement of the principal or the principal's nominee, making answer B incorrect. The parents of the juvenile should be notified and allowed a reasonable time to attend unless waiting for the appropriate adult would cause an unreasonable delay in which case the principal or his/her nominee can act as an appropriate adult, making answer C incorrect. However, if the juvenile is suspected of an offence against the educational establishment then the principal or his/her nominee cannot act as an appropriate adult, making answer D incorrect.

Investigators' Manual, para. 4.7.5   **DV = 2**

Answer 19.17

Answer **B** — The right under s. 56 of the Act can be delayed (making answer A incorrect). The delay can be authorised by an officer of the rank of Inspector or above, making answer C incorrect. Answer D is incorrect as although the authorisation level is correct, the right can only be delayed up to a maximum of 36 hours (48 in cases involving terrorism) and this 36-hour period is calculated from the 'relevant time'. The 'relevant time' is the time that DEBNEY arrives at the police station, i.e. 11.00 am, and so the right could be delayed up to 11.00 pm on the following day, making answer B correct.

Investigators' Manual, para. 4.5.6.2   **DV = 7**

Answer 19.18

Answer **D** — Code C, para. 11.4A states that a significant statement is one that appears capable of being used in evidence against the suspect, in particular a direct admission of guilt, making answer B incorrect. FLATMAN's comment to HARLOWE would appear to be a significant statement on that basis. However, para. 11.4 states that a significant statement is a statement that occurred in the presence and hearing of a police officer or a civilian interviewer before the start of the interview and this is not the case with the comment made to a civilian witness. Therefore, the comment is not a significant statement, making answers A and C incorrect. Answer C is further incorrect as a significant statement should be put to the suspect at the beginning of the interview after caution.

Investigators' Manual, paras 4.7.9.2, 4.7.9.8   **DV = 2**

Answer 19.19

Answer **C** — Code E, para. 4.13, allows for short breaks to be taken during an audio-recorded interview, making answer A incorrect. This paragraph states that if the break is to be a short one and both the suspect and the interviewer are to remain in the room, then the audio recorder may be turned off. There is no need to remove the tapes and when the interview recommences the tape recording should continue on the same tapes, making answers B and D incorrect.

Investigators' Manual, para. 4.7.9.8   **DV = 3**

Answer 19.20

Answer **D** — Section 118 states that a person will be in police detention for the purposes of the Act if (i) he has been taken to a police station after being arrested for an offence or after being arrested under s. 41 of the Terrorism Act 2000, or (ii) he is arrested at a police station after attending voluntarily at the station (answer A) or accompanying a constable to it, or is detained there or is detained elsewhere in the charge of a constable (answer B), except that a person who is at court after being charged is not in police detention for those purposes (answer D). In addition, where a person is in another's lawful custody by virtue of paragraph 22, 34(1) (a designated escort officer and answer D) or 35(3) of Schedule 4 to the Police Reform Act 2002, he shall be treated as being in police detention.

Investigators' Manual, para. 4.5.6.1   **DV = 5**

Answer 19.21

Answer **C** — Section 36(3) states that a custody officer must be an officer of at least the rank of Sergeant (answer B) however, s. 36(4) allows an officer of any rank to perform the functions of a custody officer if a Sergeant is not readily available to perform them (answer C). An officer of any rank can perform the role at a desig-nated or non-designated police station, making answer A incorrect. The effect of these sections is that the practice of allowing an officer of any rank to perform the role of custody officer where a Sergeant (*who has no other role to perform*) is in the po-lice station must therefore be unlawful. Answer D has Sergeant EDEN (i) performing another role and (ii) *out* of the police station.

Investigators' Manual, para. 4.5.5   **DV = 2.5**

Answer 19.22

Answer **C** — As long as the interview under Code C, para. 6.6 can be justified at court, the interview will be admissible, making answer A incorrect. Where a suspect is in an authorised place of detention and fails to answer questions, no inference will be drawn from that failure if he/she has not been allowed the opportunity to consult a solicitor prior to being questioned, making answer B incorrect. Answer D is incorrect as an interview under Code C, para. 6.6. can only take place if an officer of the rank of Superintendent or above authorises it. It is not necessary to await the arrival of a solicitor to take a non-intimate sample without consent for evidential purposes.

Investigators' Manual, paras 4.5.6.6, 4.13.4   **DV = 5.5**

Answer 19.23

Answer **A** — In cases where the person has been detained under the Terrorism Act 2000, the first review should be conducted as soon as reasonably practicable after his/her arrest. It must be conducted by a Superintendent.

Investigators' Manual, para. 4.5.7.6   **DV = 4**

Answer 19.24

Answer **D** — Note that the *incorrect* comment is required. Answers A, B and C are all correct statements in relation to intimate samples. Answer D is incorrect as the consent of a suspect must be given in writing (Code D, para. 6.10).

Investigators' Manual, para. 4.6.8   **DV = 6**

20 | Incomplete Offences and Offences Against the Administration of Justice and Public Interest

---

QUESTIONS

Question 20.1

A travel company employs LUCAS and KIRK as coach staff; amongst other duties, the two sell refreshments to customers travelling by coach. LUCAS suggests to KIRK that they make their own sandwiches and sell these to people using the coach instead of the sandwiches supplied by the travel firm. KIRK agrees to the suggestion.

Would this constitute an offence of conspiracy to defraud (contrary to Common Law)?

A No, because this offence involves deceiving another into acting in a way that is contrary to his/her duty.

B Yes, but you must show that the defendants were dishonest.

C No, at least three people must be involved in the conspiracy.

D Yes, but only as long as you prove that the end result would amount to the commission of an offence.

Question 20.2

McEVOY is due to be a contestant on a 'live' general knowledge TV show. When McEVOY takes part in the show his wife will be watching at home. Before the show begins husband and wife devise a plan so that when McEVOY is asked a question by the host of the show, McEVOY's wife will send him a 'text message' via his mobile phone that will contain the correct answer. If all goes according to the plan, the two will win up to £50,000.

Does this amount to a statutory conspiracy (contrary to s. 1 of the Criminal Law Act 1977)?

A Yes, the two have agreed on a course of conduct that will amount to the commission of an offence.

B No, McEVOY cannot commit statutory conspiracy if the only other party to the agreement is his wife.

C No, for there to be a conspiracy there must be an agreement with at least three people involved.

D Yes, unless the plan is later abandoned by the two.

Question 20.3

WISEDALE plans to falsely imprison a schoolboy and sexually assault him. He plans to gain access to a local school and commit the offence in the school toilets. WISEDALE buys a rucksack and places a kitchen knife, some rope and masking tape into the rucksack. He gains entry to the school and hides in the toilets waiting for his chance to commit the offence. The school caretaker catches him before the offence is committed.

Considering the law relating to attempts under s. 1 of the Criminal Attempts Act 1981, at what stage, if at all, does WISEDALE commit the offence of attempted false imprisonment?

A When he plans to gain access to the school and commit the offence in the toilets.

B When he buys the rucksack and places the kitchen knife, rope and masking tape into the rucksack.

C When he gains entry to the school and hides in the toilets waiting for a chance to commit the offence.

D The offence of attempted false imprisonment is not made out in these circumstances.

Question 20.4

KRAY arranges to handle a container load of electrical goods stolen in the course of a robbery. Unknown to KRAY, the container full of goods has been intercepted by the police who arrest the driver, return the contents to the rightful owner and substitute a container full of boxes containing old newspapers for the original container. A police officer drives the substituted container to the arranged meeting point and KRAY arrives shortly after, driving a large goods vehicle. KRAY backs the goods vehicle up to the container, opens the container doors and begins to load the worthless boxes into his goods vehicle when he is arrested.

Does KRAY attempt to handle stolen goods in these circumstances?

A No, in these circumstances the goods have ceased to be stolen and as the goods are not 'stolen' the offence cannot be committed.

B Yes, although it is 'physically' impossible to handle goods that are not stolen, this impossibility would not preclude such a charge under the Criminal Attempts Act.

C No, this offence does not exist and would be a 'legal' impossibility.

D Yes, but the prosecution would have to show that KRAY intended to dispose of the goods in order to show he had 'embarked on the crime proper'.

Question 20.5

MORRELL works in a haulage yard where large amounts of designer clothing are stored in trailers drawn by goods vehicles. MORRELL is contacted by SHACKLETON who tells MORRELL he will pay him £500 if he unlocks the rear doors of a trailer to enable SHACKLETON to steal its contents. MORRELL agrees and as the yard is closing, he unlocks the doors of one of the trailers intending that SHACKLETON will be able to steal its contents.

Considering the offence of interfering with a motor vehicle under s. 9 of the Criminal Attempts Act 1981, which of the statements below is correct?

A The offence is not committed because MORRELL is not the person who will carry out the theft.

B As MORRELL has not interfered with anything carried in or on the trailer, he does not commit the offence.

C MORRELL commits the offence as he has interfered with a trailer intending that SHACKLETON will commit theft from it.

D Motor vehicles are covered by this legislation but trailers are not, therefore MORRELL does not commit the offence.

Question 20.6

DC BROWN receives an anonymous telephone call stating that stolen goods are being stored at a house owned by GIBBS who has several convictions for theft and handling stolen goods. DC BROWN believes the information to be true. DC BROWN swears out a search warrant for GIBB's home address and during this process the magistrate asks DC BROWN what corroboration she has sought for the information provided. DC BROWN has not sought corroboration but rather than lose the chance to arrest GIBBS she tells the magistrate that the information has come from a tried and tested source who has always been accurate in the past.

Is DC BROWN guilty of an offence of perjury in judicial proceedings (contrary to s. 1 of the Perjury Act 1911)?

A Yes, DC BROWN has committed the offence although corroboration will be required in relation to the falsity of her statement.

B No, as swearing out a search warrant is not classed as 'judicial proceedings' for the purposes of this Act.

C Yes, the officer is guilty but to prove the offence, corroboration will be required to prove the fact that she actually made the alleged statement.

D No, as DC BROWN believes the information to be true she is not guilty of the offence.

Question 20.7

ROWLEY is an independent candidate for forthcoming council elections and campaigns that asylum seekers should not be allowed to live locally. To gain public sympathy and thereby votes, he causes several bruises to his face and reports the matter as an assault to DC TROMANS. ROWLEY tells the officer that he was attacked by two Iraqi men who objected to his views. ROWLEY intends his report to be taken seriously by the police but tells DC TROMANS that he cannot identify his attackers as they were disguised. As a result, the investigation only amounts to one day's work for the officer before being filed.

With regard to the offence of perverting the course of justice, which of the statements below is true?

A These circumstances do not amount to an offence, as the allegations made by ROWLEY are incapable of identifying specific individuals.

B For a charge to succeed, the prosecution must show that a lot of police time and resources were involved in the investigation; this is not the case with ROWLEY.

C Making a false allegation of an offence would mean that ROWLEY commits the offence.

D ROWLEY commits the offence but the consent of the Director of Public Prosecutions is required before a charge can be brought against him.

Question 20.8

Eighteen months ago, PROSSER gave evidence against HILL regarding an assault. HILL was sentenced to 3 years' imprisonment but is released early. HILL wants revenge against PROSSER and is walking the streets searching for him. HILL sees PROSSER's sister, AUCOTE, out shopping and approaches her saying, 'Don't think

I've forgotten your brother and the little story in court, his house will be burnt down tonight'. HILL intends to cause PROSSER to fear that harm will be caused to his property.

Why is no offence of harming witnesses (contrary to s. 40 of the Criminal Justice and Police Act 2001) committed?

A HILL commits no offence as it is over a year since the proceedings were concluded.

B HILL commits no offence as he does not intend to pervert or interfere with the course of justice.

C HILL commits no offence as the harm done or threatened must be physical and not to the person's property.

D HILL commits no offence as the threat has not been made in the presence of the person who would be harmed.

Question 20.9

CLINTON and GREEN share a flat. One afternoon, GREEN tells CLINTON about a robbery that she has just committed that netted her £1,000. The next day, GREEN goes to Spain for a week's holiday. Two days later, DC LAGRAM comes to the flat and asks CLINTON if she knows where GREEN is. When CLINTON asks why, the officer tells her that he needs to speak with GREEN about a theft committed that day. CLINTON knows that GREEN has not committed the offence because she was out of the country but is worried that she will lose her flat-mate and so tells the officer that GREEN moved out a month ago and no longer lives at the address.

Has CLINTON committed an offence of assisting an offender (contrary to s. 4 of the Criminal Law Act 1967)?

A No, because CLINTON knows that GREEN has not committed the offence of theft.

B Yes, but GREEN will have to be convicted of the offence of robbery before CLINTON can be prosecuted for the offence.

C No, because the 'positive act' of providing misleading information to DC LAGRAM must relate to the robbery.

D Yes, CLINTON knows GREEN has committed a relevant offence and has provided misleading information with intent to impede her apprehension.

ANSWERS

Answer 20.1

Answer **B** — Answer A is incorrect as the offence of conspiracy to defraud can take two forms, one is as per answer A and the other is an agreement by two or more persons, by dishonesty, to deprive a person of something which is his or to which he is or would or might be entitled [or] an agreement by two or more by dishonesty to injure some proprietary right [of the victim] (Viscount Dilhorne in *Scott* v *Metropolitan Police Commissioner* [1975] AC 819). This definition means that answers C and D are incorrect.

Investigators' Manual, para. 4.8.3.2   **DV = 4.5**

Answer 20.2

Answer **B** — Although there has been an agreement that if carried out in accordance with the conspirators' intentions will involve the commission of an offence, the offence of statutory conspiracy is not made out. This is because a defendant cannot be convicted of statutory conspiracy if the *only* other party to the agreement is his/her spouse, a child/children under 10 years of age or the intended victim.

Investigators' Manual, para. 4.8.3.1   **DV = 7**

Answer 20.3

Answer **D** — The defendant's actions must be shown to have gone beyond mere preparation towards the commission of the substantive offence. The courts have accepted an approach of questioning whether the defendant had 'embarked on the crime proper' (*R* v *Gullefer* [1990] 1 WLR 1063) although there is no requirement for the defendant to have passed a point of no return if the intention of the defendant can be ascertained. Up to point 'C', WISEDALE has not 'embarked on the crime proper'. In *R* v *Geddes* [1996] Crim LR 894, GEDDES was found in a boy's toilet of a school in possession of articles that suggested his reason for being there was to kidnap a child. His conviction for attempted false imprisonment was quashed. Even clear evidence of what he had in mind 'did not throw light on whether he had begun to carry out the commission of the offence'.

Investigators' Manual, para. 4.8.4   **DV = 2.5**

Answer 20.4

Answer **B** — You may consider that the offence cannot be committed because the goods from the container have been recovered by the police and returned to their rightful owner. Under s. 24(3) of the Theft Act 1968 this would mean that the goods shall no longer be regarded as 'stolen goods'. However, s. 1(2) of the Criminal Attempts Act 1981 states, 'A person may be guilty of attempting to commit an offence to which this section applies even though the facts are such that the commission of the offence is impossible'. This makes answer A incorrect and also answer C as the offence is not a 'legal' impossibility. Answer D is incorrect as KRAY has already 'embarked on the crime proper' by moving the boxes from one vehicle to another.

Investigators' Manual, paras 4.8.4, 4.8.5   **DV = 4**

Answer 20.5

Answer **C** — This offence is committed if the defendant interferes with a motor vehicle or trailer or with anything carried in or on the motor vehicle or trailer, making answers B and D incorrect. The defendant's intentions at the time of the interference will be that an offence (one of which is theft from the motor vehicle or trailer) shall be committed by himself or some other person, making answer A incorrect.

Investigators' Manual, para. 4.8.4.1   **DV = 5**

Answer 20.6

Answer **A** — Section 1(2) of the Act describes the term 'judicial proceedings' as including proceedings before any court, tribunal, *or person having by law power to hear, receive, and examine evidence on oath*, making answer B incorrect. Corroboration is required in cases of perjury (see Perjury Act 1911, s. 13) but not of the fact that the defendant actually made the alleged statement, making answer C incorrect. The fact that the officer believes the original anonymous information to be true does not stop her committing the offence. Firstly, an application for a search warrant may not be made on the basis of information from an anonymous source if corroboration has not been sought (Code B, para. 3.1). Secondly, the offence is committed when a lawfully sworn witness makes a statement in proceedings, which he/she knows to be false, or does not believe to be true. DC BROWN's statement on the quality and source of the information would fall into this category.

Investigators' Manual, para. 4.9.2   **DV = 6**

Answer 20.7

Answer **C** — The consent of the DPP is not required to charge with this offence, making answer D incorrect. The fact that the allegations made by ROWLEY are incapable of identifying specific individuals is immaterial if the defendant intends that the allegation be taken seriously as in *R* v *Cotter and Others* [2002] EWCA Crim 1033, making answer A incorrect. The requirement to show that a great deal of police time and resources has been expended on the investigation was raised in *R* v *Sookoo* [2002] EWCA Crim 800 but is associated with giving false details to the police on arrest, making answer B incorrect. Making a false allegation of an offence means ROWLEY commits the offence (*R* v *Goodwin* (1989) 11 Cr App R (S) 194 (rape)).

Investigators' Manual, para. 4.9.4 **DV = 5**

Answer 20.8

Answer **A** — This offence is aimed to protect those who have been involved in relevant proceedings and so there is no requirement for an intention to pervert or interfere with justice, making answer B incorrect. The harm threatened can be physical or financial and can be made to a person or to property, making answer C incorrect. It is immaterial whether the threat is made in the presence of the person who would be harmed, making answer D incorrect. The offence must take place between the start of the proceedings and one year after they are concluded.

Investigators' Manual, para. 4.9.6 **DV = 6.5**

Answer 20.9

Answer **D** — Section 4 of the Act states, 'where a person has committed a relevant offence, any other person who, knowing or believing him to be guilty of the offence *or some other relevant offence*, does without lawful authority or reasonable excuse any act with intent to impede his apprehension or prosecution shall be guilty of an offence'. The fact that CLINTON knows GREEN has not committed the theft is immaterial as she knows she has committed a robbery, i.e. she knows GREEN is guilty of *some other arrestable offence*, making answer A incorrect. The 'positive act' carried out by the defendant is about the behaviour of the defendant, not the offence which it relates to, making answer C incorrect. CLINTON can commit the offence before GREEN is convicted of the robbery, making answer B incorrect.

Investigators' Manual, para. 4.9.7 **DV = 6**

21 Disclosure of Evidence, Documentary Records and Business Documents, the Criminal Justice Act 1967 and the Criminal Justice and Public Order Act 1994

QUESTIONS

Question 21.1

DC SMART is the OIC in a case involving ELDIN who has been charged with an offence of s. 18 assault. ELDIN's solicitor makes a request for advanced information to help decide whether ELDIN will plead guilty or not guilty. ELDIN's solicitor requests a summary of the prosecution case together with copies of the statements of the proposed prosecution witnesses. DC SMART considers that providing copies of the witness statements might lead to a witness being intimidated.

What course of action should DC SMART take?

A The officer should consult with the CPS as the rules allow the prosecutor to limit disclosure of some or all of the prosecution case.

B The officer must disclose all the material requested by the defence solicitor in order to comply with Article 6 of the ECHR and the Human Rights Act 1998.

C DC SMART need not disclose any statements to the defence at this stage, as they have no entitlement to any material.

D Unless the material undermines the prosecution case, there is no requirement for the statements of witnesses to be disclosed.

Question 21.2

LUNN is arrested and charged with an offence of rape and the case goes to trial. The OIC of the case, DC ATTWOOD, accidentally fails to comply with disclosure rules under the Criminal Procedure and Investigations Act 1996, although there is sufficient credible evidence available which would justify a safe conviction.

Which of the statements below is true with regard to the effect this non-compliance will have on the trial?

A An accidental failure to disclose will not affect the trial and the accused will still have to make defence disclosure to the prosecution.

B A failure to comply with disclosure rules in these circumstances will not automatically mean the trial will be stayed for an abuse of process.

C The prosecution will offer no evidence as otherwise the trial will be stayed on the grounds that there has been an abuse of process.

D The courts are obliged to adjourn the trial in order for the prosecution to make adequate disclosure to the defence.

Question 21.3

BARBER is charged with an offence of murder and on 12 November she is committed to Crown Court for trial.

When should the prosecution make primary disclosure?

A 7 days after BARBER is committed to Crown Court.

B 14 days after BARBER is committed to Crown Court.

C 21 days after BARBER is committed to Crown Court.

D As soon as practicable after the duty arises.

Question 21.4

DS CHRISTIE is overseeing the prosecution of a series of aggravated burglaries committed by KEYWOOD. The operation to arrest KEYWOOD was intelligence led and KEYWOOD was the subject of numerous intelligence reports eventually leading to his arrest. On arrest, KEYWOOD assaulted DC POULOS, resulting in KEYWOOD being charged with a s. 47 assault against the officer. Due to the amount of material generated in the investigation, DS CHRISTIE decides to appoint a disclosure officer for the case.

Which of the statements below is true with regard to the appointment of a disclosure officer by DS CHRISTIE?

A An unsworn member of support staff would not be allowed to perform this func-
tion.
B DS CHRISTIE could appoint DC POULOS as the disclosure officer.
C Generally speaking, there is no restriction on who can perform the role of dis-
closure officer.
D There can only be one disclosure officer for each case.

Question 21.5

WATTIS has been arrested and charged with an offence of rape. You are the officer
in charge of the case and have the assistance of PC SMEDLEY who is acting as the
disclosure officer. PC SMEDLEY approaches you and asks your advice regarding the
disclosure of material that may be relevant to the investigation.

Which of the items below will you tell PC SMEDLEY she **DOES NOT** have to dis-
close as they would not be classed as relevant material?
A A draft version of a witness statement where the content of the draft version
differs from the final version of the statement.
B A written record of an interview with a potential witness.
C The identity of a potential witness to the arrest of WATTIS.
D The fact that house-to-house enquiries were made and that no one witnessed
anything.

Question 21.6

DC MIDDLEMORE and DC KHOJA receive information that HENLEY is dealing in drugs
outside a school. The officers drive to the school in an unmarked police vehicle and
park near the front gates where they can observe HENLEY. The officers witness HEN-
LEY dealing drugs and arrest him for supplying a controlled drug. HENLEY is charged
and the case goes to trial. During the trial the defence apply to cross-examine the
officers on the location of their observations in order to test what they could see.
This includes the colour, make and model of the vehicle the officers used.

Considering the ruling in R v Johnson, will the prosecution be able to withhold
this information?
A Yes, the court will follow the ruling in R v Johnson which states that the exact
location of the observations need not be revealed.
B No, the ruling in R v Johnson is based on the protection of the owner or occupier
of premises and would not apply in this case.

C Yes, although the prosecution will have to supply details of the location of the vehicle.

D No, under no circumstances can the location of observation posts be withheld from the defence.

Question 21.7

CROXTON is arrested for an offence of supplying a 'Class A' controlled drug and on arrival in the custody block he requests the presence of his solicitor, Mr JONES. Mr JONES is contacted but tells the custody officer it will be 10 hours before he can get to the police station. The arresting officer, DC ROACH, speaks to her duty Superintendent who authorises an interview without the presence of Mr JONES on the grounds that to await his arrival would cause an unreasonable delay to the process of the investigation. During the course of this interview, CROXTON's reply to all the questions put to him is, 'No comment'.

Considering only s. 34 of the Criminal Justice and Public Order Act 1994, what affect will CROXTON's 'No comment' response have on the case?

A A court could draw an inference from CROXTON's failure to provide an answer to DC ROACH's questions.

B A court will draw no inference unless there is additional evidence produced by the prosecution to prove the case.

C Should a court draw an inference from CROXTON's failure to answer questions, CROXTON can be convicted on that inference alone.

D A court will draw no inference, as CROXTON was not allowed to consult a solicitor prior to being questioned.

Question 21.8

VOWLES makes a statement to the police complaining that THOMAS assaulted him with a knuckleduster. VOWLES states that during the assault he managed to punch THOMAS on his left cheek. The next day, DC STOKOE and DC McCROW visit THOMAS's home address and arrest him for a s. 20 wounding on VOWLES. On his arrest, DC STOKOE notices that THOMAS has a large bruise on his left cheekbone. During the arrest, DC McCROW seizes a knuckleduster from THOMAS's living room. In interview, THOMAS tells DC STOKOE that he got the bruised cheekbone playing football the previous day but refuses to answer any questions relating to the knuckleduster. DC STOKOE believes that THOMAS's bruised cheekbone and the knuckleduster are attributable to THOMAS taking part in the offence.

Considering only s. 36 of the Criminal Justice and Public Order Act 1994, which, if any, of the below would DC STOKOE be able to give THOMAS a special warning for?

A THOMAS's bruised cheekbone.

B The knuckleduster recovered at THOMAS's home address.

C THOMAS's bruised cheekbone and the knuckleduster recovered at THOMAS's home address.

D Special warnings are not applicable for either the bruised cheekbone or the knuckleduster.

Question 21.9

DC MATKIN is completing a file for robbery where the defendant, ROWLETT, has denied the offence. DC MATKIN is considering what information he should include within the disclosure schedules. As well as material which undermines the prosecution case, paragraph 7.3 of the Code of Practice under Part II of the Criminal Procedure and Investigations Act 1996 requires DC MATKIN to supply a copy of certain materials whether or not he considers it to undermine the prosecution case.

Which of the below **DOES NOT** need to be disclosed under paragraph 7.3 of the Code of Practice?

A A record of the first description of a suspect given to the police by a potential witness where the description differs from ROWLETT's.

B Material which casts doubt on the reliability of a witness to the robbery.

C Information provided by ROWLETT indicating an explanation for the offence with which he is charged.

D ROWLETT's custody record.

Question 21.10

HOOD is being prosecuted for an offence of s. 18 wounding (an indictable only offence). The prosecution make primary disclosure to HOOD's defence team who, in line with s. 5 of the Criminal Procedure and Investigations Act 1996, must now provide a defence statement to the court and the prosecutor.

Although the courts can extend the period, within what time period must HOOD's defence team normally provide the defence statement?

A Within 7 days of the prosecution making primary disclosure.

B Within 14 days of the prosecution making primary disclosure.

C Within 21 days of the prosecution making primary disclosure.

D Within 28 days of the prosecution making primary disclosure.

ANSWERS

Answer 21.1

Answer **A** — The prosecution is required, on request, to supply the defence with a summary of the prosecution case and/or copies of the statements of the proposed witnesses, making answer C incorrect. The defence are entitled to this disclosure to consider whether the defendant will plead guilty or not guilty and this has no relevance to whether the material undermines the prosecution case, making answer D incorrect. However, if the OIC considers that such disclosure may lead to witnesses being intimidated or some other interference with justice, the prosecutor may limit some or all of the prosecution case, making answer B incorrect.

Investigators' Manual, para. 4.10.2.1   **DV = 4**

Answer 21.2

Answer **B** — Any failure to comply with the rules of disclosure, by the prosecution or the defence, may affect the trial. A failure by the prosecution to comply with their obligations means the accused does not have to make defence disclosure, making answer A incorrect. The court is under no obligation to adjourn the trial, making answer D incorrect. Although a failure to comply may mean the trial is stayed for abuse of process, this is not necessarily always the case (*R v Feltham Magistrates' Court, ex parte Ebrahim; Mouat v DPP; R v Feltham Magistrates' Court, ex parte DPP* [2001] 1 WLR 1293). In this case it was stated that in such circumstances the trial should proceed, leaving the defendant to seek to persuade the jury or magistrates not to convict because evidence that might otherwise have been available was not before the court through no fault of the defendant, making answer C incorrect.

Investigators' Manual, para. 4.10.7   **DV = 3**

Answer 21.3

Answer **D** — The Criminal Procedure and Investigations Act 1996 in effect only applies once a defendant has been committed/transferred to the Crown Court or is proceeding to trial in the Magistrates' or Youth Court. While there are provisions to set specific time periods by which primary disclosure must be met, none currently exist. Until such times, primary disclosure must be made as soon as practicable after the duty arises, making answers A, B and C incorrect.

Investigators' Manual, para. 4.10.10   **DV = 5**

Answer 21.4

Answer **C** — For investigations carried out by the police, generally speaking there is no restriction on who performs the role of the 'Disclosure Officer'. The role could be performed by unsworn support staff (Criminal Procedure and Investigations Act 1996, Codes of Practice, paras 2.1 and 3.3), making answer A incorrect. However, para. 7 of the Attorney General's Guidelines on disclosure states that an individual must not be appointed as disclosure officer if that role is likely to result in a conflict of interest, for example, if the disclosure officer is a victim of the alleged crime which is the subject of criminal proceedings. Therefore DC POULOS should not be appointed, making answer B incorrect. There may be occasions where the police investigation has been intelligence led and there may be an additional disclosure officer appointed to deal with the intelligence material, making answer D incorrect.

Investigators' Manual, para. 4.10.17   **DV = 3**

Answer 21.5

Answer **C** — Paragraph 5.4 of the Code of Practice for the Criminal Procedure and Investigations Act 1996 gives details of material that might be considered to be relevant material. This includes the items listed at answers A, B and D, making those answers incorrect. In *DPP* v *Metten*, 22 January 1999, the defence claimed that officers knew the identity of potential witnesses to the arrest of the offender and that these had not been disclosed. The court stated that this was not relevant to the case as it concerned the time of the arrest and not what happened at the time the offence was committed.

Investigators' Manual, para. 4.10.21   **DV = 4**

Answer 21.6

Answer **B** — In *R* v *Johnson* [1988] 1 WLR 1377, the judge ruled that the exact location of premises used to carry out observations need not be revealed, making answer D incorrect. The rule is based on the protection of the owner or occupier of premises and not on the identity of the observation post. So, in *R* v *Brown* (1987) 87 Cr App R 52, where a surveillance operation was conducted from an unmarked police car, information relating to the surveillance and the colour, make and model of the vehicle should not be withheld, making answers A and C incorrect.

Investigators' Manual, para. 4.10.24.2   **DV = 4.5**

Answer 21.7

Answer **D** — Section 34(2A) states that if the defendant has not been allowed an opportunity to consult a solicitor prior to being questioned then no inference will be drawn by the court on the defendant's silence, refusal or failure to give an account. This section was introduced because of the judgment of the European Court of Human Rights in the case of *Murray* v *United Kingdom* (1996) 22 EHRR 29. The court held that inferences being drawn from the silence of the accused when denied access to legal advice constituted a breach of Article 6(1) in conjunction with Article 6(3) of the European Convention on Human Rights (right to a fair trial).

Investigators' Manual, para. 4.13.5   **DV = 7**

Answer 21.8

Answer **B** — Special warnings under s. 36 of the Act are applicable if a person is arrested by a constable and there is (i) on his person, or (ii) in or on his clothing or footwear, or (iii) otherwise in his possession, or (iv) in any place in which he is at the time of his arrest, any object, substance or mark, or there is any mark on any such object which the officer reasonably believes may be attributable to the participation of the arrested person in the commission of an offence. This would mean that both the bruised cheekbone (a mark on the person) and the knuckleduster (an object in any place in which the person is at the time of the arrest) could form part of a special warning. However, the special warning should only be given if the defendant fails or refuses to account for the fact. THOMAS has answered the question relating to the bruised cheekbone, making answers A and C incorrect. He refuses to answer questions relating to the knuckleduster and so a special warning may be given regarding this item, making answer D incorrect.

Investigators' Manual, para. 4.13.7   **DV = 2**

Answer 21.9

Answer **D** — The material that must be provided under paragraph 7.3 includes (amongst other things): (i) a record of the first description of the suspect given to the police by a potential witness, *whether or not the description differs from that of the alleged offender,* (ii) information provided by an accused person which indicates an explanation for the offence with which he/she has been charged, and (iii) any material casting doubt on the reliability of a witness, making answers A, B and C incorrect. Answer D, the custody record, might be relevant to a case but does not form part of this requirement.

Investigators' Manual, para. 4.10.17   **DV = 3**

Answer 21.10

Answer **B** — Compulsory disclosure by the defence under s. 5 of the Act (providing a defence statement to the court and prosecutor) must take place within 14 days of the prosecution making primary disclosure.

Investigators' Manual, para. 4.10.11.1   **DV = 4**

Question Checklist

The checklist below is designed to help you keep track of your progress when answering the multiple-choice questions. If you fill this in after one attempt at each question, you will be able to check how many you have got right and which questions you need to revisit a second time.

	First attempt Correct (✓)	Second attempt Correct (✓)
1 Theft		
1.1		
1.2		
1.3		
1.4		
1.5		
1.6		
1.7		
1.8		
1.9		
1.10		
1.11		
1.12		
1.13		
1.14		
2 Burglary		
2.1		
2.2		
2.3		
2.4		

	First attempt Correct (✓)	Second attempt Correct (✓)
2.5		
2.6		
2.7		
2.8		
2.9		
2.10		
2.11		
2.12		
2.13		
2.14		
2.15		
2.16		
2.17		
2.18		
3 Handling		
3.1		
3.2		
3.3		
3.4		
3.5		
3.6		

Question Checklist

	First attempt Correct (✓)	Second attempt Correct (✓)
4 Robbery		
4.1		
4.2		
4.3		
4.4		
4.5		
5 Deception		
5.1		
5.2		
5.3		
5.4		
5.5		
5.6		
6 Blackmail		
6.1		
6.2		
6.3		
6.4		
7 Homicide		
7.1		
7.2		
7.3		
7.4		
7.5		
7.6		
7.7		
7.8		
7.9		
8 Offences Against the Person		
8.1		
8.2		
8.3		
8.4		

	First attempt Correct (✓)	Second attempt Correct (✓)
8.5		
8.6		
8.7		
8.8		
8.9		
8.10		
9 Threats to Kill, Child Abduction, Kidnap and False Imprisonment		
9.1		
9.2		
9.3		
9.4		
9.5		
9.6		
9.7		
10 Public Order and Racially Aggravated Offences		
10.1		
10.2		
10.3		
10.4		
10.5		
10.6		
10.7		
10.8		
11 Criminal Damage		
11.1		
11.2		
11.3		
11.4		
11.5		
11.6		
11.7		
11.8		
11.9		

	First attempt Correct (✓)	Second attempt Correct (✓)
12 Misuse of Drugs		
12.1		
12.2		
12.3		
12.4		
12.5		
12.6		
12.8		
12.9		
12.10		
12.11		
12.12		
12.13		
13 Firearms and Gun Crime		
13.1		
13.2		
13.3		
13.4		
13.5		
13.6		
13.7		
13.8		
13.9		
14 The Sexual Offences Act 2003, Rape and Sexual Assault		
14.1		
14.2		
14.3		
14.4		
14.5		
14.6		
14.7		
14.8		
14.9		
14.10		
14.11		

	First attempt Correct (✓)	Second attempt Correct (✓)
14.12		
14.13		
14.14		
14.15		
14.16		
14.17		
14.18		
15 Child Sex Offences		
15.1		
15.2		
15.3		
15.4		
15.5		
15.6		
15.7		
15.8		
15.9		
15.10		
15.11		
15.12		
15.13		
15.14		
15.15		
15.16		
15.17		
15.18		
15.19		
15.20		
15.21		
15.22		
15.23		
15.24		
15.25		
16 Protection of Children		
16.1		
16.2		
16.3		
16.4		

Question Checklist

	First attempt Correct (✓)	Second attempt Correct (✓)
17 Preparatory Offences		
17.1		
17.2		
17.3		
17.4		
17.5		
18 Presumptions, State of Mind, Criminal Conduct and Bail		
18.1		
18.2		
18.3		
18.4		
18.5		
18.6		
18.7		
18.8		
18.9		
18.10		
18.11		
18.12		
18.13		
18.14		
18.15		
18.16		
18.17		
19 PACE Codes of Practice, Identification and Interviews		
19.1		
19.2		
19.3		
19.4		
19.5		
19.6		
19.7		
19.8		
19.9		

	First attempt Correct (✓)	Second attempt Correct (✓)
19.10		
19.11		
19.12		
19.13		
19.14		
19.15		
19.16		
19.17		
19.18		
19.19		
19.20		
19.21		
19.22		
19.23		
19.24		
20 Incomplete Offences and Offences Against the Administration of Justice and Public Interest		
20.1		
20.2		
20.3		
20.4		
20.5		
20.6		
20.7		
20.8		
20.9		
21 Disclosure and the Criminal Justice Acts 1967 and 1994		
21.1		
21.2		
21.3		
21.4		
21.5		
21.6		
21.7		
21.8		
21.9		
21.10		

Also available to help with your revision

Blackstone's Police Investigators' Mock Examination Paper 2007

David Pinfield

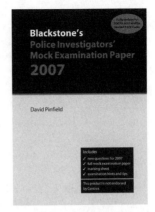

'The whole package is well set out and easy to follow with clear instructions.'
   Charlie Barton, Previously Detective Constable and Training Manager, Cambridgeshire Police

'This book can only enhance your overall chances of being successful with the NIE in your Investigators' Exam.'
   Detective Sergeant Nigel Cooper, Crime Training Manager, Essex Police

Minimise last-minute panic and ensure confidence with examination technique.

- Test your knowledge of the *Blackstone's Police Investigators' Manual 2007* by answering 80 questions in two hours.
- Check your answers and use the handy references to the relevant parts of the *Blackstone's Police Investigators' Manual 2007* to follow up your mock exam with targeted revision.
- Packed with handy hints and practical tips to prepare you for the examination day.

Blackstone's Police Investigators' Mock Examination Paper 2007 features a selection of multiple-choice questions set by an experienced question writer. Designed for use in simulated exam conditions, it will test your knowledge and understanding of the law, and your ability to answer questions under pressure.

The mock examination paper is accompanied by detailed marking matrices; allowing you to calculate your overall percentage score and recognize the areas you need to focus on. Learn where your areas of strength and weakness lie, and channel your revision into the most relevant areas of the syllabus.

For more information on this, and other Police books from Blackstone's, please visit
www.blackstonespolicemanuals.com

£14.99   Available from all good bookshops
November 2006 | c.68 pages | Paperback | 0-19-920730-5 / 978-0-19-920730-5

Please note, this product is not endorsed by Centrex